UNFINISHED IRELAND

Essays on Hubert Butler

Unfinished Ireland
is first published
in an edition of 1000 paperback copies
on 15 February 2003.

IRISH PAGES
The Linen Hall Library
17 Donegall Square
Belfast BT1 5GB

This book has received generous funding from The Butler Society.

THE BUTLER SOCIETY

Designed by Tonic and set in 11.5/13 Monotype Perpetua.
Printed in Belfast by Nicholson and Bass.

ISBN 0-9544257-0-7

UNFINISHED IRELAND

Essays on Hubert Butler

Edited by Chris Agee

IRISH PAGES
in association with The Butler Society

HMB, 1987. Photo by Albert Fenton

CONTENTS

PART III: BUTLER ABROAD

EPILOGUE

APPENDICES

So I go on believing that the strength to live comes from an understanding of ourselves and our neighbours or the diaspora that has replaced them. If we could focus on them all the curiosity and wisdom that we disperse round the world, as we focus all the rays of the sun through a burning glass on a pile of dead leaves, there is no limit to the warmth we could generate. It is easier of course to collect the dead leaves than to make sparks to kindle them. Yet I believe the life which Chekhov prophesied, "unspeakably, amazingly lovely", is not out of our reach, though it may now be a century or two farther away than he calculated.

Hubert Butler, 1985

Maidenhall, Bennettsbridge, Co. Kilkenny. Drawing by Michael Craig

INTRODUCTION

HMB, 1980s. Photo by John Carlos

FOREWORD

Chris Agee

Not long after I wrote an early review of *Escape from the Anthill* (1985), I received a letter from Hubert Butler. With his trademark swiftness of sensibility, he went straight from the opening courtesies into a compact but interrelated set of preoccupations that had evolved for more than six decades, a kind of early imaginative aquifer nourishing the unique terrain of his writing:

> I like being told that I was able "to infuse the local with the general without sacrificing the former", because that was just what I wanted to do. I must try and get hold of the *Antipolitics* of Georg Konrad. I had not heard of it.
>
> Of course I was influenced by AE, but as often happens, though I met him several times, I was too young and shy at the time and it was only later that when reading his books – like *The National Being* – that I got some good out of him.
>
> He felt he was actually *building* a Utopia on the foundation of Horace Plunkett's cooperative movement and that it concerned the marketing of butter and eggs and that the creative arts and sciences would develop when such fundamental things had been wisely regulated. But then there was the rebellion and the Civil War and the burning of the creameries and of Plunkett's house and when peace did come the cooperative movement was stood on its head and became an organisation for taking the milk away from the villages and processing it in a vast factory.
>
> In the Age of Reagan and Gorbachev and Mrs Thatcher, all this seems very remote and yet even here there are small groups thinking on these lines … (30 December 1985)

He ended with an invitation to visit Maidenhall. A second note, dated over a year later, tells me that we had arranged this visit for the afternoon of April 13th, 1987.

I never went – then or later. Something must have come up on that occasion, forcing me to bow out: I lacked a car, and the visit was timed to precede my first trip to the Soviet Union. But unaccountably, I never sought to arrange a second date. In retrospect, I can barely credit this – it outstrips my earlier par of not engaging with Allen Ginsberg, who had seated himself smilingly across from me in a Cambridge cafeteria. Missing Butler at Maidenhall now seems a colossal inattention, like funking lunch with Chekhov at Melikhovo, or skipping a chat with Frost on his front porch in New Hampshire.

Yet I am quite certain that this inattentiveness – though partly a vestige of youthfulness, and tinged too with a soupçon of shyness – had nonetheless a substantial intellectual dimension illustrative of the overwhelming response to Butler's writing before the last, Indian-summer success of his four collections of essays. This response was, in a word, *underestimation*. Even with *Escape from the Anthill* behind me, I – like so many before – underestimated the achievement, not really grasping the full measure of this marvellous writer. Notwithstanding my praise of the book, quite unstinting, I remember plainly that some scruple of historical reservation made me hesitate, and that I did not, therefore, quite carry, inwardly, the conviction of my public words. Was Butler perhaps too much the local historian, the country amateur, the last fragment or even figment of past Anglo-Irish glories? Was he, as Raymond Williams might have put it, representative of a *residual* rather than *emergent* opposition to the *dominant* grain of our "megapolitan" century, which Butler had delineated with such incisiveness?

In the Age of Reagan, Thatcher and Gorbachev, here was someone who wrote of utopian Irish creameries; obscure and seemingly vanished religious conflicts in interwar Croatia; and the Lilliputian struggle of humane community in era of an all-conquering globalization and statism. Yes – incontrovertibly – the style was magisterial, the analysis of the banal universalising of mental focus – the dangers of mass communication – unimpeachable. I thrilled (and still do) to Butler's great peroration on "escape from the anthill" (*EA* 12) and to the certitude of his prediction that "the great commensal communities" of East and West (*EA* 231), consolidated by fear and greed, would sooner or later disintegrate.

Yet the difference between *thrilling to* and *believing in* is rather like the Orwellian distinction between the malleability of politics and the permanence of principles. Was Butler's terrain entirely firm, I wondered, or was there a touch of the doomed counterattack against the dangers of the big, on behalf of the beauties of the small, using the contours of the past – the Irish village, the Greek city-state, the German princedom? Outside the throwback of partitioned Ireland, had not the division of Europe put paid to the nationalist nightmares of *Mitteleuropa* Butler once knew so intimately? Intellectual caution counselled, inwardly, a hedging of bets as to whether Butler's style (and style follows intellect) would outflank the historizing impulse.

Fifteen years after that review, in October 2000, I was gunning down the M50 on the outskirts of Dublin, heading for the Friday evening opening of The Hubert Butler Centenary Celebration in Kilkenny Castle. If, in the meantime, one of the two great commensal communities had disintegrated, the other was alive and well and in undoubted full flow all around. New shells of bright industrial sheds marched relentlessly into the moulded antiquity of the countryside – the Celtic Tiger churning up another counterpane of ancient hedgerow. The unnamed sites were being erected, it seemed, in the sure expectation of uninterrupted flows of inward investment. With Butler on the mind, it was impossible not to feel, with fine irony, that this emergent Ireland – the Ireland that had begun to recognize him – was nonetheless one, like the old, with which he would have strongly contended. Had he not once lamented the failure of the Anglo-Irish to renew themselves as a bulwark against the "new suffocating ascendancy" of international commerce? Or wondered aloud if "the great dams of Ardnacrusha and Poulaphouca, or the television mast on Mount Leinster, or the huge roads that level out villages and raths and eskers," would prove any more enduring than the choked canal and the forgotten railway cutting? "They are all linked with certain ways of life and thought," he held, "and ideas have never been as ephemeral as in the twentieth century" (*EA* 2).

An hour late owing to the bottlenecks of the New Ireland, I drove into a Kilkenny whose ancient and intimate contours seemed to vouchsafe Butler's lifelong feeling for the decisiveness of scale. The cars had slowed to a crawl through the twisty streets, the homely lights of small shops glimmered in the early dusk, and the back walls of the Castle overshadowed a scene of ivied continuity around the dark swirls of the Nore. When I reached the auditorium in the Castle, filled to capacity for the launch of the Celebration, Roy Foster in his Opening Address had just reached this apt metaphor, so true to Butler's own tone: "Hubert couldn't see a safely moored boat without wanting to rock it, and sending ripples out to the edge of the harbour and beyond." If Ireland was the harbour, then the Celebration promised to be the future's far shore where those expanding ripples would be given their fullest due to date in the local and national community – what AE had dubbed more grandly, and more dubiously, as "the national being". The atmosphere in the auditorium was electric with anticipation and occasion; and we were memorably launched, one felt, on an important public moment in the literary life of the island.

That expectation was borne out over the next two days of reflection, reminiscence, conversation and debate, both formal and informal. As Neal Ascherson would put it in his Closing Address, the symposium was "a rare occasion ... at which the 15-year process of honouring and establishing the work of Hubert Butler reached its culminating moment ... the planting out of a strong young tree, nursed up from seed since 1985, which from today stands in the middle of Ireland to give fruit and shade to readers and thinkers and other writers all over the world". From Julia Crampton's evocative welcome, Mayor Cuddihy's historic apology, and Roy Foster's stage-setting overview; through the three thematic Sessions, "Remembering Butler", "Butler in Ireland", and "Butler Abroad"; to Neal Ascherson's final reflections on "unfinished" Ireland – there was a distinct sense of the weekend possessing an extraordinary coherence, a real Butlerian tautness, with each formal contribution building the momentum, and often paving the way for subsequent reflections. The Celebration even had its moment of *opera bouffe* controversy when two Cork Stalinists, discovering that Butler was not the fellow-traveller they had somehow imagined – perhaps owing to the controversies in which Butler had been embroiled in the fifties, when he had been branded a "Communist" – changed tack, and began denouncing him for "racism", "élitism", and so on.

Naturally, the idea of a book arose – a founding document for the future study of the work and the man – and the result is *Unfinished Ireland*, the first publication dedicated entirely to Hubert Butler. Apart from the intrinsic interest of the contributions individually, this volume has a composite uniqueness that can lay claim to at least two major departures in published perspectives on Butler. One is that, for the first time, his work receives a substantial biographical frame. The second is that, within this frame, the balance and interrelations of the interests of this most multifaceted of writers comes clear with a new depth, and something like a general outline of the terrain of his writing emerges: a basic map, as it were, to his literary sensibility. Those much-adverted-to interests that even for dedicated admirers have seemed a little like *terra incognita* or *here-be-dragons* on the Renaissance map of his mental travels – for instance, the Irish Saints, or his Yugoslav investigations – are given their due, with the consequence that unexpected affinities between superficially disparate areas of the work now become much clearer.

In his wonderful recollection of a childhood close to Hubert, with its rich hint of metaphysics in the image of bees in their "undying dimension," Joseph Hone reminds us gently that those who knew Butler – to say nothing of those who loved him – will not always be with us. Given the late recognition of Butler, the absence of biographical recollection by fellow writers is especially acute, since many of the literary peers who might have responded to earlier success never reached the decade of his overdue appreciation. How fascinating would have been the insights of a Bowen, a na Gopaleen, an O'Faolain, a Rebecca West, all of whom knew Butler to varying degrees. *Unfinished Ireland* is, therefore, first and foremost a major gathering of personal reminiscence, full of the telling insights, incidents and detail that is the Proustian stuff of recollected intimacy or friendship.

It is a truism that, in some sense, every writer insinuates temperament into the work. It could hardly be otherwise. Rather uniquely, though, one feels in the tones, turns and tropes of Butler's style, the sinews of his temperament – perhaps the deeper translation of temperament is the very definition of outstanding writing – so that when this combines with the autobiographical tenor of many of the essays, the writing becomes a highly wrought pattern of thought and personality, a shot-silk of temperament-in-style. Thus the first section of this book, "Remembering Butler", gives something of the outward frame for this inward textual apprehension of personality, deepening our understanding of both the man and the work.

At the same time, the book's biographical picture will, I think, tend to realign the relative weight of various intellectual foci within the overall field of his writing. Just as the introduction of several heavy gravitational bodies will impact on the calculation of all surrounding orbits, so the gist of several of the contributions must change the way we visualize the balances within the oeuvre. Three necessary re-alignments, it seems to me, are made especially plain in the following pages.

The first concerns what might be called The Decision – that is, the decision to stay put on the Nore, and all its ramifying coherence throughout his life. It is alluded to by several of the contributions, and Butler himself gives it absolute pride of place in the opening sentences of *Escape from the Anthill*:

> These essays are not so heterogeneous as they look. They are all skewered together by a single idea. Or perhaps I should call it an obsession, a mental necessity that turned into a physical one. When I was a boy of fourteen I decided I was going to live in the place where I was born and where my father, grandfather and great grandfather had lived before me. It seemed an easy and obvious thing to do, since I was my father's eldest soon and he had a house and farm in Kilkenny… It was some time before I grasped how difficult this was going to be and noticed that not only was all my education slanted away from Ireland but that the whole island was titled eastwards. (*EA* 1)

We need to give this first and last credo due attention, for although it is frequently cited, it is equally often lost under a palimpsest of adult intellectual developments.

In 1914-15, after the outbreak of the First World War but before the Easter Rising, boarding at Charterhouse in England, young Hubert opts for certain return to Maidenhall. (Note the early single-mindedness, the awareness of ancestors, the imperial atmospherics.) Yet if The Decision flowed from a boy's "mental necessity", in what, exactly, did this "obsession" first originate? Reading Eleanor Burgess' fascinating cameo of Butler's early years, one is tempted by the idea that it owes something important to the rather unhappy boarding school experience in England. That is to say, by his own account, The Decision is, at root, about place, ancestry and land – about *home*. This first level of the palimpsest clearly undergirds the later youthful and more explicit awareness of Empire, nationalism, the fate of the Anglo-Irish, the Irish Literary Revival, and so forth, and not *vice versa*. Out of "the single idea" of staying put – opting for a small community in an era of escalating scale – what begins as a kind of adolescent metaphysics emerges as the deep-rooted localist ethos structuring his life, writing and commitments.

For many, the most surprising re-alignment occasioned by *Unfinished Ireland* will be Butler's decades-long devotion to research on the Irish Saints. It resulted in his only book-length text, *Ten Thousand Saints: A Study in Irish and European Origins* (1972), which he considered his most important work, though it was scarcely noticed in his lifetime (nor has been since). Here for the first time, Richard Crampton describes the immense scope of this linguistic investigation, and its recent prescient intersection with a revolutionary area of genetic research. Hence the exactitude of Hone's vignette of a rainy afternoon in the Maidenhall drawing room:

> Hubert returns to the fire, to a journal in Serbo-Croat, a tool in his long Yugoslav scholarship, then to a text in Irish, part of his equally long interest in the Irish Saints ... Tiring of the Yugoslav journals and the Irish Saints he reaches for the long shelf of French novels to his left. Picks one out at random. Starts to read it straightaway. I see the spine. It's Maupassant – *Madame Tellier's Establishment and Other Stories.*
>
> He glides through the three very different languages so deftly that they might all be the one language to him. He hears Archbishop Stepinac, Saint Columbkille and the chatter of the girls in Madame Tellier's Establishment – all in their original tongues. Where most of us see through a glass darkly in other languages, Hubert sees the light clearly in more than a half dozen of them.

Yes, that rare combination of contemporary Yugoslavia and ancient Ireland; but also, in the intellectual background, Greek and Latin at Charterhouse, the early translations from the Russian, and more generally, the student of literature and the scholar of language – in short, a *literary linguist* of the first order, whose multilingual gift is inseparable from the texture of his temperament-in-style.

Yet how did Butler visualize what he was at, his efforts as a writer and thinker, sitting there in the drawing room, without a published book, into his fifth, sixth, seventh decades? Christopher Fitz-Simon, who lived at Maidenhall as a wartime child, takes Butler at his oft-expressed self-description: "It was said that Hubert's absence of personal as well as professional vanity stood in the way of book-publishing, that he had assured a pushy interviewer that he was 'a country scholar' and had no wish to enter the urban literary labyrinth, especially if it involved Dublin." If *country scholar* risks striking us today as dilettantish, this was much less the case in the Ireland of his day, which had not lost sight of several independent traditions of rural cultural life now submerged by the centripetal pull of metropolitan civilization. For more than two centuries, the Anglo-Irish intelligentsia of the Big House, the rural polymath, and the scholarly manse had made enormous contributions to the study of Irish antiquities, natural science, and the indigenous language, to list the most obvious. Moreover, the Irish parish was cognate in this respect with the European. Figures such as Geoffrey Keating, Maria Edgeworth and Horace Plunkett had their rural parallels right across Europe in the likes of Gilbert White, Gregor Mendel or Peter Kropotkin. In reviving the Kilkenny Archaeological Society in 1944 – whose founders, Pimm and Graves, had correspondents all over Europe – Butler was staking his colours to this generalist and often solitary rural tradition, whilst consciously diverging from the collective juggernaut of academic specialization, whose central danger – the fragmentation of knowledge – would evolve into one of his most prescient themes.

Butler's radical overhauling of the linguistic origins of the Saints is unlikely to receive an easy ride, and even in this volume some of the faultlines of the potential response begin to emerge. For Edna Longley, *Ten Thousand Saints* "is another kind of genealogy which may really belong on the same 'Protestant-magical' shelf as Yeats's *A Vision*"; while Tim Robinson, though paying tribute to the depth and symbolic richness of the book, avers that "a resignedly syncretic agnosticism is the only rational attitude to the truth-value of the Lives of the Saints". I suspect that Butler would have admired the cultural sharpness or personal validity of these responses; but one thing, nonetheless, is certain: these were not the terms in which Butler understood his own labours. For him, *Ten Thousand Saints* was a *magnum opus*, a major work of trailblazing scholarship. "Nobody has managed to undermine in the very faintest degree," he remarked in 1956, a decade and a half before publication, "my absolute conviction that my method of approach is the right one and that 20 years from now the general scheme of my argument will be universally accepted."

In this light, Butler's very late essay, "Boucher de Perthes: The Father of Prehistory" (1987) is highly self-revealing. It is written in one of his quintessential modes – autobiography by proxy – and leavened by a marvellous shuffle of wit and discernment. Once one is aware that *Ten Thousand Saints* amounts to a linguistic prehistory of the wanderings of Irish and European tribes, the parallels become inescapable; for Boucher and Butler are simply working, it dawns, at different strata in the same field of prehistory. Whereas Butler probes the knowledge fossilized in tribal and place names, Boucher excavates the stone tools and bones laid down at a much more antique epoch, thereby overthrowing the Old Testament account of Creation:

> From 1838 onwards (Boucher) sought to convince the scientific world that man had existed thousands of years earlier than anyone had supposed: he had in fact discovered the Old Stone Age. He was met with the same total indifference as was later to be the lot of Mendel when he approached the leading specialists of his generation. (*CD* 95-96)

Not only does Butler situate Boucher in the pan-European tradition of the provincial solitary and country polymath described above; this essay also becomes one of his most sustained treatments of "the old jealousy between the paid scholar, who lacks freedom, and the independent one, who lacks status" (*CD* 103), as well as a reflection, in the spirit of Karl Popper, on the role imagination in knowledge:

> It is curious that even today the Father of Prehistory continues to irritate his spiritual children. It seems to them intolerable that fate should have selected this discursive old dilettante, who grew prize pears, wrote poems and plays, organized a swimming bath and, though a customs official, advocated Free Trade, to carry through a major revolution in geology and anthropology. Had they not dedicated their entire lives to such pursuits? And since collective jealousy is more potent than the individual kind, being laced with professional *esprit de corps*, some have almost managed to delude themselves that Boucher de Perthes never existed ...
>
> Boucher fully grasped that the knowledge to which he aspired could not be deep if it was to be wide. "My science", he wrote, "is only foresight", a form of intuition based on wide-ranging reflection and experiment in a dozen arts and sciences, and his

triumph was perhaps the last and the greatest of the old polymathic humanism … Boucher had greatness because he was a crusader for the unity of knowledge in an age when its fragmentation was already far advanced. His appears to be a lost cause but it is one that will always have adherents. Fighting his own battles, he was fighting for others too, the individualists, the provincial, the scholar who refuses to specialize. (*CD* 97-98, 106)

Nor was Butler unaware of the Popperesque value of the fantastical shelf: "it was just the fantastic element in Boucher's character, which, allied to his practical earnestness, made him assert the impossible and maintain it doggedly against the experts" (*CD* 102). It's not for nothing that *Ten Thousand Saints* is dedicated to Boucher de Perthes (an honour otherwise reserved, in the Lilliput volumes, for his wife Peggy); and if we want the self-image in the background of the diverse writings set out in the Bibliography at the end of this volume, it is of a country scholar in the radical mould of the customs officer of Abbeville, embarked on two overarching interests, one ancient and one modern.

As one might guess from the cohesiveness of Butler's sensibility, these two long-distance topics – the Irish Saints and the massacres of wartime Croatia – are not as unrelated as they would at first appear. A first flicker of why may be glimpsed in that earlier juxtaposition of St Columbkille and Archbishop Stepinac – two great prelates, one ancient and one modern. But the degree to which the two topics form a fascinating thematic continuum, across which Butler moves as effortlessly as between Irish and Serbo-Croat, can felt as the third re-alignment prompted by *Unfinished Ireland*. Like a binary star, the orbits of the Saints and the Massacres are held in some sort of overall gravitation of meaning.

First off, if his interest in the Irish Saints flows seamlessly from his localist ethos and the devotion to neighbourhood and place that informs it, the same is true of his interest in Yugoslavia, albeit in an experiential rather than ancestral way. Having lived there for three years, between 1934 and 1937, Yugoslavia, he tells us late in life, "is the foreign country I know best" (*EA* 8). Although during his stay he crisscrossed the six nations of that complex and post-imperial state, he was based in Zagreb and Dubrovnik, and it is clear that Croatia (especially its Dalmatian coast) constitutes the heart of the long Yugoslav sojourn in both emotional and geographic terms. The interpenetration of the two parishes, the Irish and the Croatian, is one of the controlling wellsprings of his work. In his reflection on Butler's relation to Christianity, Robert Tobin reminds us of how much the Balkan experience was a background benchmark for his attitudes to the Irish Churches, particularly his challenging stance on ecumenism. At the same time, John Casey is surely correct in identifying a widened sense of Irish place as the key to his genius for cultural empathy:

> Nor was it simply his temperament, his quality of sympathetic
> attentiveness, though that counts for a lot. I think he could not
> have learned and appreciated so much of another place had he not
> first educated and then enlarged his sense of place at home. And
> I think he developed here in Ireland a notion of life that is both
> an element of his style and worldview. No, not worldview —
> worldview is a perspective from afar and may be an ideological
> siren song offering final answers. Butler was sceptical of siren
> songs and final answers.

Clearly, the study of the Saints was a later part of his enlarged sense of place; and more generally, that "notion of life" is part of the imaginative aquifer never far from the surface of his thoughts. The focus on the particular, the belief in local history, the fatuousness of "the pseudo-cosmic disease": these, John Banville suggests, are part of an all-of-a-piece vision rooted in a rare authenticity of perspective; one flowing, moreover, from The Decision, though equally applicable to non-native ground.

Important as Butler is on the Holocaust, Yugoslavia was undoubtedly the central case study for his reflections on "the new passionate racism – the disease of the twentieth century". If his interest in the Saints arose from the scholarly life (one comprising his "pleasant constructive planning for the revival of archaeology" in the form of the Kilkenny Archaeological Society), then Yugoslavia was pressed upon him more urgently by his life-in-history, the crucible of his personal experience of a country that had been engulfed by a genocidal sectarianism, "the most bloodthirsty religio-racial crusade in history, far surpassing anything achieved by Cromwell or the Spanish Inquisitors" (*EA* 284).

In his illuminating overview of Butler's thinking on nationalism, Terence Brown helps us to locate the field of meaning in which the Saints and the Massacres orbit: the origins and dynamic of racial solidarity.

> Like subsequent theorists of nationalism (the Ernest Gellner of
> *Nations and Nationalism* immediately springs to mind), Butler in
> this essay ("Fichte and the Rise of Racialism in Germany," *circa*
> 1936) does not presume that racial feeling or indeed any kind of
> nationalism is a given of the human condition. It emerges as a
> consequence of circumstance. As such racial sentiment "seems
> always to have represented a transitional and regressive phase in
> the history of peoples, a disorganized period when a settled

equilibrium has been disturbed". In ancient times primitive man both in hunter-gatherer and settled communities had no need of racial sentiment. In such conditions "it is clear that the community is a spiritual rather than a material fact, and its preservation or destruction does not depend primarily on aggression or blood kinship or other physical factors ..."

In the ancient world, however, droughts, floods, pressure from other tribes, often uprooted a community and set it wandering, making it prey to feelings of "racial solidarity", until the group once again became settled and "under the influence of property, sentiment attach[ed] itself to the country and its institutions, not to race". In fact its members became civic nationalists and abandoned ethnic nationalism, in the terms recent theorists of nationalisms have frequently deployed. Yet in such peoples "the habits and feeling of nomadic life lie there still in germ, and at a threat the people" will regress to racial solidarity. Among modern nations, Butler then declares, the Germans were the first to experience and to justify such a regression, following their defeat by Napoleon's forces. At that moment (and throughout the essay an implicit analogy is being drawn with the Germany of the 1930s, reacting against the defeat of 1918) they were already "dispersed and divided" and under the pressure of conquest, all too likely to adopt racialism as a unifying force.

Here the thematic continuum between the Saints of the linguistic scholar and the elucidation of "the new passionate racialism" by the prose artist comes clear. In *Ten Thousand Saints,* the subject is the migration of tribes in Irish and European prehistory; whilst across much of the rest of his writing, there is a fugal meditation on varieties of nationalism in contemporary history, culminating in the great septet of Yugoslav essays. Unlike the current conventional wisdom, which sees nationalism as a quintessential product of the last two centuries, Butler takes a characteristically longer and more iconoclastic view, holding tenaciously, Brown concludes, "to his theory that racialist nationalism is a product of displacement and dispersal," and to the implied corollary that the contemporary phenomenon is an avatar of antique, even archaic, provenance.

There can be few writers whose work achieves such panoptic historical range through the infusion of the parish with the universal. Butler, in fact, might be best seen as an "artistic philosopher" of the various meshed levels of human being – local, regional, national, continental, global: arguing from the start that the century's human energy and focus must be shifted back to the first two of those adjectives, which sustain the health of the rest. To this already exceptional literary range, he adds temporal breadth: he is interested in the thread running from the prehistory, to the contemporaneity, of human community. Hence his interest in far-flung utopian communities encountered in both Irish and American settings, as Christopher Merrill reminds us; hence, too, the close interrelation between The Decision to stay put on the Nore, his commitment to the civic nationalism of Wolfe Tone, and his thinking on the centrality of neighbourliness as an antidote to the anthill and its mass-media ravages.

So where does one place Butler, in a writerly sense? Strangely, the question is not much ventured upon by those (in the main Irish) who have written about him. The general assumption, well-illustrated in this volume's Selected Critical Bibliography, seems to be that he is a last mellowy efflorescence of the great Anglo-Irish tradition of Swift, Yeats, Shaw and Bowen, a late scion of the Literary Revival. This of course is true as images go, and by his own account he might be described as a remnant of the Anglo-Irish intelligentsia; but there is, equally, something cramped about this mantle. Like all genuinely major writers, there is a point where the *sui generis* transcends the background it simultaneously distills. Kafka is German and Czech, but also belongs to a transnational pattern of sensibility that, like the Baroque or the Classical, cannot be reduced to a national frame. What is this wider interlacing, then, in Butler's case?

Christopher Hitchens, in his recent volume *Orwell's Victory*, ventures the following observation:

> *Nineteen Eighty-Four* is the only English contribution to the literature of twentieth-century totalitarianism, able to stand comparison with Silone and Koestler and Serge and Solzhenitsyn. It is a summa of what Orwell learned about terror and conformism in Spain, what he learned about servility and sadism at school and in the Burma police, what he discovered about squalor and degradation in *The Road to Wigan Pier*, what he learned about propaganda and falsity in decades of polemical battles. It contains absolutely no jokes. It is the first and only time that his efforts as a novelist rise to the level of his essays.

Admirers of Butler will immediately feel that Hitchens errs with that "only". As so often with the Anglo-American literary world, the Irish zone is overflown. (Particularly surprising with Hitchens, a professed admirer of

Butler). Indeed, many of those same admirers will feel almost all of Butler's work equals or surpasses Orwell's essays. One writer who has dwelt on this comparison is the American poet Martin Earl:

> Major (political) interruptions have a way of unveiling the real prescience of certain neglected authors, how their styles and what they had to say has embedded itself in our contemporary modes of reaction, often without our even being aware of it. Like spies, they spend their years mapping the blind spots, the gaps in the official versions. By uncovering the secrets of their own history they tell us something about ours. Hubert Butler combined uncommon prescience with a prose style that is born of the need to tell things as they are ...
>
> That Butler is prescient, that Butler's description of Balkan bellicosity and religious blindness does, inevitably, hold a mirror up to Ireland's own, that Butler is Orwell's heir to clear-speaking prose are all truisms which, simply for being such, must necessarily inform our initial understanding of this writer. However, beyond the surface felicities lies a subtlety of thought that surpasses Orwell's. Butler, as a writer of firm Christianity, had the more difficult balancing of paradox, and must have been challenged every step of the way to reconcile his belief with the evidence. The result is an urgency and modernity that sets him apart from Orwell. Humility and maybe a certain diffidence moved him to take on subjects which, precisely because they were of a less obvious and more intricate scale than, say, The Empire, the Spanish Civil War, and Totalitarianism, resulted in the written record of a consciousness closer to our own, a less deliberate, less monumental ego, a kind of wandering archivist who is in it for the long run.

Hitchens identifies "a power of facing unpleasant facts" as central to Orwell's ethical imagination, and the same is no less true of Butler. Little wonder that Joseph Brodsky, an ardent admirer, saw him as a "dishonesty hunter" whose most important work had to do with the successive cataclysms befalling *Mitteleuropa* in the mid-twentieth century. If Butler's Lilliputian intricacy lacks Orwell's grand historical impact, this too reflects "a notion of life that is both an element of his style and worldview" – whose very genius, and continuing power, lies in the championing of the small-scale over "a Brobdingnag of our own contrivances" (*EA* 338).

Towards the end of his contribution, with delayed astonishment, Christopher Fitz-simon wonders about Butler's long neglect: "What were the publishers *doing?*" Perusing the Bibliography, one is astounded by the earlier failure to appreciate the quality of Butler's writing, so self-confident and abundant over the four decades before the Lilliput volumes. (And such a salutary lesson in the traps of contemporary fashion and mannerism!). Thus it is the lot of certain writers to belong more to posterity than to the present, and to winter out in "the space beyond" even the most discerning energies of a culture or a period.

Looking over the whole of Butler's life and work, one senses how deeply both were marked by the brief revolutionary moment in which he came to maturity. A near-contemporary of Orwell, Butler belonged to a generation who were born around the turn of the century; who experienced the First World War and its imperial upheavals as children or adolescents; who came of age in the interwar period, which was deeply troubled across most of Europe; and who were then profoundly influenced in their forties by the experience of totalitarianism and a still more violent World War. Of the Great War's end to European empire, Butler would later write:

> Yugoslavia had been born in 1918 after the defeat of Austria-Hungary and the rise of the Succession States. For the Southern Slavs it was the fulfilment of an ancient dream of harmony between four neighbouring and kindred peoples. I was at Oxford then and there was springtime in the air. There were Serbs, Croats and Czechs, there were Irish too, all rejoicing in their new-found freedom. We all had minority problems and I was surprised that Ireland, least scarred by war, did not identify herself with the other small new states more warmly, share experiences and take the lead for which she was qualified. (*EA* 8)

It is hard to imagine Butler writing as he did if he was even five years older, or younger – that is, if he belonged *fully* either to the Edwardian war-generation, or the first generation to come of age in the new post-Versailles, post-imperial Europe. As I note in my own contribution, Butler first envisaged and then understood himself not merely as an Irish intellectual, but equally an intellectual of the larger cultural pattern to which Ireland belongs and into which it is subsumed; namely, the small nations of Europe, the so-called Succession States, that emerged out of the imperial aftermath of the First World War.

In Germany, one historian has termed this generation, in its fascist incarnation, "the generation of the unbound." Perhaps the experience of catastrophic extremism burgeoning among one's own peers, then empowered by the state, accounts for the occasional striking echo of other writers of the same generation one encounters when reading Butler. When Hannah Arendt (of whom Butler wrote) remarks that "only where men live so close together that the potentialities for action are always present will power remain with them," it might be a leaf straight out of Butler's credo, with its special blend of hope and realism. As this quote intimates, one of the most salient attitudes uniting this tough band of cognate writers is a fierce distrust of the state. Butler, Ascherson reminds us, "thought that any intellectual surrender to any state brought with it the risk of moral death." Even in his last major intellectual initiative, the founding of The Butler Society and the editing of its journal from his late sixties through his seventies, one senses the desire to escape the state-sponsored anthill by cultivating a new form of independent community. It is therefore entirely fitting (and would surely have pleased him) that The Butler Society has generously funded *Unfinished Ireland*, in whose journal the call to rebel "against the civilization of the anthill" first appeared.

In its Irish incarnation, Butler's was the generation that came of age as the old globalization of Empire, the British *imperium*, began to unravel in Ireland. Yeats was the great exemplar, deliberately choosing

> the small community, moving his heart and his body and as much as he could of his mind from London to Ireland, his birthplace. For him and a dozen other well-known Irish writers Ireland had been a larger Brook Farm, a refuge whose walls were built not by some transcendental theory but by history and geography. For a few years our most parochial period became also our most creative. (*CD* 194)

Facing the same colonial and post-colonial crossroads, Butler likewise plumped for the small community against the eastward tilt of background, education and power. The Decision, in some deep and irrevocable way, wedded him to "a notion of life that is both an element of his style and worldview". In this, he possessed a truly dissident sensibility, profoundly at odds with the civilizational grain of his centripetal century. Like many who have been marked by moments of revolutionary renewal – 1776, 1848, 1917-18, 1989 – his life and work constitute a vivifying blend of high hopes and realistic acumen. Set against the new globalization, he is a buoyant and inspiriting writer because, as he said of Chekhov, "his faith is so soberly expressed as to be proof against all disillusionment" (*ILN* 183). For even now, in the Age of Bush and Blair and Putin, there are individuals and small groups thinking along his lines.

Ireland, January 2003

Susan (Peggy) Butler, 1980s

THE HUBERT BUTLER
CENTENARY CELEBRATION

Julia Crampton

*The opening remarks of the Celebration
on Friday evening, 20 October 2000.*

Welcome to this event celebrating my father, Hubert Butler, who would have been one hundred years old this coming Monday, October 23. This weekend friends will reminisce about my father and his life. Others who never knew him will discuss his written work. I think this event, with such diverse and illustrious people taking part, would have surprised and delighted him. My mother would have considered it long overdue.

My parents were a remarkable team. It is important to think of each in the context of the other because they were a team. They were so very different, yet they complemented each other. To be the only child of such parents might seem daunting, but in reality I never was an only child. There are many here tonight, and some who will be speaking tomorrow, who considered my parents their substitute parents, or at least their mentors.

Before my grandfather died, leaving Maidenhall to my father, we lived much of the time at my mother's family house, Annaghmakerrig, now the Tyrone Guthrie Centre in County Monaghan. While we were there, a very young Joe Hone came to live with us. The Fitz-Simons, Christopher, Nick and their parents, were also part of the large household. This was at the start of the Second World War. When we moved to Maidenhall in 1941, many children whose parents were in different parts of the war-torn world came to live with us for their holidays. Among them were Eleanor Arkell whose father was in the Sudan, and the Strunz family rescued from Vienna.

My parents had a great many friends and admirers, young and old. There was hardly a day when someone did not drop in for tea on the porch, lunch or supper in the kitchen or to stay the night. Frugal of necessity, gourmet cooking was not a high priority at Maidenhall. It did not matter if the cats had chewed the ham, or if the meat was a little old. It was the company and conversation that mattered.

Staying at Maidenhall was never dull. All comers knew that that they were welcome, but risked having their heads bitten off by my gifted and strong-minded mother. If they were worth their salt, they faced the challenge. Depending upon the season one could be commanded to pick fruit, take slugs off the cabbages, feed the donkeys, make the tea, distribute flyers and stuff envelopes for some on-going interesting project or a hundred other things.

Among my father's many projects was the Butler Society that he co-founded to preserve Kilkenny Castle. The Society still flourishes and has just had its twelfth triennial rally of more than two hundred people from all over the world.

Hubert and Peggy never lost their interest in people and causes, local or world-wide. Their last crusade, though unsuccessful, with John Kirwan's help and determination, was to keep part of Kilkenny Castle as a space for local archives. Ever an organizer and leader, my mother held meetings at her hospital bedside during her final illness.

Beside the life at Maidenhall that orbited round my parents mainly under the command of my mother, my father had his other life, travelling and writing. In 1985 Antony Farrell was inspired to edit and publish *Escape from the Anthill*, the first collection of Hubert's essays, followed by four others. But his writing by no means covered all he was or did. He considered himself a market gardener. I hope the section "Remembering Butler" will fill the gap for those who did not know him. People who knew and worked with my father will, with the passing of time, become a smaller and smaller group. This meeting is, in a way, handing on this legacy, this collective memory, to those who will keep the interest in my father and his writing alive.

Joseph Brodsky, the Nobel Laureate, never met my father, ardently admired his writing, and said of Hubert: "He was, one imagines, a man of phlegmatic disposition, fond now and then of quoting Horace..." This is not my father. He was not phlegmatic! Fresh cement, however, inspired him to compose a Latin verse, not quote Horace. Joe Hone and I have hand and footprints immortalized in cement amid Latin verse. On a concrete wall surrounding a flowerbed in the garden, Hubert wrote one of his poems. The last line reads: "Fetida sub flores nostra cloaca fluit," or "Under the flowers our stinking sewer flows." So now we know where not to dig too deep.

I know Hubert would have been entertained by the Internet and all its possibilities, the ability to cross all borders, span the globe and exchange ideas freely. Type Hubert Butler into a search site on the Internet and pages and pages of information come up, ranging from references to his work on Yugoslavia; to quotes of his work used by the Canadian Broadcasting Company; to university courses making him required reading; to the on-line magazine *Archipelago*, which receives about 20 thousand hits a week. My father's essay, "The Artukovich File," is one of the most often visited archival pages in *Archipelago*.

It is extraordinary that this event is thanks to two young Americans who never knew my father or each other. They both found him through his writing. Chris Agee was one of the first people to review *Escape from the Anthill*. Robert Tobin found my father through his research while at Trinity College, Dublin. Eleanor Burgess and Rob Tobin had the idea for this event. Chris Agee then joined in and added a whole new dimension.

The sponsorship by *The Irish Times* with the support of Susan and Nicholas Mosse made the use of Butler House possible. We thank them all. *The Kilkenny People* contributed the designing and printing of all the flyers and the programmes. Thank you *Kilkenny People*, Peter Seaver and particularly Karen Doyle, the designer who has done a really beautiful job. We are grateful to The Mayor and The City of Kilkenny for making a generous contribution to help make this event a success. We also thank Paddy Friel of the Castle for allowing us to use this wonderful new space and giving the reception this evening.

Jane Wright has nobly held the fort in Kilkenny. Her family, the DeMontmorencys, have been friends and neighbours through five generations. Burnchurch, her house, is three fields away from Maidenhall.

I am so glad to see you all here. I am delighted Billy O'Sullivan and Maurice Craig are with us this evening because they knew my parents for longer than most in the audience, with the exception of my Uncle Gilbert, Hubert's only brother, who is also here tonight.

And welcome to the people of Kilkenny! Many of you knew my parents well and for many years. My father was first and foremost a Kilkennyman. I look forward to seeing you all at Maidenhall on Saturday evening, after the session "Butler Abroad".

AN OVERDUE APOLOGY

Paul Cuddihy, Mayor of Kilkenny

This apology on behalf of the people of Kilkenny
followed the opening remarks of Julia Crampton.

This evening I wish to apologise publicly for the treatment the late Hubert Butler received in Kilkenny in 1952. I wish to apologise because it is important to do so when you are in the wrong and we were in the wrong. I am not here to pardon him as he did nothing wrong.

You might ask why we need to apologise to a man who has been dead for nine years. Hubert Butler wasn't dragged through the streets or sent to Devil's Island as Albert Dreyfus was in late 19th century France. He wasn't put to death. However he was badly treated and he and his family were ostracised here in Kilkenny for a period of time.

What did he do to merit such treatment?

He told the truth about what had occurred in wartime Croatia, then part of Yugoslavia. Some people weren't able or willing to cope with the truth, so they punished Hubert Butler for telling the truth.

In order to understand fully why this happened, it is important to remember the political climate that existed in Ireland and postwar Europe at this time. The Soviet Union was expanding westward and democracy was being crushed throughout Eastern Europe. It was the time of the Cold War.

Anti-communism was rife and the "Red Scare" was real for many people. Anyone who was perceived as being anti-communist was on our side, according to public opinion.

When Tito locked up those who had collaborated with the Nazis in Croatia during the war, public opinion in Ireland and Europe was outraged when some of the people concerned were senior churchmen.

Ireland was at this time a very different society to that of today. People were inclined to be unquestioning and accepting of the *status quo*. Few people had access to second-level, never mind third-level, education. That didn't make them any less intelligent than the young people of today. Those people just didn't get the opportunities that people take for granted today. People were poor; times were bad with high unemployment; emigration was rife.

These are facts, but they are not excuses for what happened in Kilkenny.

If Hubert Butler didn't already know, and he probably did, the events of

1952 taught him the difference between having friends and acquaintances. It is important to remember that friends of Hubert Butler came from all denominations and backgrounds and they stood by him.

There were those who proved to be passing acquaintances who weren't able to – or wouldn't – stand by him.

This was to be proven when the full force of the establishment turned against him. Like another Irishman of that time, Dr Noel Browne, he stood up for what he believed was right and, like him, suffered for it.

Being a man of courage is often a lonely occupation.

However, despite his being ostracised for telling the truth, Hubert Butler rose above the controversy. While he may have been disappointed by the turn of events he wasn't embittered in the long-term. He kept his friends and kept a sense of perspective about life.

Hubert Butler didn't leave, he stayed, and was proven to be right at the end of the day.

What would Hubert Butler say to us now if he were here this evening?

If this is not presumptuous – and I apologise if it is – I think he would caution us against falling into the trap that each generation faces ... of merely exchanging one set of prejudices for another.

He might ask us to consider, and his wife Peggy certainly would ask us to consider instead: "When you leave out the names of the personalities involved in the 1952 incident, what does this episode in our history teach us about ourselves as a society?"

I think a lesson we can take from it is that all of us as individuals and as a society ought to be able to look at ourselves in the mirror and not be ashamed of what we are looking at. We have to be able to address injustice in our society and we have to stop pretending that the truth doesn't count.

Our society has come a long way since 1952. I would suggest that it has a long way to go.

Having courage shouldn't be a lonely occupation. I think that Hubert Butler would agree that a questioning society is a healthy society. I also think that we should ask ourselves this question here tonight: "Are we friends, or acquaintances, of those whom society overlooks or chooses to reject?"

In short, I believe that we should try to think for ourselves, to be willing to question our beliefs and values, and try to emulate the independent spirit of Hubert Butler. We remember here the archaeology buff, the historian, the writer, the traveller, the family man, the encourager of others, the humanitarian, and the market gardener.

Hubert Butler was all these and, what is more, he was a Kilkennyman of whom we are very proud. He remains as one whose example of fearlessly telling the truth and taking a stand for right, will be remembered for generations to come.

To Julia, as his daughter, I ask you to accept this as a full apology. I know that you will also remember the many happy times that you have spent in your family home at Maidenhall. I know too that you realise that you have very many friends here in Kilkenny.

HUBERT MARSHAL BUTLER: A CHRONOLOGY

1900	Born 23 October at Maidenhall, Bennettsbridge, Co Kilkenny to George and Rita Butler
1909-12	Bigshotte Rayles Prep School, England
1912-18	Charterhouse, England, on a mathematics scholarship
1919	Matriculates at St John's College, Oxford, as Senior Classical Scholar
1922	Graduates from Oxford
1922-26	Recruited by Sir Horace Plunkett as a librarian for the Irish County Libraries and works in Ballymena, Coleraine and Portstewart
1927	Teaches several months in Alexandria, Egypt, having travelled through Italy
1928-29	Travels in Greece, Switzerland, Austria and Germany
1930	Marries Susan Margaret (Peggy) Guthrie in June and honeymoons in Latvia, having been refused entry to the Soviet Union
1931	His translation of Leonid Leonev's novel *The Thief* published in London; teaches several months in Leningrad at the height of the Red Terror
1934	His translation of Chekhov's *The Cherry Orchard* produced at the Old Vic and published in London
1934-37	Awarded a Travelling Scholarship to Yugoslavia by the School of Slavonic Studies in London; is based in Zagreb, Belgrade and Dubrovnik; travels extensively in Croatia, Serbia, Bosnia, Macedonia and Montenegro
1935	Peggy returns to Ireland for the birth of their daughter, Julia
1938-39	Works with the Quakers in Vienna expediting the escape of Jews after the *Anschluss*
1941	Inherits Maidenhall upon the death of his father, and returns with his family; it will remain his home for the next half-century

1944	Revives the Kilkenny Archaeological Society
1947 & 50	Visits to Yugoslavia; investigates the wartime genocide under the quisling Ustashe regime in Croatia
1952	The "Papal Nuncio Incident" at a public meeting in Dublin; censured by various civic bodies for his stance on the ecclesiastical role in the Croatian genocide; is forced to resign from the Kilkenny Archaeological Society
1954	Organizes the first Kilkenny Debate
1955	Stands for Kilkenny County Council with the aim of offering "a minority voice"; is heavily defeated
1956	Visits China with an Irish cultural delegation and returns to the Soviet Union
1961-62	Travels in the American South during the Civil Rights Movement
1967	Founds The Butler Society with Lord Dunboyne and George Butler and begins his annual editorship of *The Journal of the Butler Society*
1972	*Ten Thousand Saints: A Study in Irish and European Origins* published by The Wellbrook Press, Kilkenny
1985	*Escape from the Anthill,* published by The Lilliput Press
1986	American-Irish Literary Award
1988	*The Children of Drancy,* published by The Lilliput Press
1989	Irish Book Award, Silver Medal for Literature
1990	*Grandmother and Wolfe Tone*, published by The Lilliput Press; *The Sub-Prefect Should Have Held His Tongue: Selected Essays*, published by Penguin
1991	Died 5 January in Kilkenny
1994	*L'envahisseur est venue en pantoufles*, published by Anatolia Editions, France
1996	*In The Land of Nod,* published by The Lilliput Press; *Independent Spirit* published by Farrar, Straus & Giroux, USA
2000	The Hubert Butler Centenary Celebration, 20-22 October

ABBREVIATION OF TEXTS

The abbreviations listed below are used throughout this volume whenever Butler's six books (excluding the British and French editions) are quoted, and are followed by the relevant page number. These citations are, therefore, not included in the Notes that follow several of the contributions. The full details of the six books may be found on page 202 in "Hubert Butler: A Bibliography."

CD   *The Children of Drancy* (Ireland, 1988)

EA   *Escape from the Anthill* (Ireland, 1985)

GWT   *Grandmother and Wolfe Tone* (Ireland, 1990)

ILN   *In the Land of Nod* (Ireland, 1996)

IS   *Independent Spirit* (USA, 1996)

TTS   *Ten Thousand Saints: A Study in Irish
            And European Origins* (Ireland, 1972)

HMB, with Louie in the garden at Maidenhall, 1988. Photo by Tom Crampton

PART I: REMEMBERING BUTLER

HUBERT BUTLER AND HIS CENTURY

Roy Foster

The last time I had the honour to talk about Hubert Butler in public was when I gave the address at his memorial service in St Canice's Cathedral, just across this city. Some time before, ruminating my theme, I went to visit Peggy at Maidenhall. Over a comfortable tea in the beautiful booklined room I asked her what kind of thing she had in mind. Fixing me with that well-remembered look, she enlightened me: "About eight minutes MAX", was all she said. Peggy as usual cut straight to the bone, but I'm afraid I'll take rather longer tonight. For Hubert's centenary, I want to talk about his century, as he reflected it in his life and work.

To live for a very long time is not in itself an achievement, though we sometimes talk as if it were: it depends what you do with your life. And what you do with it is at least partially dictated by the times you live through and the opportunities given to you. Hubert Butler entered the world with the twentieth century and nearly lived it out. On the day of his birth, 23 October 1900, Queen Victoria was still on the throne of a still-united Great Britain and Ireland – which she had visited a few months before. The Boer War was in progress. The Irish Parliamentary Party had just reunited under John Redmond. And two days before Hubert's birth, Arthur Griffith had founded Cumann na nGaedheal, bringing together anti-war opinion and forming the lineal ancestor of Sinn Fein. On the day of his death, 5 January 1991, the news in the papers was all about Ireland's diplomatic position regarding the oncoming Gulf War, the funding of an Irish-language television station, the Common Agricultural Policy's implications for Irish farmers, and the decision to convert the seventeenth-century Royal Hospital at Kilmainham, once the home of retired soldiers from the British Army, into the Irish Museum of Modern Art.

The news stories reflect the way that, over Hubert Butler's century, Ireland had moved not only to independence, but also – in a sense – from the periphery to the core. From being part – a central part – of the British Empire, it had become (three-quarters of its landmass, that is) an independent European republic, a process Hubert had observed and commented upon. The creation of "new" countries was a particular interest of his, and he could, with unique authority, see the Free State's birth in the same conspectus as that of Czechoslovakia or – later –Yugoslavia. In December 1943, with Europe in flux, he wrote a letter to his friend Geoffrey Taylor, literary editor of *The Bell*, who had complained that there weren't enough "facts" in an essay he had been sent:

Historical facts have that gritty, substantial feel about them only in the examination schools and their too-extensive purlieus. I discard them as building material because they are really too plastic to use except as ornament. For example, in a small state like Yugoslavia you could get a purely factual account of its creation from a dozen representative citizens, Croat, Bosnian, Slovene, Macedonian, etc., or from representatives of the various economic and religious cross-sections, and each would give a different but quite truthful picture. When Yugoslavia comes to be reorganised, facts will be so cogent and clamorous and innumerable that they will be used just as seasonings to the theoretic puddings made by the powers. Subjective considerations will weigh the most, shaped by the views of society current at the time. In 1918 the pundits of the moment, Seton-Watson, Pares, Miss Durham and others, felt queer atavistic attractions towards primitive forms of society, and were able to ignore the irresistibly dominant Austrian culture. I feel the same attraction and so have only sympathy for this astounding *tour de force*, but it is due to mental gymnastics and has nothing to do with the facts. Ireland, as a state, is the same sort of intellectual concoction, emanating probably in part, like Yugoslavia, from Anglo-Saxon brains. There are such things as real human societies, in *posse* if not in *esse*, but they are masked by these political figments, not revealed. *(GWT 46-47)*

The prescience of this doesn't need to be emphasised. It shows Hubert, at a dark and uncertain period in the history of his century, looking forward as well as back with that blend of tough realism and resilient idealism which he would come to make his own. By the time he died, the "intellectual concoction" that was the Dominion of Ireland had reorganised its status, both constitutionally and in the eyes of the world. If Ireland had become more cosmopolitan, that was an essential part of his vision too.

But not the least of the ways in which he made his life a unique and original achievement was the manner in which he established that cosmopolitanism could be practised, so to speak, at home. His early commitment (at fourteen, he tells us, the year the First World War broke out) was to staying and living in the place where his ancestors had lived – that part of the Nore Valley commanded (in its gentle way) by Maidenhall. If he left it, as he did in his twenties and thirties, to live abroad, he would return with the increment of foreign experience to illuminate Irish life. That is put much more pompously than he would have, but it is nonetheless what he did. And throughout his life and work, there is a running engagement with writers who left without intending to return. The celebrated review of Brian Inglis' *West Briton*, and the politely savage correspondence that succeeded it, is one example. But more relevant, and perhaps more characteristic in tone, is his reflection on another Irish writer who went to work in England – George Bernard Shaw. Hubert admired him on one level but – very typically – manages to relate Shaw's regrettable misjudgements and shortcomings to the fact that he left Ireland.

> It is a queer paradox that Shaw, whose international influence was greater than that of any other European writer, was yet incapable of international thinking. His tributes to Hitler, Mussolini, Stalin, his defence of the Italian invasion of Abyssinia, are appalling in their tasteless frivolity, unless one thinks of Shaw as a genius shaped like Joyce by a small community to be its gadfly but pitchforked by fate into being a World Figure. He was denationalised, a very different thing from being international; that is to say, he had no passionate regard for any particular land or people, so that there was no untranslatable residue which an intelligent foreigner could not assimilate. Hence he was popular abroad and yet had no understanding of foreign countries. He seems to have seen the Balkans, for example, through the eyes of Anthony Hope.
>
> I suppose it is idle to wonder what would have happened to Shaw had he never left Ireland. No doubt his genius would have been suffocated or cruelly cramped. And yet he carried to the end some of the stigma of the *déraciné*, and latterly he suffered badly from the pseudo-cosmic disease. That crusade for reformed spelling, for instance, has surely a rootless, expatriated sound, like Joyce's learned gibberish, O'Casey's staccato Stalinism and Yeats's intercourse with Yogis. Were these really serious experiments in literature, art, politics or religion? Or were they just the symptoms of a wild, nervous recoil from the narrow loyalties of a country which criminally failed to give nourishment to these tremendous talents? *(ILN 235-236)*

The autobiographical resonance in these rather questionable judgements is loud and clear: Hubert was preoccupied by not being "denationalised." I'll recur later to the ways in which his legacy is a prophecy about what Ireland would become at the end of the last century: one of the ways in which he was ahead of his time was in his persistent emphasis that Ireland's future would be European as well as local, that the "tilt" towards England must be corrected by adopting other angles, while remaining centred at home. And this necessarily involved, from time to time, standing at an angle to his local universe.

At the heart of Hubert's notion of being Irish, and declaring a commitment to Irishness, was an equally persistent commitment to the values of Irish Protestantism – as he saw them. It need hardly be said that this was not how some – I could almost say, most – Irish Protestants saw them: as he makes hilariously clear in an essay called "Portrait of a Minority" as well as in crossing swords with clerics and fellow-Protestants all his life, especially those who believed in not rocking the boat. Hubert couldn't see a safely moored boat without wanting to rock it, and sending ripples out to the edge of the harbour and beyond. His notion of Protestantism was not particularly doctrinal; he puts it best in the 1976 essay on Shaw which I've quoted from already. Hubert liked Shaw's definition of a Protestant as "theoretically an anarchist, as far as anarchism is practicable in human society, that is to say he is an individualist, a freethinker, a self-helper, a Whig, a Liberal, a mistruster and vilifier of the state, a rebel." At the same time he thought Shaw wasn't wrong in seeing the true nature of Irish Protestantism "distorted into conservatism and conformity by its association with an ascendancy class." He noted Shaw's expectation that under Home Rule this aspect of Protestantism would find an aggressive voice in Irish politics: but it was "splendidly argued and absolutely wrong" *(ILN* 233*)*. By acquiescence and silence, Hubert thought, battles which should have been fought for all Irish liberals had been lost, or at least let go by default.

Hubert's use of "Protestant" sometimes reflected his discomfort with the hyphenated identification "Anglo-Irish", and his repudiation of "Ascendancy": he was committed at once to affirming his tradition and descent, and proclaiming its close connection to the life of Ireland. Early on, he drew attention to the fact that houses like Edgeworthstown, Coole Park, Moore Hall and Bowen's Court, which had stood as the Big Houses of their locality, were distinct from most of their kind because they had harboured projects to create a common culture for Ireland. They connected themselves to the country at large by giving something vital to the life of Ireland, and to Irish identity. This was born out of the intellectual commitments and interests of the remarkable people who lived there – Richard and Maria Edgeworth, George Moore (father and son), Augusta Gregory, Elizabeth Bowen. In this locality, he would have added in Desart Court and Sheestown, which had backed the experiments in co-operation and the publishing ventures which he hilariously described in essays like "Anglo-Irish Twilight" and "The Auction." He also pointed out that all those houses were now tumbled into ruins.

Maidenhall survives. It is a more modest dwelling than some of these legendary houses, but its atmosphere is as distinctive and the ambition of its most famous inhabitant, whom we're celebrating this weekend, to contribute to the intellectual making of modern Ireland is a comparable enterprise to theirs. The fact that he used the label "Protestant" as unashamedly as he did raised hackles and went on raising them: though by the end of his life they were a new sort of hackles, bringing – for instance – an incoherent assault from the over-sensitised "cultural" editor of *Fortnight*. In that case, the word "liberal" seemed to add a particular odium: from the perspective of this critic, the combination of Protestantism and liberalism added up to something like a posh Unionist. This couldn't be more wrong, because for Hubert, the kind of Protestant values he enshrined were Bunyanesque: it meant bearing witness and affirming independent views. I think of Hubert when I read Yeats's superb statement in his Senate speech on divorce in 1925: "It is one of the glories of the Church in which I was born that we have put our Bishops in their places in discussions requiring legislation." No one better than Hubert, if a Bishop required putting in his place regarding projected legislation. But there is a Yeatsian parallel at work at another level here too. Chris Agee has pinpointed well what lies at the core of Hubert's work: the "ethical imagination" that is a creative imagination too.

For Hubert, the form his creativity took was, of course, writing: and writing in a very particular way, which I'll come to eventually. But for the moment I want to talk about content rather than style. As I've said, he went out into the world on his own Pilgrim's Progress and came back to Ireland. In going out into the world, he discovered his material – his calling, in a way. Aged sixteen, he had passed through Dublin still smouldering after the Easter Rising, and recognised subsequently that he was an Irish nationalist: his opinions on the subject were not altogether welcome to his family, notably his formidable mother. He has recalled this in one of his consummate little set-pieces of total recall, like a scene from Turgenev. Two Republicans arrived at Maidenhall during the Troubles and demanded money for the cause:

> My mother and I were in the porch and she danced about with fury. "I know who you are", she said to one of them. "You're Jim Connell. Take your cigarette out of your mouth when you're talking to me." He took it out and I began to scold my mother for interrupting what might have been a revealing conversation. It was only the second time I had seen a republican, and when I went back to Oxford I wanted at least to say what they were like and what their plans were. My mother answered me sharply and

> we started an angry argument. The two men looked at each other
> with embarrasment and slunk politely away. *(EA 98)*

Why this is like Turgenev, and not Somerville and Ross, is because the scene
does not resolve itself into a reassuring collusion between Big House and
disaffected tenantry: the tone, while just as funny, is bleaker and more realistic.
At twenty-one he returned from Oxford, inflamed with ideas, like one of the
characters in *Fathers and Sons*. In the years of the Irish "Troubles" up to and
including the Civil War he was a close observer of nationalism, from an "Anglo-
Irish" standpoint that was not "Ascendancy"; nor did his English education
(Charterhouse and Oxford, hilariously recalled in "A Fragment of
Autobiography") alter this. In the 1920s he came under the sway of the saintly
co-operativist and pacific nationalist, George Russell (AE) and entered the
world of Horace Plunkett, Lennox Robinson, and the Carnegie Libraries
movement; his own work in the County Libraries has been recalled at length
in a thoughtful essay. But characteristically, what preoccupied him most was the
controversy into which the Libraries movement was plunged when its
secretary, Lennox Robinson, published a short story called "The Madonna of
Slieve Dun" in a short-lived literary journal edited by Francis and Iseult Stuart
and F.R. Higgins, and backed by W.B. Yeats. The story gave offence to some
Catholic opinion-makers (though not all) and also to the Provost of Trinity,
who chaired the Libraries Board: there was a clash of threatened resignations,
and eventually the movement foundered and control of it was shifted to
Scotland. Hubert saw this – afterwards – as a mistake; Robinson's story was
not worth the loss of what could have been a potent transmitter of culture in
provincial Ireland.

I think myself that if he had read Yeats's letter trying to put backbone into
Robinson, Hubert would perforce have agreed: it is, once again, an echo of a
voice we'd recognise. When Robinson wanted to resign, Yeats told him:

> Your desire would be to escape from so much annoyance by that
> easy act but when you consider public opinion in this country I
> think you will stay where you are. You have done nothing needing
> explanation or apology. You have but claimed the same freedom
> every important writer of Europe has claimed. Neither Flaubert
> nor Tolstoy nor Dostoieffsky nor Balzac nor Anatole France
> would have thought your theme or your treatment of it
> illegitimate. Ireland must not be allowed any special privilege of
> ignorance or cowardice. Even if your resignation helped the
> Libraries for the moment it would injure them in the end perhaps

irreparably because it would injure the position of literature. We
must not surrender our freedom to any ecclesiastic.[1]

Perhaps if the Libraries movement had flourished in the form Hubert wished,
and he had taken control of it and developed it (as AE had done the agricultural
co-operative societies), we would in the long run have been the losers: for as the
Libraries movement stultified, Hubert was free to travel, to visit Eastern
Europe, and to spend two vitally important sojourns there: one in St Petersburg
in 1931, teaching English, and another in Zagreb from 1934. If his essay "Riga
Strand in 1930" is one of the most poignant observations of East European
Jewry before the deluge, to the St Petersburg experience we owe what to me is
one of his greatest essays, and one of the most moving: "Peter's Window." His
affinities with Russian culture produced his translations of *The Cherry Orchard*,
and Leonov. But above all he came to see Ireland against a background that was
distinctively European, and to believe – exactly as Yeats put it – that "Ireland
must not be allowed any special privilege of ignorance or cowardice."

Hubert's sojourn in Zagreb in the mid-1930s began the fascination with
Yugoslavia which persisted all his life, and which perhaps helped draw the
attention of the world to his writings in the 1990s. But as the shadows
lengthened over Europe he saw the dangers of totalitarianism in Western
Europe too. In the late 1930s he was working with a Quaker organisation to
help Austrian Jews to relocate to Ireland, an experience unforgettably
described in another classic essay, "The Kagran Gruppe." The opening words
convey the essence of the essay, and the man.

> I believe one of the happiest times of my life was when I was
> working for the Austrian Jews in Vienna in 1938-9. It is strange
> to be happy when others are miserable, but all the people at the
> Freundeszentrum in the Singerstrasse were cheerful too. The
> reason surely is that we have always known of the immense
> unhappiness that all humanity has to suffer. We read of it in the
> newspapers and hear it on the radio but can do nothing about it.
> *(CD 197)*

And he continued to be deeply absorbed by the question of collaboration: when
people turned their attention away from the loss of others' liberties – and their
own. It led him to reflect upon episodes which others would also ponder long
after him, such as the Jewish children shipped off from Paris to Auschwitz in the
summer of 1942. It is an unflinching confrontation of a story from which many
of us would turn away: a story which, as he points out, is full of uncertainties

and blurrings, like a fairytale or a myth of such horror that no one wants to confront the ur-version. There are, accordingly, several versions of the story of "The Children of Drancy." But it is not a myth or a fairy-tale. And part of Hubert's subject is why we turn away from the contemplation of evil, and what the banality of officialdom is allowed get away with, by depersonalising issues and removing people who suffer into the realm of statistics. "We cannot visualise them reading Babar books, having their teeth straightened, arranging dolls' tea parties. Their sufferings are too great and protracted to be imagined, and the range of human sympathy is narrowly restricted." This remarkable essay covers an enormous range in ten pages: and ends, interestingly, with Yeats. Butler rebuts C.P. Snow's rather simpleminded accusation that the sympathies of Yeats and other intellectuals with political authoritarianism lies directly behind the atrocities of Nazism.

> Yeats deliberately chose the small community, moving his heart and his body and as much as he could of his mind from London to Ireland, his birthplace. For him and a dozen other well-known writers Ireland had been a large Brook Farm, a refuge whose walls were built not by some transcendental theory but by history and geography. For a few years our most parochial period became also our most creative. If there was in Yeats a Fascist streak it derived from his disillusionment with the drab unheroic Ireland in which the dreams of the visionaries of 1916 had ended. He complained that "men of letters lived like outlaws in their own country." When he saw that Irish fascism promised to be as drab and demagogic as Irish democracy, he rapidly back-pedalled and rewrote the song he had composed for the Blue Shirts, making it so fantastic that no political party could sing it. He led the campaign against the Irish censorship and in everything he did and said he was a champion of intellectual and moral and social freedom.
>
> In all this he was an isolated figure and even in Ireland the range of his influence was very small. But in my opinion personal and parochial efforts like his did form a real obstruction on the road to Auschwitz, whereas its traffic was never once interrupted by conventional weapons. *(CD 207)*

In 1941 his father died and Hubert himself "deliberately chose the small community." He returned to Maidenhall, which became the centre of his life from then on. He focussed his writing energy on *The Bell*, working as review editor for that legendary journal, and writing some marvellous pieces for it himself. But that very year he had written a short but far-seeing essay calling for an outward-looking Ireland to take its place in a new world after the war:

> Just as our island is physically protected by the sea, there is an ocean of indifference and xenophobia to guard our insularity and save us from foreign entanglements. Whatever its political value, culturally this self-sufficiency has been and will be a disaster to Ireland as to the other small states … It is not necessary to labour the point that self-sufficiency is in fact insufficient for a national culture … Great cultures have always risen from the interaction of diverse societies. And where that interaction has been varied, easy and reciprocated, as between the city-states of Greece, or during the Renaissance, national genius has expressed itself most freely. Its flowering period has been briefer and less abundant where it proceeds from a long interbreeding between two peoples, often involuntary and conditioned by geography rather than by mutual attraction.
>
> In the eighteenth century French culture was as dominant in Germany as English culture in Ireland. In both cases the ultimate result was a bitter recoil to self-sufficiency, pedantry, mythology and linguistics. *(GWT 32-33)*

Already he had – so to speak – marched with history looking over his shoulder, from Stalin's Leningrad to Hitler's Vienna to Pavelić's Croatia, and had interrogated the questions raised in his own inimitable way. Thus he has traced the Jews of Europe from Riga in 1930, to Nazi Austria in 1938, to the transit station at Drancy in 1942. At the end of the war, the fall-out from Eastern Europe's tragic history claimed his attention once more; and the backwash, as we know, rolled as far as Kilkenny, when Hubert landed himself in hot water by calling attention to the forced conversions of Orthodox Serbs by Croatian collaborators, at a Dublin meeting which included the Papal Nuncio.[2]

Like Lennox Robinson, or Horace Plunket, or indeed W.B. Yeats, Hubert had created a seismic fallout in Irish public opinion without intending to. This did not banish him to silence. Issues like the boycott of Protestant businesses at Fethard-on-Sea in 1957, after an altercation about the education of children of a mixed marriage, galvanised him into print; to this period also we owe perhaps his most luminous essay about Irish social history, "The Eggman and the Fairies" (1960), dealing with the tragic story of the burning of Bridget Cleary near Slievenaman in 1895, by a husband and neighbours who believed she had been transmuted into a changeling by fairy intercession. Again, it's a story where others have followed in his footsteps; but even as masterly a treatment as Angela Bourke's luminous book on the subject is, to a certain extent, in Hubert's debt.[3] Both these apparently unconnected essays are dissections of rural Irish society: Hubert surgically removes a top layer to reveal the impulses and currents beneath. If nothing else, they triumphantly demonstrate that the master-essayist did not need to travel to the metropolis to find his subjects. At the same time, in the 1960s and 1970s, Hubert continued to travel and to write: China and America were added to his repertoire of impressions: his reputation in Ireland was earned as much through his long record of outspokenness, often in masterly letters to *The Irish Times*, as for what was by now an astonishing accumulation of essays, many of them unpublished, others in journals not widely read.

His "discovery" at the age of 85 came about exactly in the manner, and by the kind of agency, which both appealed to him and vindicated his own belief in local enterprise and uncompromising intellectual standards. Antony Farrell was setting up Lilliput Press from his bedroom in Gigginstown, County Westmeath, and was committed to producing a collection of Hubert's essays as his first book. He succeeded, and so did the book: once again, the ripples went far beyond the local Irish harbour. Three widely-reviewed collections followed, and two volumes of selections: accolades, prizes, interviews, critical studies. By the end of Hubert's century, he was recognised – in the USA and Britain as well as in Ireland – as one of its key commentators, who had at once kept pace with history and kept faith with his "ethical imagination", transmuting his observations of the great world-historical cavalcade, or the inexorable juggernaut, into beautifully worked and mercilessly clear-sighted essays which bear reading and re-reading. What had also become evident was the extent to which, not only his preoccupations but his judgments had been vindicated by the process of history: he had tracked what Eric Hobsbawm has described as "the age of extremes", monitoring it from a standpoint of a secular humanist (Hubert might have said, "Protestant") who had seen the value of the local and the immediate, while never losing sight of the fact that we are all – in John Donne's words – a piece of the main.

By the time he died he knew that his work had been valued; he also knew that it was worth valuing; but he had known that all along. In the most unpretentious way, he had become a sort of national icon. I was one of many who, after reading him and writing about him, sought him out: and always came away, down that swerving drive from Maidenhall, feeling the better for it. His voice still speaks with particular clarity to those of us conditioned (or perhaps disillusioned) by the various false dawns of the 1960s: but at the same time his work is pervaded by that dogged hope for a better world which affects so many characters in Chekhov. Ideal communities, whether at Oneida or New Geneva, were one of his constant preoccupations. By the time the public accolades came along, his value had been recognised by his own community, and this is certainly what meant most to him.

What he represented too, despite the gentle demeanour, the seraphic smile, the beautiful manners, was a complete preparedness to take the offensive, to carry the war into the enemy's camp, to go out and shock. There is an interesting tension here, between his chosen style of private life and his public style of engagement. The historian Eric Hobsbawm, at a symposium arranged for his eightieth birthday, declared that he thought his work would last, not because his interpretation was correct (though of course he thought it was), but because he had taught himself to write well. It wasn't necessarily an analysis one might have expected from the most distinguished living Marxist, but it points to an important truth. Hubert was – in my opinion – uncannily often in the right, but he will go on being read, perhaps for as long as Montaigne, because of his style. The beauties of his phrasing, the delicacies of his humour, the surprisingly rapid twist of the rapier make reading him a continual delight. A great deal of work went into it: he knew what he wanted to do. In that same 1943 letter to Geoffrey Taylor he described how he was developing his essay technique of "putting an idea across and working on it at the same time" and defended an essay which Taylor had found obscure: "in fact", wrote Hubert, "as I felt fairly certain where I wanted to get, and there wasn't much space, my idea was to hustle the reader (for his own good) past all the forks and turns and not picnic at each cross-roads and take him into my confidence. That would have been a different kind of journey. I was quite ready to make it, but not in that article … I usually find indirect methods the best and have sympathy with the man who gave his son a good slap so that he would remember having seen a salamander." *(GWT 46)* This is extremely enlightening: Hubert had nearly half a century of writing life left to him, but the approach was set out already. And as we read him, the sense of delighted approbation and agreement is invariably suddenly moderated by a well-placed slap: reminding us that we have just encountered something special.

Whenever one writes or talks about Hubert's work, the temptation to quote is insurmountable. Above all, perhaps, it is a question of voice: that direct, unpretentious, uniquely modulated tone which never falters or becomes strident, which asks questions of himself as well as of his readers. I might recur again to "Peter's Window", because it sums up so much of what makes reading Butler; and it is significantly an essay that ends upon a question.

His life in 1931 with the Archangelsky family and their circle is described with consummate humour and psychological insight: Kolya with his passionate, flinty "Manichaean" outlook, his mother with her agonised resentments, the Communist baroness, his friends like Lihachev and the Pole who keeps offering Hubert his aunt's bed, the Mexican Communist who combats the Russian conditions by filling her room with the perfume of lilies and jasmine: "an appalling primeval smell that was neither Slav nor Latin: Lihachev said it was Aztec." Then there is Lihachev's father, a *ci-devant* rich doctor who since the revolution has made his home a commune for all his friends and relations, but finds it lacks the sport of the old days, when they had to travel long distances to quarrel with each other. Here, as elsewhere, Ireland and Russia seem very near to each other.

In this one essay, a novel and a memoir all at once, the essence of distilled Butler can be tasted. The detail of life and relationships is conveyed in dialogue which might come out of a perfectly gauged novel:

> One day as we were queuing up outside the offices of the Lensoviet, (Kolya) tried to explain himself to me: "I am a Caucasian from Georgia, like Stalin, with the same theological background. He was a theological student. He believes like the Manichaeans that there is Good and Evil, Black and White, a dichotomy. All this which he thinks Good is Evil." He waved his hand at the Lensoviet and the long queue.
>
> "Why do you like the English so much then? They are not Manichaean. They play down all major issues of good and evil. They are loyal to small obligations, not to big ones. I can't imagine an English teacher neglecting all his classes to help the friend of friends who were once very good to him."
>
> He looked hurt, as if I had accused him of being un-English. But I had meant it as a compliment and I could not let the subject drop. I argued that social organisation works better in England, simply because the English only made superficial impact on each other. They glide about, cannoning off each other like billiard balls. They can calculate each other's reactions accurately, because they hardly ever impinge. Perhaps the reason why the Russians are difficult to organise is because they make real contact. It's like playing billiards with bull's eyes.
>
> "You forget that I am a Caucasian. That's what I hate about the Russians, always prying and enquiring about each other."
>
> I found his claim to be Caucasian as irritating as he found my claim to be Irish: "I don't think Russians could ever be detached in the tepid, unemphatic English way. You would merely isolate

yourselves."

After a pause he said, "Darya Andreyvna was catechizing my mother about you today. She thinks you are a spy and wants the house committee to turn you out. She has been to the Upravdom (the president of the house committee). Lyubotchka did her best for you. She said she thought you were a harmless idiot because you smile when you talk to her."

"I only meant to be friendly."

"Yes, but real Russians only smile at jokes." *(EA 311-312)*

Then the searchlight swings to one of his key reflections, prompted by taking part in a march to celebrate the fifteenth anniversary of Socialist Reconstruction:

Organised in processions, those whom we have known as complex individuals shed colour and character. Also there is some unconscious tabu that we violate every time we look at our friends in their public moments, which are often the moments of deepest privacy. The violation may be easy and pleasant, but it delays us for that split second between perceiving and observing. Kolya passed close by but not till he had gone did I realise that I had seen him. A column of sailors went by and I looked in vain for Lihachev. A little later I noticed a dislocation in the procession, people moderating their step behind and on either side of the baroness. She walked slowly enough for me to watch her. Her companions on either side, keeping step, held a pole from which a banner was stretched: WE ARE MARCHING TOWARDS THE CONQUEST OF TECHNICAL EFFICIENCY IN A SOCIALIST WORLD. She did not look either ironical or embarrassed. It was as if she was half asleep but sufficiently awake to enjoy her dream. She did not seem conscious of her lameness, imposing her pace with confidence on those around her.

I have thought that just as half our physical lives passes in sleep, it is perhaps intended that our mental life should be equally distributed between the assertion of our uniqueness and its renunciation. If that trance-like state of submersion in a public or collective mood bears an analogy to sleep, it would reflect our individual and self-centred lives by very simple images and phrases in dream-like sequences. In such a way, the caricatures and slogans that floated above them would complement, like dreams, the intricate, logical natures of Kolya and the baroness.

The slogans were the shadows of human thinking in which their thoughts merged restfully, just as their footsteps concurred in the broad beaten track upon the snow, and we do not expect faithfulness in tone or form or colour from shadows. *(EA 322-323)*

I still remember reading this, in 1985, and feeling so moved, so intrigued that I read and re-read the passage with mounting excitement. I subsequently tried to quote it at length in the review of *Escape from the Anthill* which I submitted to *The Times Literary Supplement*, a review which was cut down from immense length to a manageable quarter-page. But I had such a row with the editor that he took the book on holiday with him to see what the fuss was about – and was converted at once. Hubert's next collection had the lead review, from John Bayley. A handsome acknowledgement, but no more than his due.

The passage remains resonant, because it is about individualism and political commitment. At the end of "Peter's Window", the searchlight swings forward again – or one might vary the metaphor and say "telescope", because that is the image used by Hubert himself, as he re-visits the heroic city twenty-odd years later, finds all his friends disappeared, and is taken by an Intourist guide – Anna – to survey the rebuilt city through a telescope in a viewing-park above the Gulf of Finland.

I traced the Neva till it veered southwards by the Finland Station and the Summer Palace. To the north I saw the islands where I had walked with Yegunov and his dog. They were now called the Kirov islands, Anna told me, and the great highway that led to them was called Kirov Avenue. Thousands of honest men and women died because of Kirov, but their names are nowhere recorded.

I have forgotten much of what Anna told me but I am more inclined to apologise for writing about great events, which touched me not at all, than for tracing again the tiny snail track which I made myself.

Is it not obvious that when through the modern media far things are brought near, the near things must be pushed far to make room for them? Imperceptibly we become Lilliputians wandering in a Brobdignag of our own contrivances and persuading ourselves that through contact with greatness we ourselves become greater. Then something happens to jerk us back to thoughts and people of our own size and significance.

> Most of the time when I was looking through that telescope, I was thinking not of the tremendous disasters that had befallen Leningrad and all Russia, but of the small stupidities, the acts of laziness or greed I had committed myself. Why had I not given the blue rug to Kolya's mother instead of leaving it behind by mistake? Why hadn't I sent Guzelimian his fishing-rod? *(EA 338)*

Great themes of Russian history, of Irish consciousness, and of human destiny focus down to the blue travelling-rug and the fishing-rod. It is worth, perhaps, quoting an unpublished reaction to reading this essay, from Isaiah Berlin – who knew, and thought, as much about the sacrifices of humanity to abstract principle, and the scars of Russian history, as anyone. After reading "Peter's Window" in 1990, Berlin described it, in a characteristic blend of enthusiasm and sombreness, as

> absolutely delightful – touching, charming, unlike anything else, and the atmosphere is conveyed marvellously. His Russian was obviously adequate, though from time to time he does produce some non-existent forms of the language, as you might imagine. The relationships of the people living in the house are wonderfully described – I see them before me, and so do you. I fully understand why he did not send Guzelimian his fishing-rod. I think that, like me in 1945, he lived to some degree in a fools' paradise, and that his visit probably did do some of these people a certain degree of harm, which is why he didn't find them again in 1956. I was in Leningrad in the same year but did not seek anyone out – I thought I had probably done enough harm – certain[ly] Akhmatova thought I had. The only thing which astonishes me is that in spite of his foreign currency black roubles, the people he lived with had as much food and good things for their parties and lived in such relative comfort as in fact they did; by 1945, I can assure you, none of this was any longer possible, and not just because of the war; 1956 was no better. One doesn't know now. What he came across were the last relics of the old regime, lurking in the nooks and crannies of the new. Thank you ever so much for sending it to me – it made the first third of my flight to America totally happy.[4]

It is apposite to invoke Isaiah Berlin, and indeed Eric Hobsbawm, because they share with Hubert a preoccupation with nationalism in the modern age.

Berlin has written more illuminatingly than anyone about the philosophic roots of nationalism in German Romanticism; Hobsbawm has, more and more, focussed his scholarly attention on the development of twentieth-century nationalism rather than the progress of labour relations, as one of the forces driving us to the age of extremes. Hubert was, in a sense, ahead of them; early on he grappled with the relationship of religion to nationalism in Central Europe, and though he was at first over-optimistic about the fading of fundamentalist values, by the end of his life he had revised his opinion. "Religion", he had written in 1958, "which once rampaged like a shark, devouring everything which could not escape, now feeds itself like some non-poisonous jellyfish groping for plankton with sensitive tentacles" *(EA 209-210)*. In the age of the rediscovered jihad, East and West, this was a bit too much to hope for. Similarly, Hobsbawm had, at the end of the 1985 Wiles Lectures in Belfast published as *Nations and Nationalism Since 1780*, speculated that we were coming to understand nationalism, Hegelian-style, because it was now a phenomenon that was passing: but again, he had to change his mind. Hubert's relationship to nationalism was always more realistic than this; it is woven through his commentaries, autobiographical and philosophical as well as political. In "The Auction", for instance, there is a feline passage where he presents the Anglo-Irish gentry's interest in tuberculosis as a strategy for defusing nationalism in Edwardian Ireland, and implies that they saw them both as parallel infections.

> (Tuberculosis) was one of those rare and blessed battle-cries, like co-operative creameries and village halls, which appeared to have no political or religious implications. Indeed it was better than either, for often a priest wanted to consecrate a village hall or put a crucifix instead of a clock above the rostrum, and there were rumours that the creameries were used for political agitation when the farmers' boys for miles around, having taken their milk-churns from their donkey-carts, had leisure for exchanging views. But nobody could say anything of the kind about tuberculosis. When my mother had started a branch of the Women's National Health Association in Bennettsbridge, Lady Aberdeen (crusader against tuberculosis and wife of the Lord Lieutenant) had come down and talked to the Association and driven round the neighbourhood. My sister had sat on one side of her and Miss Foley, the priest's sister, on the other, and Mrs Cuffe beside the chauffeur. It was an immensely amiable, non-political, non-religious occasion. Tuberculosis acted like a love-potion, and

at the end of it we children distinctly heard Miss Foley say, "A thousand thanks, Countess, for my most delightful drive." With the savage snobbery of children, learning for the first time the exciting art of speaking in inverted commas, we had pestered each other for months and months with poor Miss Foley's over-unctuous gratitude. So now tuberculosis, which had once seemed a sordid, almost shameful secret between the doctors and the dying, was invested with dignity and importance. Now that it was made everybody's business, it attracted to itself not only the tender and the charitable, but also the ambitious and the interfering and the timid, who saw that sympathy for the sick might be interposed as a fluffy bolster between themselves and Home Rule which they saw irrevocably approaching. (GWT 17-18)

This is a pointed critique of those who take to do-gooding in order to take shelter from a coming – and necessary – deluge: in this case the national independence which Hubert believed necessary. Where "nationalism" might be taken to mean "national commitment", his commitment is unequivocal, and this stringency pervades his attack on Brian Inglis' autobiography. It is one of Hubert's most passionate pieces of polemic because, after a fair appreciation of Inglis' description of old Malahide Protestant "society", the atmosphere of *The Irish Times,* and so on, he excoriates Inglis for leaving Ireland to become "an important London journalist" instead of staying in Ireland and showing that the Southern Protestant tradition could provide more exemplars of an Irish way of life than "the handful of old country crocks, retired British servicemen, civil servants and suburban car salesmen in whom the spirit of contemporary Anglo-Ireland has its incarnation" *(GWT* 140). Inglis is a "defeatist", in Hubert's view, because he believes that in the overwhelmingly Catholic Republic, the large issues of church-state relations, and the moral law as expressed through political legislation, are "barred" from discussion by the tiny Protestant minority:

Irish Protestants constitute 25 per cent of the population of Ireland, north and south, yet those of the Republic enjoy telling each other and being told either that they have no stamina or that they would "only do harm by interfering." In this way they can free their minds from the unglamorous complications of Ireland and the dreary forms of bloodshed which they foresee. They have an excuse for whatever form of disengagement may be comfortable and for devoting themselves agreeably to what they call "wider issues" in a larger society. But for a small historic community can there be any issue wider than survival and the prevention of bloodshed?

"Outsiders only make things worse by intervening." Chicago gangsters have grown fat on this repulsive old sophistry ... moral cowardice dressing itself up in a diplomat's bemedalled frock-coat. The great Protestant nationalists did and said what they thought to be right and never argued that they could help their friends best by withholding their support from them. Nor did they consider themselves "outsiders." (*GWT* 142)

It is Hubert at his most fire-breathing, and it is not entirely fair. Not only does he elide "Protestant" and "Anglo-Irish", in a way he scrupulously avoids as a rule, but he carries out a piece of fancy statistical footwork by suddenly compressing the Protestant populations of North and South to arrive at twenty-five per cent of the whole (1962 figures), when Inglis' whole point is that he is reflecting the position of Protestants in the Republic alone. Inglis has, of course, committed most of the cardinal sins in Hubert's canon, so it is open season. The arguments are not always just, but they reflect Hubert's deep-rooted commitment to fighting for a secular constitution: and his belief that the more separate Northern Ireland became from the rest of the island, the more it would resemble what George Bernard Shaw had prophesied at its inception, "an autonomous political lunatic asylum." [5] This, it must be admitted, has its resonances forward. Again, on the subject of national culture, Hubert was ahead of his time: in that notable essay called "The Barriers", written in 1941, he argued for exchange of ideas, celebration of diversity, and acknowledgement of difference, anticipating the approach of initiatives like the Cultural Traditions Group in Northern Ireland in the early 1990s.

The problem of a struggling national culture is thus an international one. It can preserve itself only if the spiritual channels by which it can communicate with foreign cultures are kept free and its intercourse is equal and reciprocal. In Ireland intercourse with England only was possible and that could not be on equal terms. Anglo-Irish culture, which should comprehend all literature from Swift to Edgar Wallace in translation, could never become the focus of a nation. The same might be said of the old Austrian civilization, on which the Succession States of Eastern Europe tried to base their new national cultures. It was too strong and powerful to be assimilated. As soon as this was apparent, they dedicated themselves, like Ireland and the new states of the Baltic, to cultural self-sufficiency. Their only contact with each other was through consuls and diplomats, tourists and bagmen, and always in the interests of politics or commerce. There was none of that easy social intercourse by means of which the cultural centres of the Middle Ages were nourished. These little states were formed to protect and foster small cultural units. They failed. Everything that was unique and spontaneous in their national life was smothered behind the barriers reared to protect it. *(GWT 33-34)*

Hubert Butler's century is over now, but in the Ireland of 2000 there is no shortage of issues which reflect closely upon his preoccupations and which he, in a sense, taught us to think about. One need go no further, regarding the sort of ideas I've just quoted, than the speech of Síle de Valera in Boston last September, as Fianna Fáil Minister for the Arts, arguing for the erection of just the kind of cultural barriers, and expressing just the kind of suspicion of European influences, which Hubert so often combated. And, regarding the necessary secularisation of the state, one thinks of him when one hears – as I recently heard – of a current exercise in a Dublin institution of higher education where first-year history students are given extracts from works of history and asked to guess the religion of the author – and therefore their supposed "bias." He should indeed be living at this hour: not only because his work is coming into the kind of recognition it deserves, but because the controversies and problems in Irish life which Hubert went out and jousted with are still around us.

Some come dressed in the old fustian, like Ms de Valera or that confessionally-minded Dublin history lecturer: others appear in new ways. This symposium will in all probability take them in, but one might indicate questions like the civil rights of refugees, the reversal of emigration, the future of "green" politics, the revelations of political corruption, and the binge of national commemorations that dominated national life from 1995 to 1998 – often based on ideas of "national memory" which relied on the mechanisms of psychobabble and feel-good populism rather than historical or philosophical enquiry. When an *Irish Times* columnist can postulate as a profound mantra the message that "we must remember what we never knew", you are free to judge it as either an emotional truth so profound that it transcends rationality, or as self-indulgent idiocy.[6] I have a notion which side Hubert would be on, and I wish he were here to clarify the case for keeping "false memory syndrome" in the place it belongs.

His own memory stretched over this turbulent century both in personal and historic terms. His sense of the need for secularism, his observations of fundamentalist politics, his redefinition of the real message of Wolfe Tone deserve to be remembered as we confront the most immediate of all those crises which loom around our own "small community" – the state of what used to be called the national question as the peace process staggers into a new reverse. He was very conscious of "the border" – it's a recurring image in his writing – and not just because he had a lot to do with setting up the Tyrone Guthrie Centre at Annaghmakerrig in his wife's ancestral home, a stone's throw from the border with Northern Ireland which he had seen come into being. In 1955 Hubert wrote about the border, in a manifesto that was never published, for a magazine that never got off the ground:

> A pessimistic Ulsterman once told me that there were not enough borders and that in his opinion we should make a few more down South. A period of appalling cosmic boredom was ahead of us and the only hope was to diversify it a bit by interposing frontiers. They might delay the passage of the mass-produced standardized ideas and emotions with which we are being overwhelmed.
>
> I think he was wrong. Borders do not keep out vulgarity and stupidity. The only way of keeping them at bay is to have an intelligent and vigorous public opinion. At present there is, south and north of the border, an almost unbelievable spiritual stagnation. A dumb stupid antagonism breaks into an occasional muffled snarl or jeer. Where there is disagreement there should, at least, be the stimulus of conflict. It is from challenge and response that civilizations have risen in the past. Why are our differences so unfruitful?
>
> Here is one reason. Too many people would sooner be silent or untruthful than disloyal to their side. From cowardice they keep their private opinions suppressed till they have a chance of becoming public ones. Then they burst out with the force of an explosion. What should be said is blurted. There are clarion calls and crusades and political landslides and united fronts, but the art of free controversy was never so neglected.
>
> Timid or stupid people often enjoy times of crisis. They can suspend, for the country or the cause, those careful discriminations which tire the brain and do no good to the career. *(GWT 65)*

These are among the most characteristic words Hubert ever wrote. Constitutionally incapable of being either timid or stupid, he devoted himself to thinking tirelessly about careful discriminations and cared very little about his career. He broke taboos, notably the taboo whereby criticism of official thought-control in Ireland was so often left to liberal Catholics because Protestants felt it was bad form – like poor Brian Inglis – to refer to the public position of the Catholic Church in independent Ireland. But in that same 1955 essay, Hubert was equally scathing about Catholics within Northern Ireland who preferred to bide their time and hope for a quiet takeover through demographic change – instead of confronting the nature of the state and exploiting its potential for pluralism:

> "Time is on our side," they are saying. "We breed faster than they do, and Ulstermen with imperial responsibilities are leaving Ulster or neglecting it. The Province has the artificial vitality of the garrison town and no organic life. If ever the pipeline were cut, it would perish. Fermoy is ours today, Enniskillen will be ours tomorrow." That, no doubt, is how the Britons exulted when, after the Romans left and for a few short years before the Saxons came, they surged back into Verulam and Caerleon. It is an argument as sound as it is hateful. Yet few southern Irishmen would wish to absorb Ulster like greenfly invading a neglected tree, like Poles pouring into German Silesia or Czechs into Sudetenland. Ulster would no longer be of value to Ireland if she were robbed of her rich history, her varied traditions. If she gives up these, which link her to the rest of Ireland, and becomes a mere imperial outpost, she will deserve the fate of Breslau and Fiume and Konigsberg. On the other hand if she keeps her Irish character the border will slowly cease to be a menace and an anxiety. Either it will become meaningless and will drop off painlessly like a strip of sticking-plaster from a wound that has healed, or else it will survive in some modified form as a definition which distinguishes but does not divide. *(GWT 67-68)*

Nearly half a century later, the time has come to pay attention to this, as to so many of Hubert's formulations. His acuteness and prescience about Ireland, about Europe, about Ireland in Europe will ensure his continuing influence; but, as I've tried to outline this evening, that perception, those preoccupations, are based on philosophic foundations and literary genius which put him in a far greater tradition than simply that of political commentator or historian. In an age where the intellectual market is dominated by vast, distended, catch-all histories, churning out words which say nothing at all, Hubert stayed in his few fields along the Nore, and in essays which often covered fewer than ten pages said more about world history than the most inflated blockbuster or television series. The view from the front porch of Maidenhall is emblematically Irish, but it stretches far beyond the water-meadows, the river, the distant ruined Norman castle and much older Celtic church: west to American utopias, east to Sarajevo and Riga Strand, sweeping through lost memory, failed aspirations and great hopes, like the telescope trained on the Nevsky Prospekt in "Peter's Window."

An expanded version of this address appeared in The Irish Story: Telling Tales and Making It Up in Ireland *(2001).*

NOTES

1 See Daniel J. Murphy (ed.), *Lady Gregory's Journal* (Gerrard's Cross: Colin Smythe, 1978, 2 Vols) Vol 1, pp. 563-566.

2 See Hubert Butler, *The Sub-Perfect Should Have Held His Tongue*, and Appendices to *Escape from the Anthill*.

3 Angela Bourke, *The Burning of Bridget Cleary* (London: Pimlico, 1999).

4 Isaiah Berlin, letter to Roy Foster, 22 January 1990, copyright with the Isaiah Berlin Literary Trust (quoted with the Trust's permission).

5 Quote by Paul Arthur in *Political Quarterly* 79 (2000) p.128.

6 See John Waters, quoting the Native American artist Jimmie Durham, in *The Irish Times* 11 October 1994.

HUBERT THROUGH THE SEASONS

Joseph Hone

Since I grew up in Maidenhall with Hubert, I have vivid images of him. Perhaps I can resurrect some of them.

Let me choose a precise day, a morning in late summer 50 years ago. He's shaving, sees the warm day coming up outside, no wind. Ideal – for what? I think I know his thoughts that morning. A few hours later – yes, he's there. I see him now. A tall, slightly awkward figure, an old pair of flannels, belted with an older tweed tie, a ragged honey-smeared green flannel shirt, buttoned to the wrists, gloves, smoker bellows in hand, a felt hat – and a bee veil. He's dabbing furiously over one of the open beehives on the front lawn.

The sun is hottish, the bees angry. I can hear their distant outraged hum. From the safety of the porch, I see Hubert very clearly. Now, entering some Einsteinian space-time continuum, the historic past, in which Hubert and his bees lived, has not gone. He and his bees and that late summer day have long since been removed into another plane of existence, where the day continues, with his life, where he is active and available.

Despite the all too clear evidence of organic decay in our lives – now I can suspend belief in that decay. Somewhere Hubert and his bees are still at it, living in a hidden parallel world, where he can move to and fro in time, from that morning on the front lawn, in his old belted flannels, the bees an angry swarm above his head.

And so – an hour later, I am still there, wary in the porch, and Hubert is digging out the small honeycombs from their waxy beds in the hive, the hives, right down the line. And then the same with the larger honey frames, from the last hives.

And now it's tomorrow and the frames are in the oak-barrelled honey separator in the pantry, the handle turning. The honey is spinning out inside, the whole room dripping with honey. And I have the smell – the thick sweet smell. Hubert's turning the handle, I'm turning it, we're all turning it. Now it's next day, and the same, and finally the bottling of it.

And as the year, that particular year, begins to turn, falling into September, it's autumn. Hubert is shaving again, and I'm sure I know his thoughts now. It's apple time. The risen fruit – red-cheeked, yellow, brown. The early Worcesters and James Grieve, the Conference pears in the main garden, the Coxes in the big orchard. The chip boxes to get ready in the basement, the pickers to pick, Joe to be persuaded to join in. Hubert, like me 50 years later, can smell those

Maidenhall apples, the tart-sweet odours, as he shaves. Another day, taken out of time, where he lives again, and is about to storm the orchard, in that other undying dimension.

Winter. The drawing room. There is always a fire. He is in the high-backed red covered chair. Legs crossed, slippers. He's older now. It's winter. The face longer, thinner, sculpted, eyes a paler blue. Gazing at the fire a moment. Returning to his book. A book of the Saints. His face like one.

But in a winter long before – I'm about 12 – the two of us are out in the yard stables, with the big cross-cut saw. Hubert is feeling suddenly energetic and I've been press-ganged again. There's been a gale, trees down in the inches. There's the huge pile of wet branches behind us. We start off at quite a pace, getting through the mossy bark easily enough. But soon the teeth are getting stuck in the wet wood. The saw wrenched out – fumbled in again, and stuck again. I say "It's pretty useless, isn't it?" The rain is pelting down outside. There is his frustrated determination then – "No, let's go on." Another minute or two. Stuck again. Another five minutes – and we pack it in. Rain. Rain and wind. Hubert returns to the fire, to a journal in Serbo-Croat, a tool in his long Yugoslav scholarship, then to a text in Irish, part of his equally long interest in the Irish Saints. I bring the tea in. Peggy is away. The house is empty. No TV then, or radio. No electricity. Lamplight. I'm reading an old cricket book, *The Fight for the Ashes, 1932-33*. There is nothing to do but read and listen to the rain. And the spaniels snoring by the fire. Tiring of the Yugoslav journals and the Irish Saints he reaches for the long shelf of French novels to his left. Picks one out at random. Starts to read it straightaway. I see the spine. It's Maupassant – *Madame Tellier's Establishment and Other Stories.*

He glides through the three very different languages so deftly that they might all be the one language to him. He hears Archbishop Stepinac, Saint Columkille and the chatter of the girls in Madame Tellier's Establishment – all in their original tongues. Where most of us see through a glass darkly in other languages, Hubert sees the light clearly in more than half a dozen of them.

But winter sometimes when the house is full. A party, a celebration, or the Kilkenny debates. People are arriving, by chance or to stay. The "Pope" O'Mahony bustling in out of the blue, having hitch-hiked all the way from Dublin, his hands full of muddled books, papers, letters, magazines – "an outrageous article, Hubert, I had to show it to you at once." Such is his brio as he crosses the drawing room that half the papers fall. I pick them up. Some are wads of blank notepaper, headed the Hibernian or the Shelbourne Hotel. "You must write a letter to *The Irish Times* at once, Hubert – an outrageous slur on that decent Anglo-Irish family. Here, I've written a letter for you." And he hands him a letter, on notepaper headed "The Kildare Street Club."

And the next afternoon the arrival, in a little black Ford, of Myles na Gopaleen, driven down from Dublin for the debate. Hubert, Peggy and I are out on the gravel to welcome him. Myles is next the driver, a small suitcase on his lap. But he can't open the door. A smile – he waves vaguely at Hubert, like Marie Antoinette in a coach. Hubert pulls the handle, Myles pushes. And suddenly Myles flies out onto the gravel, all in a heap, the little cardboard case flown open, spilling its only contents on the gravel – a pair of dirty pyjamas and a half-full bottle of Jameson. The dogs start to worry at the tasty pyjamas. The bottle rolls slowly to a stop. But Hubert has seen nothing. "Myles, how nice to see you. I think you're in the Green Room."

An earlier winter. We children are up on the top floor playroom, at lessons – of a vague sort – with Miss Goulding, the acid ogreish yellow-haired governess. There is a big red felt screen by the door. Suddenly heavy footsteps charging up the stairs. The door flies open, the screen falls with a great crash. And Hubert is there, thundering in stage left, vengeful, fire-breathing, a figure in a pantomime come to save hero and heroine from the wicked witch. "How dare you tell the children not to speak to the maids, Miss Goulding! How dare you say it was vulgar to speak to them. You will take your notice at once."

Uproar! Joy! No more lessons. Miss Goulding leaves that afternoon. The garden boy takes her to the Bennettsbridge station in the pony and trap. The pony and trap are abandoned at the station and she takes the garden boy on the train with her to Waterford, for the boat to England. The Guards are called. A great buzz in the house. The sensation continues. The two of them are found taking tea in the Adelphi Hotel. The garden boy is brought back in some confusion. But Hubert has promoted his liberal ethic in a most palpable, unforgettable way.

Spring, years later. I've come into the drawing room for some reason. Hubert is writing at the desk by the window. But he's not writing. He's lost to the world, gazing over the lawn, the valley, across the river to the mountains beyond, the Blackstairs and Mount Leinster to the left, half hidden in cloud. I wonder what he's writing? I think I know now.

"I have lived most of my life on the Nore … In 60 years the view has changed very little. Looking across the river towards the Blackstairs and Mount Leinster, I can still see the same stretch of cornfields, nut groves and mountain slopes. Beside the woods of Summerhill and Kilfane I can spot the round tower of Tullaherin and Kilbline, the 16th century castle of the Shortalls. There is only one new cottage in sight."

Spring, and the daffodil-picking, lush gold carpets of them, all over the lower lawn, but planted in various patterns in previous years, circles, spelling out people's initials. Picked, they must be counted and bunched in dozens for the country market. "Joe, we need help with the daffodils." Joe is not too keen. The stalks, greasy with sap, will get my hands all sticky and why not leave the daffodils nicely on the lawn where they are? "Oh, Joe, do stop talking rot."

Spring turning to summer, and Hubert is in the humour now, abandoning Archbishop Stepinac, Saint Columkille and Madame Tellier. For the bees and their hives this year are to be loaded up on a lorry and taken up to the gorse and wild flowers on the mountains across the valley.

But a woman, a journalist, is coming from England to see him. She upsets the bee-moving business. But Hubert, always polite and welcoming, drops everything and welcomes her – big, a very big, masculine hearty woman with short cropped hair and rapid-fire dismissive talk, in a throaty gin-and-tonic voice. Miss Tracy. Honor Tracy she's called. She's a real sight, a tornado. She's writing a book about Ireland. And by the odd bits of talk I hear of it – not a complimentary book. To be called "Mind you I've said nothing." A book of the ice age years in Ireland.

But it's summer now, good hot weather, and Miss Tracy goes for a swim in the river. She returns, pleased as punch with her exertions. I'm in the pantry, by the hotpress. She has a wet bathing costume with her, or what remains of it. It's torn asunder, a shambles of dripping wool. It's Peggy's old costume. I hear Peggy's voice to Hubert in the drawing room later. "She just took it – without asking – and forced herself into it. It's ruined." "I think perhaps it might be better, Peggy – if we say nothing."

It's still summer and we're all out on the upper lawn having tea under the big maple tree by the swing and the tennis court. Hubert, in his felt hat – which he wore in the most unnecessary circumstances and lost when it was needed – is leaning across the tiny low table looking at a book, which James Delahanty, sitting on the grass, is passing up to him. I can't quite see the title of the book. James was as bookish as Hubert. Booksellers everywhere did well out of his ironmongery shop in Kilkenny. Peggy and Julia are poised, on chairs, in summer dresses, with tea cups delicately raised. There's someone else there, and I can't make out quite who it is. It might be me. The scene is frozen suddenly. The book stays half way up to Hubert's hand, the teacups half way to their lips. The dappled sunlit patterns through the maple leaves are stilled. It's high summer, set in amber now, at Maidenhall under the maple tree, by the swing, near the tennis court.

Autumn again, rumours of fruit once more. And another woman is coming to tea. She's tall, gangly, straggles of ash hair, unruly in the breeze as she gets out the car. A lackadaisical air, a sort of seeming hauteur. So perhaps for this reason, waiting behind Hubert in the porch, I'm nervous of her. I'm introduced. "Elizabeth, this is little Joe." "Ah," she says. "I ku-ku-know your fe-fe-father. Or is he your grand fe-fe-father?" Horror of horrors, for I have to say something. "I de-de-don't ku-ku-know." We both of us — Elizabeth Bowen and I — have a terrible stammer. "She's a novelist", Hubert tells me later. "Is that why she st-st-ammers so badly?" I hope never to be a novelist, my stammer is bad enough already.

Autumn, and Hubert is togged out again, the old flannels, felt hat and bee veil, a cloud of furious bees about his head, and the smell of burning corrugated paper from the bellows smoker. And the oak-barrelled honey separator must be got up from the basement. And now I'm turning the handle again, the honey flowing. Soon I'll be going back to school in Dublin. The awful school in Ranelagh. And I don't want to go. I want to stay here, turning the handle, listening to the honey flow. But I must go.

And now, 50 years later, all this is gone. Hubert, the people, the bees. But no, they're not gone. They're just down the road from us, at Maidenhall — available in that other undying dimension, that parallel universe which runs with ours, across the divide, where the bridge is love.

And Hubert, this morning, is happy. There's been stormy weather. A few trees down in the recent gales, a lot more wet wood to be cut for the winter. He'll be looking for me, with that damn great cross-cut saw. I must go.

EARLY YEARS

Eleanor Burgess

"I believe that it is in the first 25 years of our lives, that our characters are shaped and our tastes formed", wrote Hubert in his "A Fragment of Autobiography." Hence it seemed important, on this occasion, to try to resurrect his first quarter-century, though of course not from memory. Instead, while keeping in mind his dislike of any speculations about himself, that he did not personally authorise, I have mostly made use of his letters to his mother, with whom he was to have a love/hate relationship.

She was a very intelligent and practical lady, closely involved in village affairs and devoted to her ducks and chickens. She taught the children English and French while their father taught them maths and their grandmother history. Hubert's subsequent academic success at school indicates the good grounding he had received.

Content with each other's company Hubert and his sisters lived an almost self-contained life on the top floor of Maidenhall. (Gilbert was not born until 1910.) There were quarrels and jealousies particularly between Hubert and Cicely, his elder by 20 months, but he had found working with her on her magazine, *The Magpie*, both creative and enjoyable. In retrospect Hubert considered he had had a happy childhood until this idyllic life ended abruptly when, just before his ninth birthday, he found himself "dumped" in Berkshire at Bigshotte Rayles Prep School. He was stunned and thought his parents had given him away. However his first letter written from there does not give that impression; in fact, it ends with the words "it is very nice here."

When viewed from a middle-age perspective he blamed his misery and loneliness and particularly the breakdown of the happy family relationship on his being sent to school. But, none of his letters from school reveal his unhappiness. Schoolboys wrote about events not their feelings and Hubert was no exception. His letters also contained messages to the rest of the family and enquiries about *The Magpie*. He proudly told how he came top in an arithmetic exam with 52 out of 75 marks, the next only getting 21.

In the summer term of 1913 he successfully sat the exam for a maths scholarship to Charterhouse. But there trigonometry lost its mystical, numinous quality. For him it had provided an alternative, abstract world when he had stopped believing in Heaven. Now disillusioned, his interest in maths waned, to be replaced by Greek and Latin. His sense of isolation increased. There was no one with whom he could talk and share his ideas. Apparently his happiest moment there was when his house, Verites, went on fire.

All the same, in the classical sixth form he won all the available prizes and on the strength of his rendering part of Shelley's *Adonais* into Latin in Lucretian hexameters, he was encouraged to try for a scholarship to Balliol. He failed, perhaps because at the *viva* when asked what he most admired about Virgil he replied truthfully that he did not like him at all. However he had set his heart on Balliol, and his pride was mortally wounded, although he did succeed with the top scholarship to St. John's. There he made friends with Tyrone Guthrie who invited him home to Tunbridge Wells, thus fortuitously causing his auspicious first meeting with Peggy. They were married in June 1930 and here we are celebrating the outcome of this happy partnership of over 60 years.

To return to Charterhouse and the autumn term of 1918. Hubert was expecting to have to join the army but the war ended 19 days after his 18th birthday, so his deliberations as to which regiment to join were redundant. He certainly did not want to stay on at school and so, with the family farm in mind and his interest in growing things, he went to Reading University to study agriculture for two terms as a stop-gap. Here he did feel happy and free, largely through getting to know his distant cousin, Willi de Burgh, Professor of Philosophy, who had a profound influence on Hubert. It included stimulating his interest in Russia, its culture and language. Hubert described their walks together: "Mr B walks very fast and erratically, plunging along through marshes and streams with torrents of conversation like a fountain." Hubert spent much time at the de Burgh home where, among other things, he was introduced to jazz: "I can't say I feel jazz-mad. I don't know anything about the jazz but should imagine it is only a very passing craze and from all accounts you could get quite satisfactory lessons from any intelligent farmyard animal ... I am quite content to be a wall-flower and watch the family's antics: but Mr de Burgh likes it." He was definitely enjoying life: his letters contain many touches of humour. "It was odd that Wellington College should get burnt down the day after I went to it. I got such good practice at Charterhouse!"

He went around on an old bicycle that was prone to punctures and chain trouble. As part of his course he cycled to Windsor to see the King's farm: "I have brought back many hints for brightening and improving the dairy at home: stained glass windows and mosaic ceilings supported by ribbed columns with the milk in costly and hideous vessels, Sèvres or Dresden or Staffordshire ... (and) coats of arms on the butterpats." This expedition had not helped his leg which was suffering from three diseases. He had strained his thigh somehow getting into the bath. "My legs got in before I was ready to follow: then a great bite on my ankle ... and eczema on my toes. I took them with difficulty to the chemist to be diagnosed." His subsequent letters give amusing accounts of how he and his landlady coped with the problem until, in July, he left Reading.

He kept in touch with the de Burghs and eventually they introduced him to the Zinovievs who taught him Russian. Before this he had set the pattern for his language learning when holidaying with the de Burghs in the Alps on the French/Italian border. "I am enjoying it immensely: I am so much more independent than in our little Belgian trip (with Cicely in 1920) and feel myself understanding much more and am far more stimulated by what I see." He was not too pleased when one of his Oxford friends turned up: "As I had counted on a fortnight's immersion in French ways and customs." He got to know the "delightful" French family who ran the hotel. "We do a lot of things together even dancing. It isn't so distasteful in practice as in theory, as bar the eldest kitchen maid I am *quite* the star performer ... after two dances I have already begun to feel less British and stuck-up."

At Oxford, his mind moved on from Latin verse, his interest in the Classics gradually diminished, though he always retained an affection for Lucretius. Passing through Dublin in 1916, on his way to school, within a week of the Easter rising, and seeing the still-smoking ruins, he had become an Irish Nationalist; so, what could he do for his country? In the vacations he visited Kilteragh. AE's utopianism and particularly Sir Horace Plunkett's ideas on cooperative agriculture had a lifelong influence on Hubert. Meanwhile his academic career suffered. On 1 December, 1920, he wrote: "Mods are in March and I think I am only fairly safe for a first." Then he goes on to describe an "amusing" dinner at The Irish Society, where they entertained Yeats and Plunkett. "Yeats sat enthroned at the head of our table looking very distinguished and exceedingly bored with tortoiseshell spectacles. All the other lions were planted round him in the usual absurd dinner-party way. So most of us could only look on and admire, while Yeats and Plunkett chatted to each other, which they found difficult as they were deaf in the wrong ears. Yeats was far too dignified unfortunately to give a speech of more than four or five sentences, though I believe he is extraordinarily good if roused. Plunkett spoke more pleasantly and affably for about half an hour ... He gave the Sidney Ball lecture this afternoon and got a good reception."

A year later, being "very much at odds with life" Hubert was apologizing for a "hysterical" letter he had just written. "The truth is I was feeling very low about Greats. I am afraid they are not my subject. As you know I allowed myself to slide while I was in Ireland ... and besides I do not think that I can ever be sufficiently absorbed in Aristotle for a first and a fellowship, as I had hoped." The hysterical letter started with his views on the political situation at home. These were very much at variance with his parents', and consequently a major cause of his alienation, particularly from his mother. "I am really glad that the

Irish business is settled at last. It may mean a readjustment of power in the country, in which our class will probably suffer, but I don't believe that it is to anyone's interest that we should be removed. In fact it seems to be more in line with Sinn Féin's programme to offer inducements to stay. I think you know that I have always held heresies about our qualifications for power ... So as an Oxford Olympian I shall not be sorry to see the rise of a governing class drawn from rather different ranks. Our day was done, I think, about a century ago." He ends the letter with a plea for help: "by believing in me, not as a wage earner which I will never be, but a person with far wider sympathies than is usual, hampered by very great shyness. Don't talk to me of 'jobs', because quite honestly if my only use is to be paid for executing someone else's plans, which I disbelieve in, probably I will fling myself into the Isis."

Having contemplated abandoning his studies, he spent the Christmas vacation in London. "I think I shall go back to Oxford this term, mainly because, like most Irish people, I find it more comfortable to postpone or misinterpret important decisions. But partly too because I think the philosophy side of Oxford work would be very useful to me later ... though I believe if I was sincere with myself I would throw it up immediately. But how can a person of my muddled morals and education ever be sincere? I know my assumed helplessness will annoy you very much. You and Cicely have always liked lucid and emphatic propositions and programmes, with at any rate the appearance of clarity ... I know I have been a fool of the first water, I have heaped abuse on you for not being what it was not in your nature to be ... and probably wounded you very much ... The only possible solution of such domestic *impasses* where, as with me, congenial friends are not to be found, is to separate ... I believe that such a separation, mutually agreed to, would in the end lead to far more love and respect between different members of a family, than enforced clan gatherings." Hence his lifestyle and travels during the next two decades. On May 4th, 1922, two days after the Republicans had captured Kilkenny Castle he sympathized: "Poor Kilkenny one somehow hadn't anticipated it indulging in these vulgarities or anything more improper than choir festivals or subscription dances. I am dreadfully sorry for you all, as I know in the centre of it, however much one jokes, it must be a constant anxiety to you." He also explained why he was happier now and that "it was good for me that I never got to Balliol." This his last extant letter from Oxford ends with the hope, that "Ireland might someday create something if it settled down."

He left Oxford with a disappointingly bad degree but thankful to have found his "set", for he was keen to take part in creating the Ireland his new friends envisaged. In the cooperative village AE saw the library as the intellectual centre, whilst the creamery was to be the economic one. Encouraged by

Plunkett Hubert joined the Carnegie County Libraries. He started at Ballymena to learn the trade before moving to County Derry. He bought a motor bicycle. "I think it will prove economical to have one if I have to do a lot of travelling though I don't expect to like it much. I should much prefer to walk!" He was not altogether content to be so far from Dublin. "What I want is leisure to write and some occupation that will fill up the working part of the day, something to write about and someone to fight and someone to talk to occasionally. That is why I want near Dublin ..." Nor did he like being treated as an office boy. "Unless they are either more intelligent or more virtuous I don't see that there is any call to serve under one's social inferiors. I am not worrying in the least about the next step as I know I shall always be able to get a job as good or better than this... and in any case all I want is to be left alone and to have leisure to write ..." Rather than through a job, his ambitions would be satisfied through his writing, "as I know it is immeasurably my most valuable and important side." He contemplated resigning and continued to confide in his mother: "I shall be rather sorry to have to give it up though not very, as it has been absolutely inadequate intellectually, as I haven't even been my own master ... If I went into the Civil Service, it would only be because I was in a temper, and because I had absolutely given up hope of leading the sort of life I wanted to, so I hope it won't come to that. I know I have a genuine talent for writing, though I am afraid it is a dreadfully Henry James type of character analysis that could never be remuneratively popular ... I am afraid I should probably not do any good unless I took to writing seriously ..."

Hubert did finally leave the library service after its headquarters was moved to Scotland. He left Ireland and for the next 15 years was able to pursue his chosen lifestyle, travelling widely and becoming familiar with certain European countries and their languages, until, in 1941, he inherited Maidenhall, where he settled down to his writing.

A COUNTRY SCHOLAR

Christopher Fitz-Simon

I'm to talk about my reflections of Hubert Butler at the time when I was a student – a critical time (in both senses) for a young person: I have to think myself back into a mode of being utterly obnoxious. I'd much rather talk about much earlier memories of Maidenhall. I'll only give a minute, therefore, to Sounds: first, the sound of Hubert's voice, recounting the story of Sinbad the Sailor, as projected by the Edwardian magic lantern on dark evenings: terrifying images from the Arabian Nights, interspersed with equally terrifying slides of the Archdeacon's widow upside-down in a Bath chair in 1911.

And the sound of voices – Hubert with the two Army officers in the dining room – Commandant Ahern, and Captain … Clohessy, I think. The pair of them cycled out from Kilkenny Barracks every Thursday for tuition in Russian. In return, they gave Hubert grinds in Munster Irish. Well the sounds which cleft the night air – eclipsed consonants clashing off sliding diphthongs – would have caused any agent of Churchill's MI5 who happened to be passing on the Ennisnag road, to meditate on the possibility of a definite *coup*.

I was eight at the time. Not until I was 15 or 16 did I actually read anything that Hubert had written. He was a "Writer", that was well-known: my grandmother had once said that he was "a very learned man"; "but amusing too", she'd added, removing from "learning" any taint of tedium. Well there was this piece in *The Bell*, called "Nurseries of Writing" – I think Peggy Butler had sent a copy to her mother at Annaghmakerrig, where we were perching: I should explain that while my father was on active service with the British Army we roosted with relatives here and there. *The Bell*: A-rated stuff, I supposed. Obscure. But I took it up, and was astonished by the vibrancy of allusion, the conciseness, the immediacy. And, by the wit: in every sense. I convinced the rather supercilious teacher who had charge of the school library that a subscription to *The Bell* should be ordered. As it happened, Hubert did not contribute very often; in fact, it was pretty well impossible to find his work, unless one were to subscribe to a whole rake of periodicals, from *The Twentieth Century* to *An Cosantóir*.

Well, at that time I felt mildly ashamed that in all my visits to Maidenhall since the 1940s I had failed to grasp that as a writer, amongst other things, Hubert was out of the ordinary. When I entered Trinity a couple of years later I noticed a poster at Front Gate advertising the Inaugural Talk to be given by

"Hubert Butler" to the D.U. Christian Union. A dozen students clutching cups of tea and Marietta biscuits awaited the speaker in a room at the top of No 6, their chief converse being of a new member who had recently been saved for Jesus. Or by Jesus. I slunk into a shadow, of which there were fortunately several, aware that I was a vulgar intruder from the painted stage of the Players. Hubert arrived, spoke lucidly and engagingly on the origins of religious conflict in Croatia and Serbia, of which, naturally enough, I knew absolutely nothing, and which I found fascinating in his level assimilation. When questions were invited, there were none. I am a complete coward about raising my hand at the back of a lecture-room. There was one of those terrible silences, terminated by a hasty and utterly inadequate Vote-of-Thanks-to-the-Speaker. Here was, I thought as I sidled down the staircase, a wise and experienced commentator, and what had to happen to him but find himself in a room peopled with South Circular Road fundamentalists and members of the Trinity College Mission to Belfast? And what about the University? Why was Hubert not engaged for a series of lectures, as a Visiting Professor, perhaps? We certainly could have done with him in the School of Modern Languages, where the poet Donald Davie, and Hubert's friend Owen Sheehy-Skeffington, were beacons in a somewhat dispiriting ocean. Why, indeed, was he not lecturing at LSE, or at Berkeley for that matter? The Reading Public could also do with his work: but where were his books? What were the book publishers *doing*?

When I was 20 or 21 I became editor of the undergraduate "literary" magazine *Icarus* – I believe we published the earliest student work of Michael Longley, Derek Mahon and Brendan Kennelly – and there was a tradition of inviting an established author to contribute a piece to each issue. I'm sure I was intent upon obtaining kudos for *myself* when I invited Hubert to be guest contributor, and he generously sent a translation of a wonderful story by Ivo Andrić, of whom, I confessed, I had never heard. (Andrić wasn't awarded the Nobel Prize for Literature until some time in the sixties, I think, so his name was unfamiliar in the West.)

Neither I, nor indeed hundreds of much better informed people, had any idea of the widespread – if elusive – distribution of Hubert's work, nor did we know of the high regard in which he was held in a number of discerning coteries in a number of widely separated countries. What was most frustrating – when I was a student – was that there were no books. Edmund Wilson, and E.M. Forster, and Elizabeth Bowen wrote books, which we could easily find in the library if we couldn't afford to buy them. Alaistair Cooke, whose *Letter from America* Hubert listened to religiously on Sunday mornings (he didn't go to church), wrote books.

Well, I came across a superb article called "Peter's Window", set in Leningrad in 1931 on the eve of Stalin's purges. (Roy Foster dilated upon it brilliantly last night). The incidental detail – of people, and places – creates a thick wodge of atmosphere – Balzacian, I suppose, in its controlled glee – which lifts the piece pungently above anything which might be described as, either, a *belle-lettre*, or a merely perceptive piece of political journalism. "Peter's Window" is tantalisingly short: that, indeed, is one of its main virtues – nothing is superfluous. When I read it first in some magazine or other I thought there was a substantial book in it; certainly Hubert's stay of several months in the Soviet Union, would, one thought, have occasioned an exceptionally absorbing book containing several further scenes from the sad *Comédie Humaine* of Leningrad. – And just think how exciting – how illuminating! – it would be, now, to take down from the shelf his (alas, unwritten) books on Yugo-Slavia.

It was said that Hubert's absence of personal as well as professional vanity stood in the way of book-publishing, that he had assured a pushy interviewer that he was "a country scholar" and had no wish to enter the urban literary labyrinth, especially if it involved Dublin. He also "hated academics." I never heard him say that, but such was reported, and this resulted in a situation where all kinds of unsociable behaviour were ascribed to him – annoying to hear when you knew what an agreeably sociable and hospitable person he was, and how the doors of Maidenhall were permanently open to all who chose to come.

I thought, if Hubert disliked the unmannerly town so much, he should, in practical terms, engage a professional agent to undertake the rude business of dealing with publishers, distributors, reviewers – his brother-in-law Tyrone Guthrie used the William Morris Agency, and books sprang from his biro in spite of his intense schedule of theatre productions around the world – but of course I didn't think it my place to suggest such a thing: another way of saying that I lacked the courage of my conviction; but perhaps his peers had made the same suggestion without success.

A question continued to irk, however, and it was this: if you are retiring enough, or modest enough, to believe that your work is not of sufficient interest to be placed before the wider public as, for example, a book every couple of years in the manner of Wilson or Forster or Bowen, why then trouble to publish it at all? We had occasional pieces of immense perspicacity in reputable magazines of comparatively small readership, and we had occasional talks on the radio – never more than one or two a year, certainly nothing like the weekly bulletin of Alastair Cooke. (I thought that Hubert was superior to Alastair Cooke: Hubert's voice was more mellifluous, his verbal illustrations were more vivid, his approach to the kernel of his argument less … upfront.) Quality, not quantity, you will be saying. But surely, I thought, as a callow (whatever that may mean) student, quality need not *dis*qualify quantity, and I felt that Hubert had the capacity for both.

As to university lecturing, I felt that the student body of Ireland and beyond would have appreciated the absence of cant, as much as the presence of an unconformist erudition and a far-flung experience. I felt that students would have enjoyed hearing a man who patently denied the stereotypical labels which the unknowing might have – and possibly did – attach to him: "reclusive", "recondite", "standoffish." If only he could have overcome the dislike, or distrust, or whatever it was, of Academia, and admitted that within those groves or thickets there must have walked some students worth addressing (granted, the showing by the D.U. Christian Union was not too promising), and admitted to himself that there were professors – like Dr Skeffington – who should not be written off because of their calling.

Well, time passed, and the book *Ten Thousand Saints* issued from the Wellbrook Press in Freshford, demonstrating that Hubert meant what he said about supporting local enterprise. And then, years later, as everyone knows, Antony Farrell of The Lilliput Press (at that time, appropriately, based well away from Dublin) collected a large body of Hubert's occasional writing, in the handsome volumes which contributed more than anything else to the wider public's discovery and appreciation of his work. These books are sensitively edited, handsomely designed, professional. When they appeared during the last years of Hubert's life, I could not help recalling the time of which I've been speaking, when there were no books, and, as a student, I believed that was a huge loss.

I think it important that at a gathering of this kind, where scholars who are going to perpetuate Hubert's work are present, certain confused perceptions be set at naught. The Hubert Butler that I knew in the 1950s was not aloof, snobbish, biased, proud, exclusive: had he been any of those things, the following would not have happened. There was an annual Beer Festival in Kilkenny, which took place in a huge marquee where pints were lowered to the sound of a Bavarian brass band, alternating nightly with more local popular groups. Someone had given me two tickets. I had no intention of going, but when I enquired in the Maidenhall kitchen if there was anyone to whom I could dispose of them, who should say that he would take the tickets, but Hubert? He didn't like driving, so I went along. Now I'm not fond of beer, and I don't know if Hubert was, but he certainly downed several Smithwicks in the big tent to the accompaniment of the Nevada Showband; and, while I was consulting my watch and glancing covertly towards the tent-flap, he was looking around the jolly throng, smiling, taking it in. Enjoying. I believed Hubert to be *non-persona-grata* in Kilkenny due to the Incident over the Papal Nuncio, but I must have been wrong, for here were solid members of the local establishment coming up to him and saying in genuinely friendly fashion, "You're very welcome to the Festival, Mr Butler." And he was too.

KILKENNYMAN

Peter Smithwick

Hubert Butler was born at Maidenhall on 23 October, 1900, according to *Burke's Peerage* – or on 25 October, according to the Register of Births, in which his father's occupation is given as gentleman. His father, George Butler, was High Sheriff of Co Kilkenny for the year 1901 and so it fell to him to proclaim the new King, Edward VII. *The Kilkenny Moderator* recorded the event:

> King Edward VII was proclaimed at the Courthouse, Kilkenny, on Tuesday at 12 o'clock. The 3rd Berkshire Regiment, accompanied by the band, was drawn up in command of Major Hay and the Royal Irish Constabulary under County Inspector M.A. Allen and District Inspector R.J. Harrison. The balcony of the Courthouse was occupied by a great number of ladies and gentlemen. A fanfare of trumpets having been sounded, Mr George Butler, J.P. High Sheriff, Maidenhall, read the proclamation and the troops presented arms. The Regimental colours were unfolded and the band played "God Save the King" and three cheers were given for His Majesty.

In 1904 the King and Queen visited Kilkenny. Hubert, knowing nothing of any King except Herod, told his father he thought he would be safe as he was now in trousers. His father told this anecdote to the Bishop and the Bishop told the King, who was greatly amused. A year or so later, Hubert went to the annual Children's Fancy Dress Party in Kilkenny Castle dressed as … an Irishman.

So the Kilkenny into which Hubert was born was one still dominated by a small élite group from whom power was already slipping. His mother foresaw no future for him in Ireland and urged him to make a career elsewhere. There is little doubt that had he pursued an academic career either at one of the English universities or at Trinity College Dublin he would have achieved fame, and a financially secure exile. That he chose not to do so was a generous gift to Kilkenny and to Irish life generally.

I first knew Hubert soon after he returned to Kilkenny in 1941. The war years with cars off the road restricted activities but in 1943 he was one of the group which started the Kilkenny branch of The Irish Film Society. In 1944, with the help of other interested Kilkenny people, he helped to resurrect the local Kilkenny Archaeological Society which had been dormant for many years, and ensured that it had high standards of scholarship. In 1946 he commissioned O.G.S. Crawford to take extensive photographs of Kilkenny. He was appointed to the National Monuments Advisory Committee of Kilkenny County Council in 1950 and took a keen interest in spending its minute budget wisely.

In 1952 came the affair of the Nuncio. Chris Agee will deal with this subject in his contribution, but I must say something about its local effect. The County Councillors and the Members of the Corporation reacted with great anger. The previous August they had made the Nuncio a Freeman of the City and the resplendent ceremonies gave a flash of colour in the drab 1950s. There was a real fear of Communism throughout the Western world and the average Irish Catholic saw events in Yugoslavia as a wicked Communist government persecuting blameless Catholics for their faith. I need say no more except that Hubert's analysis was entirely correct. One Councillor said it was regrettable that the remarks against which they protested should have been made by a Kilkennyman. He was sorry that Mr Butler was a Kilkennyman. Another said that everyone in Kilkenny, irrespective of creed or class, regretted that a Kilkennyman should use those insulting remarks. Hubert stood his ground and explained his position with great clarity on the question of wartime Croatia. He resigned as Secretary of the Archaeological Society, as he thought this course would best preserve the harmony and good will which had always characterized the working of the Society. His resignation statement was a dignified apologia, free of rancour, but the truth is that he was forced out. There is a clear implication in the County Council and Corporation debates that Hubert had no right to speak. As a gentleman – and as a Protestant – he was only a Kilkennyman – and an Irishman – on sufferance. His duty was (I exaggerate, but only slightly) to support the Hunt and the Church, wear a poppy each November, and keep quiet about politics unless he felt moved to praise the new State for its tolerance of Protestants.

Hubert was not prepared to be a Kilkennyman on those terms. He weathered the storm and within a short time he set up the Kilkenny Arts Society – which staged some fine exhibitions – and in 1954 started a series of annual debates. The first was on Partition, and he invited three Unionist speakers to Kilkenny. This was greeted by one correspondent in *The Kilkenny Journal* as "an insult to the patriot dead." In the North, however, the Unionist speakers were accused of "a surrender of Lord Craigavon's hard-won fight." Hubert was pleased at being simultaneously accused of both.

In 1955 he stood for the County Council as he felt it the duty of Protestant Irishmen to play a part in the public life of the County. He emphatically did not agree that Protestants should keep their heads down. He was defeated, but achieved a creditable vote.

Apart from the Kilkenny Debates, Hubert took a public stand on many local issues. He campaigned *for* the retention of the old bridge of Durrow, *against* the modernization of the bridge at Thomastown, *for* the coordination of local archaeological societies, *for* a local museum and *for* a County archive. He spoke with great clarity and wisdom at several public meetings opposing the Amendment to the Constitution which was called the "Pro-Life" Amendment.

Hubert was a unique Kilkennyman. Fortunately, he lived long enough to be acclaimed as such. His place in our history is now secure.

EDITING THE MASTER

Antony Farrell

There was a fairy-tale element to my meeting Hubert Butler (I'll be personal here in a way that Hubert would eschew, but forgive). As a deracinated young Irish editor, I had cut my teeth in London publishing during an exilic 1970s after reading history at Trinity College, Dublin, returning to Ireland the day Margaret Thatcher began her baleful reign in Britain. I was raising a family in County Westmeath and re-engaging with Irish life and culture when, in my capacity as reader for a Dublin publishing-house in early 1983, I came upon this treasure-trove, this Aladdin's Cave of manuscript material which bore the imprint of an utterly inimitable voice. With all the excitement of a Schliemann uncovering Troy, I submitted an enthusiastic report to Seamus Cashman at Wolfhound Press based on the sheaf of essays that I'd read, pressing for publication, but it wasn't for him. I was already on my way as a publisher with Tim Robinson's numinous *Setting Foot on the Shores of Connemara*, so a vehicle was established in The Lilliput Press, and we were hungry for material.

I telephoned Maidenhall, and a voice answered. Might I speak to Hubert Butler? There was a pause. "Do you mean Mr Butler?" the voice came back. I surely did, and I made my journey south from Mullingar through the midlands that weekend. I was greeted by a serene, silver-haired man, as old as the century, steadfast in gaze, erect, who welcomed me into a house of the middle size perched on a hill overlooking the Nore. Through the modestly pillared porch, a darkened interior was animated by two people, Hubert Butler and Peggy, his wife. We drank sherry in a sitting-room library shelved from floor to ceiling with worn and cherished books, the freight of civilization, and the fruit of a lifetime's engagement with it. We then lunched frugally among favoured cats on produce from the garden, seated by an east-facing window under a leafing horse-chestnut in the upstairs kitchen, and began a conversation that was to last almost ten years. Food never tasted more nourishing.

That weekend – the first of many – we sketched out possibilities of publication, an ad-hoc programme, as Peggy explained the background and isolation that Hubert had experienced since the 1950s and the time of the ban. She brought me to meet one of Hubert's oldest friends in the neighbourhood, Stanley Mosse, who spoke vividly of his feeling for the Butlers and of his support for the work. And over that spring and summer we worked on selecting and composing the material that came to make up the first book of essays, *Escape from the Anthill*, the initial batch I'd seen being added to with every visit as Hubert unhurriedly drew out from desks and drawers typescript drafts and off-prints of essays and compositions ranging from the local to the universal, from the flax-mills on the Nore to the Kirov Islands north of Petersburg. The essay-titles alone – "The Deserted Sun-Palace", "The Eggman and the Fairies", "Influenza in Aran", "New Geneva in Waterford", "Grandmother and Wolfe Tone", "The Invader Wore Slippers", "In the Land of Nod" – gave hints of the riches and enchantments to come and yielded other volume titles. We borrowed *Escape from the Anthill* from an unpublished piece, so emblematic was it of everything the work represented, and Hubert built an introduction around it.

Hubert Butler in person possessed the most equable temperament of any man I'd ever met, and my engagement with him was not with one but with two people. Peggy and Hubert were a team if ever there was one, and their palpable devotion and loyalty was a lesson in living; I never felt in talking to one that I did not have the entire confidence and trust of the other. Peggy, or Susan as she was formally called, was a considerable personality, as any who knew her would testify, and was herself sister of the formidable Tyrone Guthrie. She lived for Hubert, and he could not have thriven without her. She both protected and encouraged, and she always knew that one day he would come to be recognized. She was Vera to his Vladimir Nabokov, and no cloying handmaiden. She was astonishingly well-read, curious, open-minded and worldly: watching the nine o'clock television news on RTÉ was a ritual, her knowledge and love of nature an education, her Art-Deco script or eye for a flower arrangement or bedspread an aesthetic delight; above all, she was the wit behind her husband, her turn of phrase, her acuity, her clarity and originality of vision became Hubert's, as they were always her own. Between them, they were truly unillusioned yet consistent and buoyant in outlook, on the world, on their neighbours, on events, on the life of the mind. They were intertwined like some of the older apple trees in their garden. Without each other there would be no centenary to celebrate.

Editing (which comes next in the dictionary to edify, "to benefit spiritually", and was perhaps nearer the mark when reading or preparing Butler for publication) was a matter of gathering and arranging, harvesting or garnering the work, much of which had lain fallow for up to fifty-five years. There was an imperturbable confidence about the procedure, unparalleled in any other author I came to know, unique in an unpublished octogenarian. The earliest and most moving piece by Hubert, "Riga Strand in 1930", didn't surface in typescript until we were preparing the second book of essays, *The Children of Drancy*, and was written on his honeymoon in Latvia, when he and Peggy stopped off en route by steamship up the Baltic to the Gulf of Finland and Petersburg, or Leningrad as it then was, preparatory to a teaching stint there: this period was memorably set down "Peter's Window," a haunting evocation of that twilit city and its peoples between the wars and before the onset of Stalinism. So the patterns of the writing became established, following an autobiographical thread as we interleaved literary criticism with travel writing, essays on the Balkans, Yugoslavia, China and North America, and on Irish history, society and place. "Even when these essays appear to be about Russia or Greece or Spain or Yugoslavia," Hubert wrote, "they are really about Ireland. The post to which I am willingly tethered still holds firm and I have grazed around it in a sufficiently wide circle. Close-cropped grass comes up again fresh and sweet, and whoever comes along next may find my patch slightly improved." We continue to be fed by that remarkably fertile patch, those "men and women" that he addressed, "who are surely more important than the systems in which they imprison themselves."

The first volume of essays, *Escape from the Anthill*, was published in May 1985, creating a groundswell of instant support, and confirming our hopes and those of his most constant supporters such as the late Shevawn Lynam, Joe Hone and Maurice Craig, who furnished an exemplary foreword to the book. On the day of publication a full-page encomium appeared in *Image* magazine written by Eoghan Harris, who said, "To follow Hubert Butler is to enjoy the hair-raising frisson of history passing by." Two days later, in the Saturday *Irish Times*, Dervla Murphy spoke of the "unique distillation of the Anglo-Irish spirit" and described the essays as "all flawless gems", and so the work rippled out into a receptive world. Monk Gibbon reviewed the book in the *Irish Independent*, Chris Agee described his stumbling on "an Irish talent of European stature" in *The Linen Hall Review*, Roy Foster alerted wider intellectual circles in *The Times Literary Supplement* – all of them sharing their discovery and responding instinctively and generously to the spirit and content of this extraordinary writer. Many Butlerians went on to become "vast friends", in Peggy's phrase, and three key publisher-editors abroad took up the torch by publishing editions of the essays over following years: signally, Paul Keegan of Penguin Books in London, Samuel Brussel in Paris who elicited an essay on Hubert from the late Joseph Brodsky, Elisabeth Sifton of Farrar Straus & Giroux in New York. Butler had truly arrived.

In his library-sitting-room at Maidenhall, which should be preserved like Tolstoy's or Turgenev's (Maidenhall in ways was as close as I've got to what Coole Park meant to Yeats: a Coole Park on the Nore), Hubert wrote in civil-service duplicate books, transferring copy in second drafts to his typewriter with its small pica-face, double-spaced on foolscap paper with two or three copies in blue carbon for interlining and commentary. He would make corrections in a careful hand on a board across his knees by the fire, with Peggy opposite immersed usually in her own reading but ready for a lightening-quick response or observation when Hubert wanted to test a phrase or an idea. I would descend for weekend work on a Friday evening to be offered a sherry or whiskey and a square meal before we began shuffling papers and debating arrangements – with breaks taken for the nine o'clock news, Saturday excursions to the garden or walks to the river-bank with the dogs, the Sunday newspapers, the occasional visitor – as each of the four volumes took shape and fell into place like delicate jigsaws or game of bezique, around us the tools of our trade in Hubert's reference shelves: his 1935 *Chambers* multi-volume encyclopedia, his books on Russia and the Balkans, local Irish history, his novels and volumes of poetry encompassing the best that was thought and said in Irish and English letters over previous centuries, as we worked adding to that golden store, spinning a world-wide web of connectivity. There was an inexpressible ease and gentleness and rigour about the process, consideration for the reader and clarity foremost in minds of author and editor. Sentences and paragraphs fell from Hubert's pen like turf-footings, the shaped deposits of carefully layered thought, self-incubated and debated, waiting to find its moment of release. His gift for arresting metaphor was exhilarating, his syntax and grammar faultless; he did tend to over-punctuate but he taught me that the obtrusive Oxford comma had its place where ambiguities arose, as in the sentence (not one of Hubert's), "she looses her breath, and pants."

Our human contact was renewed every two to three weeks over a period of ten years; after Hubert's death the editorial reins were taken up by Peggy as we annotated letters together until her own death at Auteven Hospital on 21 December 1996. Between them, they'd became surrogate parents to me, and their absence breaks my heart, but their virtual presence here gives me huge cause for joy, knowing that their combined work, and Hubert's spirit, will continue to inhabit and to nurture us wherever there are books to be read.

Lilliput has further, unseen work by Hubert Butler which will appear in the coming years to form a fifth, concluding volume of his writings, *The Appleman and the Poet*. These include a lecture of uncertain provenance given to the Folklore Society at London University about tribal ancestors and the Irish Saints; a 1949 paper in *Antiquity* on "The Dumb and the Stammerers in Early Irish History"; more material on the Balkans and Russia and, most importantly, a selection of remarkable Letters Home sent between 1916 and 1980 to his mother, Peggy and family during his travels in Russia, North America, China and Israel. This will combine with a biography in preparation, and a new Butler Reader that will take the place of Roy Foster's anthology and Elisabeth Sifton's, as both these volumes go out of print along with the individual collections published by The Lilliput Press.

Lilliput owes Hubert Butler at least part of its standing in Irish cultural life; my publishing company is a portion of his legacy, and we are privileged to be here.

FROM THE BUTLER ALBUM

Photographs 1900-1926

Left to right: HMB with sister Cicely, circa 1901-1902

HMB, circa 1902-1903

*Left to right: sister Cicely, brother Gilbert, HMB
aged 10, sister Joan, circa 1910-1911*

HMB aged 13, circa 1913-1914

HMB, either at far left or far right, aged 17-18, British Army Officer Cadet
training camp, Charterhouse, England, circa 1917-1918

HMB at Oxford, circa 1921-1922

HMB, in the drawing room at Maidenhall, Christmas, 1983

PART II: BUTLER IN IRELAND

BUTLER AND THE CHURCHES

Robert Tobin

Perhaps the best way to begin a talk about Hubert Butler and the Churches is to say that even though he was not much of a churchgoer himself, he seems to have felt strongly that the rest of us ought to be. This is not at all to say that he was personally indifferent to the Churches or that he felt they had ceased to matter. In fact, he was probably more engaged intellectually and morally with the matters of institutional religion on this island than most people, Protestant or Catholic. And when I speak of Hubert Butler and "the Churches," I do not mean only the Church of Ireland and the other Protestant denominations. As a self-conscious member of the religious minority in Southern Ireland, Butler was acutely aware of the majority Church and took an active interest in how it functioned both here and abroad.

Even so, it would be misguided to conclude that he was a particularly religious man. His writings make clear that he was not. And as one observer has pointed out, his "'real religion' was a dream of local co-operative community." [1] He did not hold conventional Christian beliefs and cannot be taken as typical of the Church of Ireland community from which he sprang. He tells us in "A Fragment of Autobiography" of his euphoria at reading the Victorian novel *Robert Elsmere* and his conviction from an early age that he, too, was a "Free Thinker" *(CD 216)*. And yet never did he perceive that a rejection of some of his Church's theological claims meant he was exempt from its social teachings, nor did he ever labour under the delusion that he could slip the bonds of his own conditioning in the language and thought of Christian culture. As his admirer Joseph Brodsky perceptively noted, whatever his personal ideas, "he couldn't help being concerned with the fate of Christendom, whose natural son he was." [2] Perhaps in the twentieth century more than in any other, Christendom has suffered shocks that have gone to its very marrow. Amidst all this uncertainty, what Butler has left us is not so much a theology as it is an ecclesiology – a vision of how the Christian Churches should relate and continue to function – first and foremost in Ireland, but also all over the world. And so even if he stayed home on Sunday mornings, Butler was far from uninterested in what was being preached from the pulpits and thought in the pews.

That he should be permitted to have this rather exceptional attitude to his own Church was to Butler one of its crowning glories. To him all Churches should be "protectors of the individual soul" *(CD 181)* and ought not only to acknowledge but even encourage the sort of free inquiry to which he was devoted, even if such searching did not guarantee an entirely stable or unanimous membership. As he commented to a Church of Ireland leader in the late 1950s, "I am a heretical person, but ... I shall go on calling (the Church) mine simply because I was born and educated in it and haven't yet been thrown out." [3] Similarly, reflecting upon the great variety of religious movements within Protestantism in the United States, he wrote that "I am a child of the Reformation [,] and the man who questions inherited belief and starts on some independent search for God will always have my sympathy however lonely and ridiculous he may often appear. If he transmits the questioning spirit to his offspring and his friends, his absurdities are likely to be corrected." [4] Here is a faith in the community itself, in its ability to discern the lasting from the ephemeral, the prophetic from the spurious. Of course it is also another affirmation of what Butler throughout his writings likes to call the "the right to private judgment," for him the very cornerstone of all Protestant thought and practice. Looking back nostalgically at the Church of Ireland as it was before the Union, he maintained that "we criticized our clergy and their doctrines as sharply as they criticized us" — an arrangement that led to "that healthy and open mutual criticism" which in his own day he regarded as so sorely lacking in all the Irish Churches *(EA 133)*. In his essay entitled "The Bishop," he paints an admiring and humorous portrait of Robert Fowler, the late eighteenth-century Bishop of Ossory, who in his youth seems to have devoted as much time to his own love affairs as he did to the affairs of the Church. Even so, Fowler went on to become a much-beloved figure among Protestants and Catholics alike because of his humanity and tolerance. The writer honours him as one of the last of his kind before the Established Church was swept up during the next generation in the enthusiasm and severity of the Evangelical Movement *(EA 32-33)*.

In truth, Butler, like many of his fellow Protestants, held a rather romanticized view of the eighteenth century, which as it receded into history became the Eden from which their ancestors were expelled after the betrayal of the Union. For this and other sins the Established Church was eventually disestablished in 1869, and after a further half-century of uncertainty and anxiety, the Church of Ireland found itself an independent, minority denomination in the overwhelmingly Catholic Free State of Ireland. While he may have loved it for its non-interference in the realm of private judgment, Butler could be scathing about his Church's failure to intervene more effectively in the realm of Irish public life after Independence. More than once he indicted his fellow Protestants for "our amiable inertia" *(EA 116)* and in later life refused to sign what he termed the "toady letters to *The Irish Times*" which some of his co-religionists occasionally circulated claiming how well Southern Catholics had treated them and assuring their counterparts in the North that they had nothing to fear from a united Ireland.[5] Rather than devoting their energies to what he saw as gratuitous and ultimately self-destructive gestures like these, Butler urged Protestants to do the hard work of fashioning and articulating a coherent point-of-view of their own. At one moment in the late fifties he even asked himself whether there was really such a thing as Protestant thought left in Ireland. There were basic questions that had to be tackled:

> How can we best show our love for our countrymen without betraying our principles [?] Where can we make concessions, where should we stand firm? It seems to me that there is no such speculation going on anywhere but the most abject and rudderless floundering and muddle. [6]

It was precisely because of this apparent lack of conviction about their own beliefs and their reluctance to ask awkward questions or to take the dissenting part on social issues that Butler discouraged Southern Protestants from being overly ecumenical. This is an important point, because it is one where his ideas are liable to be misconstrued. His stance on ecumenism developed very much within a particular time and place. He had observed how the conflict between Catholicism and Orthodoxy in the Balkans had led to sectarian atrocities during the Second World War, and he remained skeptical about subsequent attempts by church leaders to gloss over what was clearly a pathological relationship stretching back over generations. With a characteristically pithy phrase, he remarks in an unpublished piece that "scores of Archbishops have embraced in front of TV cameras, discreetly silent about the bloody carnage that has raged."[7] His devotion to truth, however painful it might be, would not permit him to accept such gestures at face value.

In Ireland, he concluded that ecumenical activity between the Churches tended to sidestep rather than to confront essential differences, differences that could not be resolved without one side or the other conceding vital parts of its tradition. The Irish Catholic Church demonstrated little interest in genuine compromise with its Protestant counterparts, and in a country where they were very much in the minority. Butler felt Protestants were fully justified in being at least as frank in their opposition. As he wrote to his friend Myles Dillon in the spring of 1962, "without professional anti-Catholics none of the heresies and schisms, to which we non-Catholics are so devoted, would have endured a year."[8] It scarcely needs saying that this sort of candour did not go over well in Ireland; however Butler did gain respect from many Catholics for his integrity and forthrightness, as evidenced by the many letters of support he received over the years. Ultimately, ecumenism was for him typical of the twentieth century's general devotion to "isms" and in its abstract ambitions was a poor substitute for neighborliness, that lynchpin of his localist ethos. He saw no reason why Protestant and Catholic neighbours could not live in harmony together, all the while respecting their fundamental differences in matters of religious practice. He was not so naive as to think tensions would never exist, and however much his experiences in the early fifties might have disappointed him, in the end they confirmed rather than discredited his faith in a workable and even symbiotic relationship between Catholics and Protestants. "We should be necessary and complementary to each other like two halves of a broken plate," he argued, "each concavity matching a convexity, each NO a YES; but the two halves will never become one if we try to sandpaper away all the awkward projections, which are necessary to its wholeness." [9]

In practical terms, undoubtedly one of most awkward of these "projections" was the issue of mixed marriage between Catholics and Protestants in Ireland. As a result of the *Ne Temere* decree issued by Pope Pius X in 1908, the Church's teachings on marriage were to be more rigidly enforced than heretofore. This meant that a mixed marriage was only valid in the eyes of Rome if performed by a Catholic priest. [10] In order to gain approval for the mixed marriage, the couple must also agree to raise any children as Catholics. This final stricture is probably what offended Irish Protestants the most; under the circumstances, it appeared to them as just another way that the Catholic Church was attempting to eradicate them from the island. Surely the most famous example of *Ne Temere* leading to open sectarian conflict in the South was the Fethard-on-Sea Boycott in 1957, sparked off by a dispute over whether the young daughter of a mixed marriage should be educated at the local Catholic or Protestant school. When the mother indicated that she would like her child to go to the Protestant school, the parish priest intervened. Then the young Protestant wife left town, taking both her small children with her up to Belfast. Soon a boycott of all Protestants in Fethard-on-Sea, social and economic, was organized by the Catholic clergy and continued with the tacit approval of several bishops. Not surprisingly, Butler was incensed, but not just with the Catholic hierarchy. He was also angered by what he saw as another example of the Church of Ireland's failure to stand up for the minority perspective in the face of obvious persecution. His frustration was compounded by the fact that even staunch Catholics like Eamon de Valera had come out publicly opposing the boycott, and still the Church of Ireland leadership remained circumspect. The following year he wrote that he "wondered again whether there was much use in my trying to maintain links … with a community that has ceased to believe in itself, and seems always to prefer amateur 'diplomacy' to principle." In the same letter he makes it clear that he does not think mixed marriage at that time to be advisable for Irish Protestants, but again he tempers his own principle with pragmatism: "we can't stop mixed marriages in a mixed community but we can prevent them being made on unequal terms." [11]

So the question arises: do Hubert Butler's views constitute a form of bigotry? Certainly there are some who have chosen to understand them as such. He himself was conscious that taking a strong Protestant stand required a sense of moderation and discipline: in his first book he writes that "the once intoxicating doctrines of the Reformation compounded of indignation and compromise are chemically unstable. They decompose easily into bigotry and flaccid benevolence" *(EA* 43). Occasions like the Papal Nuncio Incident and the Fethard-on-Sea Boycott were rare enough that they must regarded as exceptions to the neighborliness in which Butler had so much faith. And yet he never relaxed his guard against the Catholic Church's influence over Irish life, for to him it exerted "the soft, irresistible pressure of an uncompromising philosophy" *(ILN* 118). He certainly would have been saddened but not surprised that just last month (September 2000) the Vatican issued a document entitled *Dominus Iesus*, which effectively undoes thirty years of Anglican-Catholic dialogue by reiterating the pre-Vatican II stance that no churches outside the Roman tradition can be considered constituent parts of "the true Church of Christ". [12] While undoubtedly Hubert Butler lived by what Roy Foster has rightly called his "assertion of a privileged separateness," [13] that separateness was not, to my mind, finally rooted in sectarian prejudice so much as reasoned opposition. It is true that if all of us were to assert that same sense of separateness, the Churches he valued so much could not continue to exist. Still, he made his contribution while sitting home at Maidenhall, and the Christendom all around it was never far from his thoughts, or from his love. As he asked himself in a piece entitled "Christian Neighbourliness":

> How could one call oneself a Christian Irishman, linking together two badly shattered and often conflicting ideas[?] To call oneself Irish means to give my first loyalty to the country in which I was born and wish to go on living. To call myself a Christian means to love one's neighbour as oneself. That is basic Irish loyalty, basic Christianity. There is no difficulty in reconciling them. They are utterly complementary. [14]

NOTES

1   David Stevens, "Protestants in the Republic," *Culture in Ireland: Division or Diversity?: Proceedings of the Cultures of Ireland Group Conference 1991* Ed. Edna Longley (Belfast: Institute of Irish Studies, 1991) p. 142.

2   Joseph Brodsky, "Appendix: On Hubert Butler," *In the Land of Nod* by Hubert Butler (Dublin: Lilliput, 1996) p. 268.

3   Hubert Butler, letter to C. Roberts, "Chairman of a large Church of Ireland meeting in Kilkenny," 27 June 1958, Ms. 10304/442, Hubert Butler Papers, Trinity College Library, Dublin.

4   Hubert Butler, "Sandwich Boards and Table-mats" (c. 1960s), Ms. 10304/323, Butler Papers.

5   Hubert Butler, "A Petty People" (1950s), Ms. 10304/99, Butler Papers.

6   Hubert Butler, "Are Protestantism and Unionism Synonymous?" (September 1957), Ms. 10304/164, Butler Papers.

7   Hubert Butler, "A few weeks ago I read in the Irish Times...," Ms. 10304/105, Butler Papers.

8   Hubert Butler, letter to Myles Dillon, 17 May 1962, Ms. 10304/597/523, Butler Papers.

9   Hubert Butler, "Ecumania (Rough Draft)" (c. 1960s), Ms. 10304/140, Butler Papers.

10 Desmond Bowen, *The Shaping of Irish Protestantism* (New York: Peter Lang, 1995) p. 360.

11 Hubert Butler, letter to C. Roberts, Butler Papers.

12 Patsy McGarry, "Vatican Position Saddens Church of Ireland Bishop," *The Irish Times* 20 September 2000, p. 2.

13 Roy Foster, "For the Meeting of Hearts," *The Times Literary Supplement* 6 September 1985, p. 980.

14 Hubert Butler, untitled/archived as "Christian Neighbourliness," Ms. 10304/444, Butler Papers.

BUTLER AND NATIONALISM

Terence Brown

One of the most poignant, yet unsettling of Hubert Butler's essays is his short evocation of the social ambiance of Riga Stand in 1930 which stands at the head of his second Lilliput collection, *The Children of Drancy* (1988). A text of the Great War's aftermath, it reminds one of the atmospherics of the opening section of T.S. Eliot's *The Waste Land*, published eight years earlier, with a cosmopolitan caste of Eastern Europeans cast up on a shore where history had so recently been at its terrible full-tide. Eliot's poem had been moodily attentive to the *déraciné* voices of those left behind as the waters of empire subsided, following the cataclysm of 1914-18. Butler in "Riga Strand in 1930" brings more of a realist's eye to social anomalies to be observed in the young and fragile Latvian republic that had carved out a temporary space and peace for itself after the deluge. For, Butler remarks (intrigued by a social mix lost on departing Russian officers and merchants frustrated by "the petty officialdom of a young nation, proud of its new independence and snatching at all opportunities of asserting it", CD 3):

> All the same Riga Strand must have a fascination for more leisured visitors, who have time to be interested in the past and the future of the small republics which rose from the ruins of the Russian Empire. It is the holiday ground not only for the Letts but for all the newly liberated peoples of the Baltic. There one may meet Estonians and Finns, Lithuanians and Poles, bathing side by side with Germans, Russians and Swedes, who were once their masters. (*CD* 4)

For all the sane good spirits of Butler's prose reflection, as compared with Eliot's neurotic nostalgias, "Riga Strand in 1930" does in fact share a precise preoccupation with Eliot's early verse: the role of the Jews in European culture. It is difficult not to read this early essay (unpublished, as far as I know, until its inclusion in *The Children of Drancy*) in the light of Butler's subsequent writings, especially the searching and heart-breaking "The Children of Drancy" with its exacting appreciation of the numbing scale of genocidal atrocity. In so doing we may, I think, risk misreading what is being said in "Riga Strand" and therefore miss especially how this essay relates to his analysis of nationalism, which remained consistent throughout Butler's career. Let us examine what

Butler had to say of the Jews in this early piece.

Most of the essay expresses a genial visitor's relish for a certain down-at-heel social levelling in the new, insecure Lativan republic; a slightly discordant note sounds, however, when Butler remarks:

> ... the fashionable specialists have no prodigal Caucasian Princes to diet in the sanitoria, they have to haggle with Jewessess about mud-baths and superfluous fat. The disinherited have come into their own, the Jews have descended like locusts on Riga Strand ... for them it has the fascination of a forbidden land. (CD 8)

Perhaps that egregious simile ("descended like locusts") is a moment of free indirect style, in which we can take amused pleasure at the discomfiture of a fashionable and prejudiced specialist. However, the extended set of gloomier reflections with which the essay concludes suggests that it is Butler himself who reckons the Jews of Eastern Europe a people of a diasporic consciousness, among whom certain forms of separatist self-definition could take hold. The nature of Jewish identity and self-awareness is raised in a passage which must be quoted at length:

> As the evening grows colder the strand empties and a group of boys come out of the pinewoods where they have been collecting sticks, and build a bonfire on the shore. The rest of the sand sinks back into the night and they are islanded in the firelight. As the flames burn higher it is easier to see their keen, Jewish faces. They have not yet lost the colours of the Mediterranean, though it may be many generations since their ancestors travelled up from Palestine to the shores of the Baltic. The leaders are a woman with loose black hair and a Messianic youth of seventeen. Are they making speeches or telling stories? The eyes of twenty boys are fixed, black and burning in the firelight, on the woman as she cries passionately to them in Yiddish. Three or four boys reply to her and they sing strange, unhomely Eastern tunes. Only a few yards away are the cafés and sanitoria but in the darkness the sand seems to stretch away interminably and the Jewish scouts seem to be the only creatures alive on the shore, a nomad tribe, camping in the desert. They are of the same race, the same families perhaps, as the predatory blondes in the beach costumes, but the spirit that fills them now is alien from Riga or from Europe. Persecution has hardened them and given them strength to

survive war and revolution and even to profit from them and direct them. Perhaps it is they who will decide the future of Riga Strand. (*CD* 11)

In the lurid light of the flames that were to engulf European Jewry a short decade later, it is possible to read this passage with its images of fire, sanitoria and "predatory blondes", with its reference to persecution, war and revolution, as mysteriously prescient of the awful fate that awaited young people such as these glimpsed at evening in the Latvian pinewoods. Yet as a document of 1930, Butler's "Riga Strand in 1930" was, arguably, evoking Jews in the kind of terms which shortly thereafter would make them vulnerable. (Perhaps that is why Butler, with his finely tuned moral antennae, did not publish this piece at the time). They are in their persecution-forged hardness "alien" in spirit from contemporary Europe; and the passage dramatizes their presence in Riga as that of a displaced desert people far from their Mediterranean home: "a nomad tribe camping in the desert". Their songs are "strange, unhomely Eastern tunes"; we can't be sure if they are "telling stories" or "making speeches", but they may be about to "profit by ... and direct events". Even a sojourn of generations in northern Europe, and familial ties to those among whom they live, do not mean they have been assimilated.

Why did Butler write in this way in 1930, even if he chose not to publish what he had written? The question forces itself on us, even if posing it might seem otiose given the moral certitude and sheer personal courage of the writer's later activities as antagonist of Nazi anti-semitism in Vienna in 1938-39 and the alert sensitivity of his writings to its gross, particular abominations. For the mature Butler unambiguously believed that "Hitler had brought into the world misery such as no man had previously believed possible" (*ILN* 197) and had lived his life in that implacable conviction. So what was he really thinking of when he wrote of the Jews on Riga Strand in the way he did in 1930? Answering that takes us, I believe, to his analysis of nationalism which he presented in its most explicit form in an essay of *circa* 1936, "Fichte and the Rise of Racialism in Germany". In that posthumously published essay, the nature of Jewish identity was once again raised, this time as a part of a complex argument in cultural history and in relation to a general theory.

"Fichte and the Rise of Racialism in Germany" was first published in *In the Land of Nod* in 1996. It would in fact have been, had it been published in the mid-thirties when it was written, a contribution *avant la lettre* to the study of nationalism that has gone on apace in the academic world since the 1970s. This of course received added impetus from the re-emergence of the nationalistic politics Butler understood so intimately in Central and Eastern Europe, following the disintegration of the Communist world after 1989.

Butler's 1930s reflections on the subject of nationalism began with a distinction, now familiar enough in the literature, between two forms of the phenomenon: "till recently it has been to nobody's interest to draw distinctions between patriotism and nationalism, for the two sentiments, deriving indefinably from land and people, seemed to be two complementary aspects of the same emotion" (*ILN* 67). He then immediately complicates the matter by identifying a third category of analysis, one which is not a matter of land and people but of "loyalty and devotion to common traditions, history, social and political institutions" *(ILN 67)*. This latter category is fundamentally different, Butler suggests, from the other two, being dependent on individuals rather than collectivities and on "thought" rather than "instinct". As such it is fragile and easily overwhelmed by the other "two more primitive sentiments" (*ILN* 68). It is the "more primitive" forms of the phenomenon that interest Butler in this essay and in particular "the attainment or recovery of solidarity through racial sentiment" (*ILN* 68).

Like subsequent theorists of nationalism (the Ernest Gellner of *Nations and Nationalism* immediately springs to mind), Butler in this essay does not presume that racial feeling or indeed any kind of nationalism is a given of the human condition. It emerges as a consequence of circumstance. As such racial sentiment "seems always to have represented a transitional and regressive phase in the history of peoples, a disorganised period when a settled equilibrium has been disturbed" (*ILN* 68). In ancient times primitive man both in hunter-gatherer and settled communities had no need of racial sentiment. In such conditions

> It is clear that the community is a spiritual rather than a material fact, and its preservation or destruction does not depend primarily on aggression or blood kinship or other physical factors. It is only when the spiritual continuity of the tribe is fatally interrupted that these assume importance. (*ILN* 69)

In the ancient world, however, droughts, floods, pressure from other tribes, often uprooted a community and set it wandering, making it prey to feelings of "racial solidarity", until the group once again became settled and "under the influence of property, sentiment attach[ed] itself to the country and its institutions, not to race" (*ILN* 69). In fact its members became civic nationalists and abandoned ethnic nationalism, in the terms recent theorists of nationalisms have frequently deployed. Yet in such peoples "the habits and feeling of nomadic life lie there still in germ, and at a threat the people" (*ILN* 69) will regress to racial solidarity. Among modern nations, Butler then declares, the Germans were the first to experience and to justify such a regression, following their defeat by Napoleon's forces. At that moment (and throughout the essay an implicit analogy is being drawn with the Germany of the 1930s, reacting against the defeat of 1918) they were already "dispersed and divided" (*ILN* 72) and under the pressure of conquest, all too likely to adopt racialism as a unifying force. In that, for all his "reputation for solid domesticity and love of material security" (*ILN* 72), the German, like "the homeless Jew", has remained a "racialist" (*ILN* 72). For neither Jew nor German have had the good fortune of the Irish, whose material and historical circumstances have to a large extent kept them free of "any idea of racial solidarity" (*ILN* 73). The Germans and the Jews, so the argument of this essay runs, as peoples share more than they can conceive. In a terrible irony, Butler observes of German depredations on Jewry in the 1930s: "German racialism has exterminated its most capable interpreters" (*ILN* 75). And the modern Germans have succumbed to "a homeless ravening passion hungering for eternal triumphs and universal empire" (*ILN* 83).

So the Jews of Riga Strand are nomads in whom a spirit of racial nationalism could burgeon, as it had done among the Germans of Fichte's day and in Butler's own. In the context of Butler's thinking about nationalism in the 1930s, therefore, they are by no means to be seen as exhibiting an essential Jewishness that is to be deprecated. Rather they remind one what dispersal and a nomadic experience can do to a people. It can foment a latent racialism, which can flare up under stress and persecution.

In "Fichte and the Rise of Racialism in Germany" Butler identifies the French, the Swiss and the Irish as peoples in whom patriotism ("which kindles a binding sentiment for their native land", *ILN* 72), rather than racialism, has predominated. In the Irish case, this was in part because the Anglo-Irish, who invented Irish patriotism in their "idealization of a country rather than a race" (*ILN* 73), did not mingle easily with the mass of the Irish population. Yet they managed to impose some of their patriotic values with their language on the people. And as property owners they developed too "an intimacy with the unchanging earth which its too easily detachable cultivators found it more difficult to entertain" (*ILN* 73). The second part of that rather surprising sentence indicates that Butler was aware, for all his faith in Irish patriotism, that the modern Irish could fall victims of racialism too. For they also were a "scattered ... people" (*ILN* 73). ("Too easily detachable cultivators" as a reference to Irish emigration is an uncomfortable evasion of grim experience, masked as sardonic irony).

Butler held tenaciously to his theory that racialist nationalism is a product of displacement and dispersal. In 1963, in a talk entitled "Wolfe Tone and the Common Name of Irishman", he continued to value a patriotism which "concerns our country and not our blood" (*ILN* 34). Indeed by 1963 he had come to the view that the racialism that had so deleteriously affected the Germans and the Italians in modern times was not nationalism at all, but racialism *pur sang*.

> So-called Italian and German nationalists of thirty years ago were racialist and anti-nationalist. Hundreds and thousands of men, who lived for centuries under the same hills, beside the same lakes, were all at once told that they were aliens. In their thousands, Germans were rejected from the Tyrol and Slavs from northern Italy. What had this to do with nationalism, which is comprehensive and based on neighbourliness and shared experiences and common devotion to the land in which you live? It has nothing to do with racial origins. (*ILN* 35)

And the essay expresses a fear of the kind of dispersed society modernity has created, in which a diasporic version of national identity can all too easily replace the patriotism of a Tone:

> We can keep in touch with like-minded people by post in disregard of the person next door; we can get all the support for our views by turning a knob on the radio. That is why nationalism as Tone conceived it, that is to say a concentration of affection for the land in which you live and the people with whom you share it, has become in our day a delicate and fragile plant. It implies an intercourse with your neighbours which is direct and personal, whereas nowadays we need not bother with our neighbours, particularly if, as most people do, we live in cities; there are dozens of impersonal, indirect ways of bypassing our neighbours and being adherents of some remote community. (*ILN* 35-6)

Sixteen years later Butler returned to his theme in "Divided Loyalties" (first collected in *Escape from the Anthill*, 1985, where a revised version of the essay is dated 1984). There he compared his own sustained feelings for Ireland with the short-lived early twentieth-century emotions of a cousin Theo and the young Eric Dodds (subsequently Regius Professor of Greek in the University of Oxford). Their nationalism had been skin-deep, his more deeply-engrained, based as it was on his ownership of land: "if you are heir to some trees and fields and buildings and a river bank, your love for your country can be more enduring" (*IS* 97) than that of such as cousin Theo and Dodds "who had not an acre between them" (*IS* 97). Yet this essay of old age is touched with a valedictory, pessimistic note too as it records the passing of a way of life, the life of a minor gentry in Ireland, who might have been a bulwark against the forces of international commerce, if enough of them had been able, (like Butler himself it can truly be said), to extend their love of place to a dutiful love of country. For Butler, as old as the century in his eighty-fifth year, ownership of a "few acres of Irish soil" could give "an unreasoning obstinancy" but only "the illusion of security" (*IS* 97).

There is in those final phrases something of the quintessential Butler spirit – a sure grasp on the precise limits of a situation, whatever sentiment might hope for, which made him so refreshingly clear-eyed a writer. For he certainly knew that in modern conditions racialism, or ethnic nationalism, that had so besmirched 1930s and 1940s Europe, could be a threat in his own country as the patriotism he so valued and in fact represented in his good mannered yet exacting way, faded with the social conditions that had nurtured it in a vital few. His analysis of nationalism, implicit in the vivid essay that stands at the head of his oeuvre, and returned to throughout his career, challenges us to be aware of dangers that may lurk in a nationalism in the early 21st century which can invoke a globalised Irishness, a disapora of putatively shared identity, but which can involve wilful ignorance of our immediate neighbours in their sometimes difficult human particularity.

This is a revised and expanded version of the original address.

THE CITY

In memory of James Joyce and Trieste

You said: "I'll seek some other land, far off, with sails unfurled.
I'll find some worthier town than this and some serener clime.
For here ambition foiled is like a crime,
the quickening impulse of the heart is dead,
and sluggish thoughts entomb the past like lead.
Whichever way eyes glance or footsteps go,
the embers of a burnt-out ardour glow,
the scorched and broken years into the ash-pit hurled."

You'll find no other lands, my friend, speeding with sails unfurled.
Your city will go with you. Through its streets and squares
You'll still be strolling, as you strolled, despite your prayers.
You'll age beside the hearth you once held dear,
Thinking familiar thoughts. No ship will steer
Your heart, new-fallowed, to a virgin strand.
You wrecked your life in this poor, stubborn land.
It's wrecked beyond repair for all the world.

Translated, from the Greek of C.P. Cavafy, by Hubert Butler (1948).

BUTLER AND THE IRISH LITERARY REVIVAL

Edna Longley

This will be a brief glance at a large topic. It's no exaggeration to say that Hubert Butler's lifework was founded on his unusual decision to follow the gospel of a literary movement. Of course, the Irish Literary Revival was more than literary, and Butler's achievement further extends its meaning. First, I want to stress that when Butler invokes the Revival he speaks not just as an apostle but as a creator: a contributor to its continuing force. It is intrinsic to his autobiographical meditation on history that he should, at many points, reconceive the Revival's philosophy. In particular, Butler works creatively on relations between literature, culture and community. Second, I will suggest that Irish (Catholic) ambivalence about the Revival provides a significant context for some of Butler's difficulties. Here his "marginality" can be seen as representative and expressive. Finally, I will argue that all this gives Butler a significance for contemporary Irish cultural criticism which has been too little recognised (certainly by the academy). Here his marginality can be seen as central.

As Robert Tobin shows in his fine dissertation "No Absentee: Hubert Butler and the Irish Protestant Conscience", "Butler's moral genealogy" depends on the trinity of Standish O'Grady, George Russell and Horace Plunkett. These names mark the spot where the Revival impinges on practical affairs, on social models and political theory. To quote Butler's account of *The Irish Statesman*, they constitute a "bridge between literature and social endeavour, between Coole and Kilteragh" (*EA* 153-4). Not that Butler excludes the Revival's mystical dimension. *Ten Thousand Saints* is another kind of genealogy which may really belong on the same "Protestant-magical" shelf as Yeats's *A Vision*. Again, Butler's celebration of Ernest Renan identifies with Renan's Celticism, his belief in "those excellences which the Celt had once contributed to European civilisation: their gifts of imagination and of poetry, their defiance of the orthodox in thought and feeling" (*CD* 114). Nonetheless, when Butler discusses Revival writers it is usually in the context and in the mode of cultural politics. Thus he praises Yeats's "arrogance" in staying and stand against divorce: his defence of "Protestant values." Butler applies to Yeats favourite terms that characterize those values – terms that might surprise people who over-emphasize Yeats's irrational leanings. He calls him "an individualist and a Whig and a Liberal and a freethinker" (*ILN* 233). If Butler brings Yeats closer to himself by bringing him closer to George Bernard Shaw than Yeats might have liked, his insights light up all three.

A crucial act of cultural defence by Butler himself is his championing of the Revival in the polemical essay "*Envoy* and Mr Kavanagh." Here he asserts, for instance: "The Anglo-Irish were not only the cruel step-mothers of Gaelic civilisation, they were also the indulgent nurses and governesses of Irish literature in the English language" (*EA* 157). Elsewhere Butler reconnects the Revival with older patterns of Irish Protestant intellectual activity, such as antiquarianism and local history, which Yeats had strategically obscured even while remaking them for his own purposes. Thus Butler attaches – but does not confine or reduce – the Revival to its class and religious origins. Hence, perhaps, the fact that Butlerian Celts combine "poetry" with protest. They personify a robust "defiance of the orthodox" rather than ethereal "revolt against the despotism of fact". Butler's directness is salutary in that he faces the sectarian subtext which has driven attacks on the Revival since the 1890s. He pioneers a language whereby the issues might be admitted, articulated and debated if not resolved. That language, as in "*Envoy* and Mr Kavanagh", can become *enragé* as well as *engagé*, but it is above all critical and dialectical. It invites us to stand on open ground and argue back. In "Wolfe Tone and the Common Name of Irishman" Butler writes: "We may even come to be grateful for sharp expressions of opposition and only disturbed when, as in totalitarian countries, dissent is dead and every emphatic 'Yes!' does not meet its equally emphatic 'No!'" (*ILN* 47). Of course, this in itself amounts to a secular translation of "Protestant values" at their best. Butler's mantra "the right to private judgment" upholds not only "conscience" but liberty, critique, and liberty of critique. He reaffirms and reinvents the Revival's critical dimension together with the Enlightenment premises from which it derives. Further back (disputing the tenets of Thomas Merton's *Elected Silence*) Butler sees the "most precious legacy of the Reformation" as "our belief that authoritarianism in spiritual matters is an evil far greater than the disorders to which the abuse of private judgment has often led" (*ILN* 130).

Irish literary criticism was in a bad way during the mid-twentieth century. On this contemporary witnesses and retrospective commentators agree. In his valedictory editorial for *The Bell* (April 1946) Sean O'Faolain regrets that he has not published "more articles on literature, and on aesthetics and technique." But, he claims, "nobody could or can produce a purely literary magazine in Ireland today."[1] Despite his powers of "judgment" in another sense, Hubert Butler was no literary purist either. While his essay on *The Bell* credits O'Faolain with a literary mission akin to Yeats's ("not merely making a magazine but shaping a literature or calling it into being"), the title of that essay is "*The Bell*: An Anglo-Irish View"; and it chiefly features the journal's services to cultural inclusiveness: "we remnants of the Anglo-Irish 'intelligentsia' would have been nobody's children, had O'Faolain's *Bell* not taken us under its wing" (*EA* 148). Butler's house-and-family sense of *The Bell*, like the nurses and governesses in his *Envoy* essay, recasts Yeats's "ancestral houses" which symbolize the nexus between cultural and literary tradition. For Butler, an Irish journal could never be merely a literary magazine or little magazine. It was "a sortie from a besieged city", a crucial agora, a critical forum on the state of the nation (*EA* 154). This conviction shapes the voice of his essays. Butler speaks as one member of a community arguing with the others, a local man who criticises his neighbour as himself. Vocal structures and shades, of course, can also be an oblique form of rhetorical insistence, as in Butler's use of the first-person plural: "We must find some way of living together and I think Tone's way, the way of generous inconsistency, is still the best" (*ILN* 47). On one of the few occasions I met Hubert Butler I gave him a copy of a new journal (*The Irish Review*) with which I was (and am) editorially involved. He looked through the list of contributors, and then suddenly asked: "Where are the Anglo-Irish?" This was not just a literal enquiry nor exactly a rhetorical question, more an anguished metaphysical exclamation. In any case, it lamented a voice seemingly absent from the contemporary agora.

All this explains why Hubert Butler's concept of literature can tend to the utilitarian or instrumental. For example, "Nurseries of Writing" (1951) – that metaphor again – proposes that *The Bell* should foster regional writing less as "a source of entertainment and inspiration" than as "a means of self-expression, self-criticism, self-adjustment. In Ireland it is this second function which tends to get ignored" (*CD,* 143). By the same token, the mid-twentieth century Irish critic probably needed to defend literature more than to analyse or evaluate it. Censorship was not the only issue. Speaking in Russia (1956) Butler referred to a forty-year "aggressive campaign against the English language which has weakened the prestige of Anglo-Irish literature" (*ILN* 202). Although Butler's *Envoy* article attacks that journal's confusion of criticism with abuse, he understands why the urgency of his message made the messenger so breathless: "It was as though he raced through the enemy's lines, bearing some tremendous news, and at last collapsed raving among his friends, whom in his delirium he mistakes for the philistines. His lips are frothing, his pulse racing but he can only stammer out a few baleful familiar syllables, 'Mr Smyllie', 'Austin Clarke', 'Radio Éireann', 'Faugh!' He gives a last belch and dies pillowed in his own vomit, his message undelivered" (*EA* 155). That powerful image of a root-problem of Irish criticism exemplifies one means of overcoming it (inventive parable).

Butler's *Envoy* article also illuminates the problem of criticism more broadly. Patrick Kavanagh's scattergun attacks on the Revival, to which Butler is replying, do not simply reflect Kavanagh's own prejudice. They denote a long-standing reluctance to base either Irish literature or criticism on such a suspect and heretical foundation. In 1955 an outside observer, Donald Davie, was surprised by the failure of Dublin poets to assimilate Yeats's later work. And he ascribed this to "the lack of any continuous and self-respecting tradition of literary criticism", to the way in which "positions gained are silently abandoned, questions are left in mid-air, issues are left unresolved" – in fact, the antithesis of Butler's own intellectual practice.[2] Butler phrases the problem this way: "The Anglo-Irish contribution to letters is today ... a chief focus of psychological disturbance" (*EA* 156). His own literary contribution may still disturb in this sense – although the present occasion seems far from a revisionists' retreat. Yet a recent historical study of Irish criticism[3], which betrays the usual difficulty with the Revival – with nurses and governesses, perhaps – does not mention Hubert Butler. Again, Butler appears in *The Field Day Anthology of Irish Writing* (1991) under "Autobiography and Memoirs" but not under "Cultural Criticism." Ironically, an editorial headnote confuses Horace Plunkett with Count Plunkett.

The Irish Literary Revival may not be over yet. Something dead would hardly be so vigorously attacked by contemporary nationalist academics, who have translated earlier modes of hostility into a "post-colonial" idiom. For example, a recent book, *Joyce and the Anglo-Irish*, packages and approves Joyce as a Catholic writer whose "text splits away from revivalism ... is *devoted* to an undermining of revivalism's status as cultural nationalism and to a displacement of the Yeatsian Protestant tradition from the round tower of Irish literary culture."[4] Such crude reductiveness is given currency by the problem of criticism, by the problem of writing Irish literary history since 1922, by reluctance to look in certain places for continuity, dialectic and reinvention. This makes Hubert Butler a key figure among those writers who stayed or returned. Partly in a fascinating counterpoint with O'Faolain, partly through his intimate feeling for a great act of "collective creation", he helps us to track the Revival's dynamic up to the present day (*EA* 153). Catholic comment on Protestant critics often (self-revealingly) misconceives "the right of private judgment" as being "individualistic" in an introverted, anti-communitarian, wilfully perverse manner. Butler exemplifies how "private judgment", as the principle of dissent and the ethic of criticism, can operate to collective public ends. As we have seen, he is a critic who really believes in criticism: in argument, debate and dialectic, in "sharp expressions of opposition". His criticism typically deplores the absence of such values in other critics – in most academic criticism, for example. Thus he admires F.R. Leavis's study of Lawrence because, although "irascible and donnish", Leavis "is right and courageous, and maybe only an academic can nowadays effectively draw the teeth of academicism" (*ILN* 219). "The Sense of Evil and the Sense of Guilt", Butler's analysis of the soft spots in Graham Greene and Stephen Spender, wonderfully proves his point that *English* literature sorely misses the cold eye of the *Anglo-Irish*. And if Irish critics either fear to stick their necks out or alternatively collapse into their own vomit, English critics, as Butler notes in a comparative essay on Edmund Wilson and E.M. Forster, conspire in "friendly reticences and decencies of intercourse" (*EA* 185). Of Greene and Spender he writes: "Their art and their reputation would not, I think, survive a real *kulturkampf* in which first principles were not only invoked but applied" (*EA* 173).

This judgment is informed by Butler's Eastern European experience as well as his Irish experience, and it implies his own contrasting practice as a holistic critic for whom literature, "Coole", can never be enough. He signals his involvement in "a real *kulturkampf*" (not an admission that every Irish intellectual is prepared to make). Hubert Butler ultimately appears less marginal than does the Ireland of his time: an Ireland which gravely lacked (as it may still lack) discursive writers able to think about literature and culture in their deepest relation to darkest history. The Irish Free State, so to speak, enters the Second World War in Butler's writings – not only in "The Children of Drancy" or "The Invader Wore Slippers." Contemporary Irish cultural criticism, which sometimes boasts its European credentials, will not have grown up until it has fully assimilated Hubert Butler. In "The Barriers" (1941) Butler cleverly invokes the Revival's "first principles" to argue that the Free State would be less British, more independent, in cultural complexion had it not allowed Irish writers to leave and to influence countries other than Ireland. He criticises isolationist "indifference and xenophobia" by adjusting the gospel of Revival cultural nationalism to wartime conditions and hence to Ireland's longer-term European horizons. Here, as so often, he is himself the creative "interpreter" of "the national life" for whom he calls:

> It is a strange time to maintain the theory that a distinctive culture cannot exist without cultural intercourse, but since the mainspring of our freedom was not political theory but the claim that Ireland possessed and could develop a unique culture of her own, it is seasonable to examine this claim … A nation cannot be created negatively by elimination or strategic retreats into the past. It must crystallise round the contemporary genius that interprets it. The interpreters will be those who can see the national life as well as live it. (*GWT* 32-3)

NOTES

1 See *Signing-Off* (April 1946), reprinted in (ed.) Sean McMahon, *The Best of the Bell* (Dublin: The O'Brien Press, 1978) pp.120-3.

2 See Donald Davie, "Reflections of an English Writer in Ireland", *Studies* 44 (1955) pp. 439-45.

3 Gerry Smyth, *Decolonisation and Criticism: The Construction of Irish Literature* (London: Pluto Press, 1998).

4 Len Platt, *Joyce and the Anglo-Irish* (Amsterdam-Atlanta: Rodopi, 1998) p.232.

THE KILKENNY DEBATES

Proinsias Ó Drisceoil

Edward Said might well have been thinking of the essayist, Hubert Butler, when he delineated for the intellectual the role of "heightening consciousness, becoming aware of tension, complexities and taking on oneself the responsibility for one's community. This is a non-specialist role, it has to do with issues which cut way over professional discipline." [1]

Hubert Butler's work as an essayist and as a founder member of a number of societies in his native County Kilkenny are complementary and many of his best essays arise directly from his organizational involvement. [2] In 1944 he had revived the Kilkenny Archaeological Society, but by 1952 he felt obliged to resign his membership following what was alleged by the Society's president to have been an insult by Butler to the Papal Nuncio and thus to the Pope himself. This referred to a meeting of the International Affairs Association of Ireland at which Butler referred in the Nuncio's presence to the forced conversion during World War II of 240,000 Serbian Orthodox to Catholicism. [3] These conversions had been carried out by the Croatian "Quisling", Ante Pavelitch, with the collusion of Archbishop Stepinac, then the subject of heroic admiration in Ireland because of his imprisonment by Tito.

Butler "felt that the honour of the small Protestant community in Southern Ireland would be compromised if those of us who had investigated the fact, remained silent about what we had discovered" and he was prepared to endure popular ignominy and denunciation by all of Kilkenny's local authority bodies as a result (*EA* 270-283)

Those members of the Kilkenny Archaeological Society sympathetic to Butler became the core of the Kilkenny Arts Society and its sub-committee, the Kilkenny Debating Society. "It was started a year ago by old Lady Bellew and a local farmer's wife ... except for Lady Bellew the entire committee is Roman Catholic ... I was asked to join the committee ... but I was credited with rather extreme views on freedom of speech ... and I thought the committee would be in stronger position without me", wrote Butler in a letter of March 1954. Although not formally identifiable, Butler was the most influential member of the Debating Society, a discrete and effective backroom organizer. The gap between the Arts Society and culture as popularly practised in Kilkenny was notable. A letter published in local papers from its secretary, "S. McGrath Bourke, B.Arch., M.R.I.A.I., A.R.I.B.A." announced its annual Art Exhibition as "no provincial 'arty' show", offering as proof the fact that exhibition would include work by Henry Moore. [4] Those seeking drama rather than art in Kilkenny at this time were confined to productions by a variety of Catholic schools and organizations: *Kevin Barry*, and *The Dawning of the Day* at the Boy's Hall; *Eire, Handmaid of the Eucharist* in nearby Callan; and in the city's theatre, with a cast of nearly two hundred, *The Message of Lourdes*, a play in three acts.

Butler's experiences during the Nuncio controversy had left him with an enduring sense of the extent to which "parochially minded people neglect their parishes to pronounce ignorantly about the universe, while the universalists are so conscious of the world-wide struggles of opposing philosophies that the rights and wrongs of any regional conflict dwindle to insignificance against a cosmic panorama" (*EA* 272). Thus when he came to arrange a debate in 1954 under the auspices of the Kilkenny Debating Society, between Ulster Unionists and southern anti-partitionists, he wrote to Colonel W.W.B. Topping, the principal Unionist speaker suggesting the lines on which he wished to see the debate proceed,

> I believe that a clear, friendly statement of the Protestant standpoint re clerical interference – after all we don't allow our own clergy to interfere – would be valuable here too and would not be resented. That is the core of the matter for us Southern Protestants, our right to judge for ourselves. It is more important than political allegiance and the economic aspect. [5]

Reactions to the proposed debate – the first of its kind since partition – was swift. The Ulster Loyalist and Democratic Unionist Association, a predecessor of the Democratic Unionist Party, passed a resolution deploring

> the action of the government and the Prime Minister in particular, in permitting Mr. Topping, MP, the Unionist Chief Whip and Mr. W Douglas, Secretary of the Ulster Unionist Council to attend, as representing Ulster Loyalists, the debate organised by Kilkenny Debating Society … We maintain that no useful purpose can be served in debating partition with men holding extreme views for the destruction of the British Empire … The appeasement policy, the sale and betrayal of Ulster must stop.[6]

A protest meeting was called for the Ulster Hall and telegrams of protest were sent to Lord Brookeborough, the Grand Master of the Grand Orange Lodge of Ireland and to the chairman of the Ulster Unionist Council. The matter was raised in the Northern Ireland Senate, where the visit was defended by Senator Bradley, while the leader of the house, Colonel Gordon refused to be drawn.

In Kilkenny opinion was divided. The liberal *Kilkenny Journal,* edited by the husband of one of the Debating Society secretaries, Mary Kenealy, reported the proposed debate factually and without emotion. (The connection between the *Journal* and the Society resulted in its remaining silent throughout the controversy). The rival *Kilkenny People*, which had led the attacks on Butler during the Nuncio affair, felt no similar need for restraint. An article entitled "Dramatis Personae", giving details of the careers of the speakers, was hedged between two patriotic ballads, while editorials and anonymous correspondence, much of it suspiciously close to the editorial line, became more and more virulent as the weeks passed:

> Frankly we believe the debate will serve no useful purpose. It will, of course, provide entertainment, which seems to be its primary object, but those people outside the society who hope to be present will pay 5/- for the extravaganza. One thing is certain, there has already been so much controversy over the matter in the six counties and so much abuse has been poured by the Unionist speakers that it seems impossible that the more bigoted section of the Orange Order will be in any way convinced by what is said in Kilkenny...[7]

An IRA veteran living in Cheltenham wrote to *The Kilkenny People* to say "surely the people of Kilkenny are not forgetting Michael Collins, James Connolly and the other Irish patriots who did so much to keep this kind of thing out of the country." One "Bearna Baoghail" wrote saying that "the holding in Easter Week of an event as that advertised by the Kilkenny Debating Society is tantamount to an insult to our Patriot Dead. It is to be hoped that the 'show' will not go on." [8] In less serious vein, *The Irish Times* of 4 April printed a cartoon showing one of two men passing a poster advertising the debate remarking: "The rumour has it that as soon as they get across the Border, they're going to throw themselves on our mercy and seek political asylum ..."

The travel writer, Richard Hayward, and Eoin "the Pope" O'Mahony, vice-chairman of the Anti-Partition Association, were asked to make contact with Unionist and nationalist leaders. Also to speak were the president of the Irish Association, Joseph Johnston, Mary O'Malley, a nationalist councillor in Belfast who was also a member of the Irish Association and Arnold Marsh, a Protestant nationalist who was principal of Drogheda Grammar School. Hayward was to be a principal speaker but was anxious to speak without taking one side or the other!

As the Unionists were not prepared to debate on a Sunday,[9] the debate was fixed for Friday, 23 April, in the City Technical School, with the Chief Executive Officer of the Kilkenny Vocational Education Committee, Dr Richard Walsh, acting as host. A number of motions were proposed and such was the interest in the debate that a change at Unionist insistence from the motion "That Ireland's best interests are with the United Kingdom" to "That partition ought to be abolished" was front page news in *The Irish Times*.[10] In fact neither was debated, the final motion being "That Ulster's best interests lie with the United Kingdom."

Finding a suitable chairman proved even more difficult. W.B. Stanford refused lest it affect his chances of winning the Senate seat for Trinity College.[11] Seán Mac Bride would not participate if Ernest Blythe, who was willing to act as chair, were to be selected.[12] Finally, Professor Myles Dillon, a leading Irish scholar at the Institute for Advanced Studies and a brother of James Dillon who was to be a minister in the new government, agreed. It was to be a task requiring diplomacy. For example, Colonel Topping requested that his twenty minutes be exclusive of time lost due to booing and cat-calling.[13] Security arrangements were extensive and an armed Special Branch presence was provided.[14] Robert Jacob of Waterford humorously speculated that "the gunmen may move in and dynamite the Henry Moore after they have purged the debate of its principal speakers and promoters." [15]

A major difficulty became the huge demand for tickets and arrangements were made to accommodate part of the overflow on the window-sills outside. McBride and Topping were both experienced members of the Bar, but Topping threw McBride by concentrating on the inadequacies of the South rather than addressing the motion proper. Having referred to the former's "attractive though non-Gaelic accent", he went on to relate how "on the way down, having lunch and a cup of tea here and there," he had enquired as to the meaning of "An Tóstal", an off-season tourism festival then in progress, but could find no one to explain the word. "We in Ulster would not accept what was virtually a dead language in substitution for a language which was their official language." He wished to make one thing clear: "he yielded to no one in his claim to be a good Irishman and was as good an Irishman as anyone in Kilkenny or elsewhere." While English or Scottish identity was not incompatible with being British "over here the choice had to be between being Irish or being British and they said in the North of Ireland that the price of being divorced from being British was infinitely too high." Dublin "was known to be subservient to the authoritarian precepts emanating from the Roman Catholic Hierarchy." The 1951 Mother and Child Scheme had adequately justified Loyalist fears, as did film, book, and radio censorship. The South had seceded from the United Kingdom and it was this and "not, as is sometimes fantastically suggested, a mixture of gerrymandering and a British army of occupation" which determined the attitude of "the Ulsterman". Catholics in the North had "the same rights that we demand for ourselves as Protestants ... but we cannot help seeing what is happening down here."

In reply, McBride defended the rights of the Catholic hierarchy to make representations to government and stated that "the second last King of England

was deposed as result of the views of the leaders of the Church of England …
I wonder did it not occur to him that the government of the Six Counties was
run by the Orange Lodges." With regard to the Mother and Child Scheme, "if
Colonel Topping had the same experience as I had of Noel Browne, he might
not have regarded him as such a good argument." On the question of national
identity, McBride argued in terms of natural loyalties.

> If Colonel Topping was an Irishman, and he was quite certain that
> he was, why then should he choose to give his allegiance to
> another country. That seemed to run completely contrary to the
> usual course of human nature. A multi-lingual society was
> common all over the world – most notably in Switzerland, the
> best run country in Europe. Britain's real reason for enforcing
> and maintaining partition was that she required the industrial and
> ship-building potential in time of war – Britain was largely
> responsible for the imposition of partition. Britain maintained it
> by financial, political and military power.

Hubert Butler, who anonymously reported the debate for *The Manchester
Guardian*, described William Douglas as having endeared himself to the
audience "by his easy geniality and strong Ulster personality," and not least by
losing his notes! In a statement which was to be strongly contested by the
nationalist M.P. Cahir Healy, Douglas quoted the M.P. as having praised the
fairness of housing allocation in Belfast. Apart from that "all they wished the
people of the Free State was 'Good luck, God bless you and leave us alone!'"

Eoin O'Mahony and Arnold Marsh made a number of economic arguments
and O'Mahony went on to refer to what he termed "the new plantation of
Ulster" – the domination of higher education opportunities in Northern
Ireland by English people. Joseph Johnston detailed the work of the Irish
Association, while Mary O'Malley in a brief but balanced and thoughtful
contribution, described the existence of "two types of working classes in the
Six Counties, the privileged and non-privileged." As a member of Belfast
Corporation she had experienced "clearly defined acts of discrimination"
against her co-religionists "but it would not be fair at all to compare it with
fascist and totalitarian regimes." Richard Hayward concluded the contributions
from the platform with a generalised call for mutual respect.

None of the anticipated trouble materialised and Dillon was able to
conclude the meeting by citing the debate as an example of free speech. As an
Irish scholar, he was anxious to disassociate himself from any desire to impose
the Irish language on an unwilling Northern Ireland, "since I have never yet met
any Gaelic scholar of eminence who supported the present campaign." [16]

There was widespread coverage of the debate. Eoin "the Pope" O'Mahony described *The Irish News* as having "sulked" and *The Ulster Herald* as "venomous."[17] *The Belfast Telegraph* reported the debate on its front page, while *The Northern Whig* and *The Belfast Newsletter* also carried reports. Southern papers, including *The Irish Times* and *The Catholic Standard*, also gave it coverage. There was disappointment at *The Irish Times'* reporting, of which O'Mahony commented that it "does not like McBride or me and this may explain their attitude. Symillie [the editor] would not do anything unless he were asked to speak or at least advise."[18] Due to McBride's participation, the debate could not be broadcast by Radio Éireann until after the election then in progress – although it was subsequently broadcast on two occasions. Butler was disappointed at the complete absence of Kilkenny Protestants from the debate. All of his active supporters in the Archaeological Society were Catholics and in a letter to Topping he referred to the fact that

> all the local Prods (sic) while fighting themselves in the British forces and getting jobs for their children in England, accept the Soldier's Song as the anthem of the country, stand up in the cinema etc, etc. In fact not many will be at the debate and I doubt if a single one will speak. They have given up any hope of influence, other than indirect, here and are resigned to disappearing genteelly.[19]

In a letter to O'Mahony, he referred to

> an extraordinary paradox, that in fact all the proper West Britons abstained completely and even refused to put up Topping and Douglas when asked. Have you ever reflected that a real imperialist won't even fight for his own cause in Ireland. His attitude is that of the Republican prisoner who "won't recognise the court" and so keeps a "dignified silence". I wonder if the Northerners would abstain in a united Ireland?[20]

The debate had cost the organisers money and not all the participants were like "Don Quixote O'Mahony who did all his extensive travelling hitch-hiking and walking, instead of in a smart car and sent in no expenses at all."[21] More pressing was the controversy in *The Kilkenny People*, to which Butler persuaded Johnston and Marsh to write in defence of the debates. (Like himself these were intellectual southern Protestants of mildly nationalist disposition).[22] Cahir Healy wrote to say that partition was non-debatable and virulently denied the statement attributed to him by Douglas.[23] This debate continued until August when Healy declared the correspondence closed. The content of this argument may have had little impact in Kilkenny but the letters were reprinted in the

Omagh newspaper *The Ulster Herald* where Healy's points based on a religious head count in Enniskillen meant more.

Butler entered the controversy with just one letter and that under the nom-de-plume, "Protestant Anti-Partitionist." In it he criticised the incursion "into local Kilkenny politics" of William Douglas who, using information sent to him confidentially by prominent Debating Society member, Shelia Leahy, had used his 12th of July speech to attack the treatment of Protestants in the city.[24] *The Kilkenny People* editorial counter-attacked Douglas, reporting him as saying "while I was in Kilkenny I was informed that Protestants get one in five hundred Council or Corporation houses, that Protestants are not employed by the Corporation or County Council … that Protestant radiologists and nurses are not employed in the county hospitals, that Protestants librarians are not employed in the city and county libraries, and that there is not a Protestant member of the Civic Guards in Kilkenny." The editorial hinted threateningly that Protestant businesses in Kilkenny "would find it difficult to exist without Catholic support" if they did not reject Douglas: "We feel sure that the Protestant population of Kilkenny will be eager to refute Mr. Douglas's charge." [25]

The City Corporation unanimously condemned Douglas, and various Protestant employees were cited to show how false his charge had been. More bizarrely it was claimed that Kilkenny Corporation in effect took the alleged Unionist view of housing allocation since they had as a tenant a Protestant single mother who had been selected ahead of a Catholic family of ten![26] In August a Methodist former resident wrote to the local press praising the tolerance he had experienced in Kilkenny,[27] but Douglas in a follow-up letter asked if Protestants did not apply "because they would not be considered for local authority positions and they knew it."[28]

Butler suffered public disapprobation on account of Douglas's accusations, and although he knew who Douglas's informant had been, he chose not to expose her, and take the blame himself. Sheila Leahy, Douglas's correspondent, was a founder of the Kilkenny Arts Society and was a teacher and Irish language enthusiast. She wrote privately to Butler apologising for the fact that he and not she was blamed for Topping's speech on discrimination against Protestants in Kilkenny:

> I sounded a few of the poorer Protestants round Kilkenny and they said that all Douglas's allegations were only too true … I fret and fume with the rage of impotence because I dare not show my hand … I feel so concious (*sic*)-stricken too because no matter how you gloss over it, I have thrown suspicion on you and perhaps I am not so brave that I would really want to unmask myself. Soon I will call on Mrs. Kenealy and tell her that if the

K.A.S. wishes to survive the blast, we will have to have "holy" lectures and pictures for the winter. [29]

Ironically, Butler was accepting approbium for views he did not in fact hold on the subject of discrimination against Protestants in Kilkenny:

Everyone thinks – or those who don't know me think – that I was the informant but I wasn't as I haven't ever found that such discrimination does exist. Anyway it was very tactless of Douglas as of course it focuses blame on the Kilkenny Debating Society. [30]

Leahy wrote to *The Irish Times* of 6 October 1954 in response to a letter from Alasdair MacCába, advocating North-South co-operation, citing the Kilkenny debate as an example of what MacCába was advocating:

The great success of the debate proves that the educated majority of the Irish people want reconciliation … Since (it) was successful every effort was made to belittle its importance and to suggest it was the effort of the handful of pro-British ex-Unionists. Yet the organisers were all Irish nationalist by birth and tradition.

The Kilkenny People's attack on Leahy also served to cover an attack on Butler, always a popular target of the paper's editor:

We are gravely suspicious that somewhere behind the scenes somebody was conscious that a platform should be provided here for the expression of views antagonistic to the religious and national sentiments of our people. [31]

Leahy replied to this attack accusing the paper of "reactionary nationalism" and of forgetting the fact that in a united Ireland "the Orangemen" would be twenty-five per cent of the population and would have to be accommodated. [32] Butler thought of asking *The Irish Times* to publish a hostile attack on *The Kilkenny People* but desisted at the behest of Mary Kenealy. He was particularly concerned at the fact that *The Kilkenny People* had inherited the goodwill of the Protestant *Kilkenny Moderator* "and still maintains many of the subscribers" but "is hostile to this debate and the conciliatory spirit in which it originated." [33]

In fact popular interest in the controversy was on the wane and by September it had become a dead issue. Interest in partition was slight in Kilkenny and at the end of 1954 the city's branch of the Anti-Partition Association was disbanded, the few remaining members (the most active of whom was Tyrone-born Owen O'Kelly, also secretary of the Archaeological Society) going on to form a branch of Liam Kelly's Fianna Uladh.[34] Partition had not been an issue at the general election and afterward ceased to be an issue of primary consequence.

In subsequent private correspondence Butler gave his own view on partition:

> My own conviction is that a United Ireland is only a question of time and can be brought about by peaceful methods simply because the interests economic and cultural of the two halves of the country will ultimately draw us together: I think it would be hugely to the advantage of the Protestant minority in the South, for example, if there were strong Ulster representation in the Dáil. Very few Protestants think on those lines.[35]

Ironically, it was the advent of television, rather than opposition from more local forms of politics or media, that led to the ending of the Kilkenny debates, which continued annually until 1960 and were revived for single debates in 1966 and 1971. No debate in the years after 1954 burned with the passion which surrounded the debate of that year. The topics tended to be international and intellectual ("In the Atomic Age, Small Nations Stand Alone", 1955; "Is Free Trade the Answer?", 1957; "Is the Press Abusing its Freedom?", 1958; "That Our Schools Fail to Educate for Modern Life", 1959; "That Rhodesia's Declaration of Independence Is Justified", 1966). Even a debate on the language revival ("Should Ireland Revive Her Language?") in 1956 with speakers as distinguished as Seán Ó Faoláin, Myles na gCopaleen, Cecil Woodham Smith, Seán Ó hEigeartaigh and David Greene failed to similarly engage the popular imagination. Butler was prompted to revive the debates in 1971 by a Radio Éireann re-broadcast of its recording of the 1954 debate, possibly done in the interest of public education at the early stages of the "Northern Troubles."[36] The topic for the 1971 debate was entry to the Common Market, a not insignificant choice given that the eventual overwhelming vote in favour of entry marked the terminal decline of the very irredentist nationalism of which the opposition to the Society's partition debate had been a notable instance.

Butler's analysis for *The Manchester Guardian* had to await this vote and related social, educational and economic developments before the argument he put forward won wider acceptance and intellectual support:

> Ulster of the Six Counties means more than some land that has to be grabbed back from the grabbers ... It is an intricate human problem. How has a large dissident community to be reconciled to the rest of Ireland? What concessions will be asked and what

can be granted if this is to be achieved? … If it is really as disgraceful as *The Kilkenny People* said to expose the Marble City to the contamination of Colonel Topping, what hideous contamination lay ahead if the anti-partitionist dream was realised? Dáil Éireann would have to listen for years on end to those remarks … There would be rows of Colonel Toppings… and they would be by no means the worst … As the preliminaries for the debate had shown, (there) were yet more irreconcilable Orangemen, to whom Topping and Douglas were mere mealy-mouthed Quislings prepared to debate the undebatable border with Papists and gunmen.[37]

NOTES

1   Edward Said, "Europe and Its Others, An Arab Perspective" in Richard Kearney, ed., *Visions of Europe* (Dublin: Wolfhound Press,1992) p.197.

2   See, for example, "The Referendum", *Grandmother and Wolfe Tone*, pp.77-78, or "Portrait of a Minority" in *Escape from the Anthill*, pp.270-282.

3   The controversy is described by Butler in "The Sub-Prefect Should Have Held His Tongue" (1956), collected in *Escape from the Anthill*.

4   *The Kilkenny Journal* 3 April 1953.

5   Hubert Butler, letter to Colonel Topping, 12 March 1954.

6   Ed Maloney and Andy Pollak, *Paisley* (Dublin: Poolbeg, 1986) pp. 66-67.

7   *The Kilkenny People* 7 April 1954.

8   *The Kilkenny People* 24 April 1954.

9   Eoin O'Mahony, letter to Hubert Butler, date unknown.

10 *The Irish Times* 9 April 1954.

11 W.B. Stanford, letter to Hubert Butler, 26 March 1954. Publicly, Stanford gave examination pressures as his reason.

12 Eoin O'Mahony, letter to Mary Kenealy and Sheila Leahy, 23 March 1954.

13 Butler Papers, Trinity College Dublin, typescript of a report to *The Manchester Guardian*.

14 Butler Papers, typescript of a report to *The Manchester Guardian*.

15 Robert Jacob, letter to Susan Butler, date unknown.

16 *The Irish Times* 24 April 1954; *The Kilkenny People* 1 May 1954; Hubert Butler, typescript

of a report to *The Manchester Guardian*.

17 Eoin O'Mahony, letter to Susan Butler, date unknown.

18 Eoin O'Mahony, letter to Hubert Butler, 18 May 1954.

19 Hubert Butler, letter to Colonel Topping, 12 April 1954.

20 Hubert Butler, letter to Colonel Topping, 12 April 1954.

21 Hubert Butler, letter to Mary Kenealy, May 1954. A party for the speakers had cost the Butlers £15. Susan Butler, however, only claimed 35/-, this being the amount she spent on whiskey, which she considered an inappropriate drink for such an occasion.

22 *The Kilkenny People* 15 May 1954.

23 *The Kilkenny People* 24 May 1954.

24 *The Kilkenny People* 24 July 1954.

25 *The Kilkenny People* 17 July 1954.

26 *The Kilkenny People* 31 July 1954.

27 *The Kilkenny People* 7 August 1954.

28 *The Kilkenny People* 7 August 1954.

29 Sheila Leahy, letter to Hubert Butler, 5 August 1954.

30 Hubert Butler, letter to Martin Hanratty, 16 June 1954.

31 *The Kilkenny People* 19 June 1954.

32 *The Kilkenny People* 19 June 1954.

33 Hubert Butler, letter to *The Irish Times*, date illegible. The letter was not sent. Butler is likely to have been particularly conscious of the period spent by Standish O'Grady as Editor of *The Kilkenny Moderator*.

34 *The Kilkenny People* 27 November 1954.

35 Hubert Butler, letter to Martin Hanratty, 16 June 1954. Hanratty appears to have had connections to Irish-American politics and, possibly, to the IRA.

36 Hubert Butler, letter to Raymond Crotty, 19 January 1971.

37 Butler Papers, typescript of a report to *The Manchester Guardian*. Butler seems to have been unhappy with the sub-editing of the report (letter to Eoin O'Mahony, 14 May 1954).

WORKING ON THE SAINTS:
CLUES TO THE IRISH GENOME

Richard Crampton

I

Widely acclaimed as one of the great Irish essayists of the twentieth century, the erudite Hubert Butler ranked *Ten Thousand Saints: A Study of Irish and European Origins* (1972) – his investigation of the origins of 10,000 Irish saints, 15,000 ancestors and heroes, and 50 tribes, as well as the early invaders of Ireland – as his most important work.[1] In the decade following his death, the new science of human population archaeogenetics has scanned Irish and European prehistory using genetic diffusion of the pre-Neolithic male Y-chromosome of the haplotype 1 variety.[2] Coordinated analyses of DNA, linguistics and archaeology have now fortuitously verified Butler's prescient research into the Irish and European tribal jigsaw. Butler had anticipated how DNA would link Irish, Basque and other European genomes, and in the process showed where to direct further genomic research in Irish and European prehistory.

Why and how did this remarkable foreshadowing occur? Butler notes, "The Irish repeatedly insisted that their ancestors had come from Thrace, Spain, Northern Europe and the Caucasus ... we must look to the ancient pre-Celtic tribes of Europe in order to learn the origins of the Irish people, its tribal and ancestral names" (*TTS* 80-91). Ireland's westernmost European location made, therefore, a good base for the collection and examination of names, puns and stories in order to solve the intricate linguistic, historical, geographic, archaeological, topographical puzzles of prehistoric tribal wanderings. Likewise, Ireland's westerly position would later lead to the DNA analysis of Basque-Irish links that, by chance, would confirm Butler's work.[3] Thus Butler's accurate forecast from pre-Celtic and Celtic linguistics would match the following prediction of the geneticist David McConnell (based on seminal studies by Daniel Bradley, Steven Whitehead and Patrick Cunningham in the late 1990s):

> Ireland, with a rich archaeology, as a peripheral island, may have preserved exceptional evidence of its early gene pools and so may be able to contribute important pieces to the genetic jigsaw of Europe. Ireland has one of the largest stores of pre-Celtic relics and artefacts in Europe, and the modern gene pool of Ireland (with Scotland and Wales) may best represent a European pre-Celtic gene pool dating to 9000 years ago.[4]

Subsequently, in 2000, DNA analysis of the diffusion of the inherited male Y-chromosome, involving thousand-year old Irish paternal family lines, provided data that would authenticate Butler's linguistic, archaeological and anthropological work a generation earlier. [5]

II

Returning to Kilkenny in 1941, Butler expanded his interest in local prehistory, geneaology, anthropology, geography, agriculture, botany and archaeology, and systematically explored Irish and European tribal origins. An adept linguist with a classical education, he taught himself "ad hoc Irish"; borrowed, collected and read widely in Irish and European anthropological and archaeological texts and journals; and revived the Kilkenny Archaeological Society that had been founded by John Prim and James Graves in the 19th century. During the next 31 years of the pre-computer era, he travelled widely in Ireland and Europe, exploring many archaeological sites; assembled a large and carefully cross-referenced database on three-by-five-inch file cards; analyzed it; and made numerous tables, indices, glossaries, charts and maps. He published two articles as well as *Ten Thousand Saints*, and devised a compendium of the origins of Irish and European heroes, ancestors, tribes and saints. [6] His various indices include 392 saints; 736 ancestors and heroes; 334 Irish tribes and their ancestors; 265 Continental tribes and their ancestors; and 124 historians and historic figures. His glossary of Irish tribal puns correlates 50 Irish and Continental tribal names with 103 clusters of tribal folk names and 648 commonly used tribal pun elements. [7] This text, among his papers held by Trinity College, Dublin, further contains three tables of variants of yet another 197 elements which help to track Irish and European tribes and ancestors.

On the basis of these data, Butler hypothesizes that early Irish ancestors and saints fit a pattern. Ancient genealogic practice, he argues, melded ancestors. Like those of the Greeks and Hebrews, Irish tribes made punning stories to keep genealogy intact (*ILN* 247-262). Over twenty-five thousand ancestors, heroes, tribes and saints came punned from Irish, Latin and, rarely, English. Butler codifies pun-biography anecdotes about them in order to reveal ancient tribal names and origins. Thus, the names of saints – a Christian by-product of the dying art of ancestor-making – reflected the composite ancestors of composite tribes. Later, the celibate saints of the Irish Christian era would end this practice of punning on the ancestors of tribes (*TTS* 36-61).

To savour Butler's methods, one must first scrutinize the definition of the pun: "a play on words using a word for two or more meanings, or using two or more words of the same sound with different meanings" (*OED*). Notable Irish punners include Swift (*A Modest Defense of Punning*, 1716), Sheridan (*Ars Punica*, 1719), Joyce and Butler. The former pair communicated in puns, like their prehistoric predecessors, as discerned by Butler. At a *Finnegans Wake* reading during the 1966 PEN Congress in New York, Butler and his friend Padraic Colum shared the discovery of Joyce's pun of "moyles and moyles" regarding the River Liffey, which derives from "Silent, O Moyle, be the roar of thy waters" (*ILN* 207-208). In particular, "homonymble" puns and games (*Encyclopaedia Britannica*, 1975) help us understand Butler's methods. For example, the French "pas de leur eaune que nous," a pun on the American admonition "paddle your own canoe," illustrates mixed language punning. Butler detected names of prehistoric tribes between or among words, glossaries, dialects and languages. The invented punned stories of ancestors or heroes fortified memories of tribal genealogical narratives as shown by this "homonymble" pun:

> How can a man escape from a solid, sealed room, containing only him and a table, in a dense forest? He rubs his hands till they are sore (saw). Then he saws the table in half. Two halves make a whole. He crawls through the hole. Then he shouts till he is hoarse, and gallops away.

From similar punned stories about heroes, ancestors and saints, Butler elucidated Irish and European prehistoric tribal amalgamations and wanderings that turn out to correspond closely to recent discoveries about genetic diffusion in Ireland and Europe.[8]

To see how Butler worked, let's invent two neighboring prehistoric Irish tribes named Cramps and Tons that merged. They concocted their ancestor Crampton. The newly-named Crampton tribe settled by a bend (*cramp, crimp, crump*) of a river at a site they fortified (*town, ton, dun*). Tribal elders told a bizarre story with puns to solidify, preserve and recall genealogy. Narrators described the ancestor Crampton as very cramped, crimped or crumped hiding under a ton of wheat. The puns translated non-Gaelic words (*Crampton*) and syllables (*cramp* and *ton*) as if they were Gaelic. The ancestor Crampton was thus Gaelicized to Dunlop, a fortified palace, and the merged tribe's habitat became Dunlop village at the river's bend. Centuries later Christian monks neatly ended this antique, invented, oral and traditional story of the ancestral genealogy of the prehistoric Crampton tribe. They recorded martyred Saint Dunlop suffocated beneath a huge mound of grain near Dunlop village where today a shrine, holy well, rath, field or hilltop still bears the saint's name. Butler's method thus involved reworking the mnemonics, starting with punned

Dunlop names, anecdotes, word elements, glossaries and sites to bring to light the original pair of tribal names.

In Chapter Four of *Ten Thousand Saints*, "How Ancestors Were Made," Butler illustrates the way tribal ancestors were combined, and proffers the Irish-Basque connection. "Thus when some Celts and some Iberians in Spain became 'Celtiberians', an ancestor appeared, Celtiberius" (*TTS* 47). On his map of Iberia, the Vascones and Vescitani, whom Butler considers antecedents of the Basques and Gascons, lived northeast of the Celtiberians. Linguistics joins the Vascones and Basques because the letters *v* and *b* interchange. The aspirated *b* (phonetically *v*) reflects the genitive of *b* and hence, for example *Corcu Baiscinn*, would yield *Corcu Bhaiscinn* or *Corkovaskin* when Anglicized to designate "people of Baiscinn." The Corcu Baskin tribe who lived in Corcovaskin, in southwest Clare, just north of the Shannon, were said to be Basques. Butler suggests they were "Vascones, who left their name to the Basques and the Gascons, and who covered in classical times the same Pyrenean region where the Basques were located" (*TTS* 152). The DNA determination of a 94% Basque association with Munster has, therefore, confirmed Butler's argument.[9]

Furthermore, the Basques and Gascons connect by more than Butler's illumination of the shared *sc* sound in placenames, such as in Gascony next door to the Pays Basque and the Pyrenees. Gascon differs from other Occitan dialects because the pre-Celtic linguistic influence came from the Basques, the Gascons' non-Indo-European neighbours. Gascon and Basque names interrelate through the phonetic interchangeability of the Frankish *v* or *w*. The modern French *gu* is a commonplace of French morphology, moving, for instance, from the antecedent of *war* to the modern *guerre*, or from the antecedent of *to watch* for to the modern *guetter*. The French *Guillaume* likewise relates to the English *William*. These linguistic mutations from *v* to hard *g* (Vascone to Gascon) as well as from *v* to aspirated *b* (Vascone to Basque) illustrate the type of element Butler used to identify the origins of the names of heroes, ancestors and tribes. From an archaeogenetic point of view, these word elements imply that a future sampling of contemporary Gascon DNA should confirm more of Butler's arguments about the pre-Celtic links among the Irish, Basque and other European genomes. Since the *sc* sound also connects to non-Indo-European and pre-Celtic usage, Ligurians, Occitans and other descendants of the ancient Gauls likewise merit DNA sampling.[10]

Butler also examines prehistoric tribal names older than the thousand-year-old male-inherited Irish surnames tested for DNA signatures.[11] In his Foreword, he modestly remarks that

in a preliminary way I have grouped the ancestors and saints with different continental tribes, which I believe must have come to Ireland. My groupings must often be wrong but about some I have a dogged certainty. We know that the Brigantes and Menapii reached Ireland, so I hold that their neighbours the Veneti must also have come. They were famous seafarers and left their names wherever they settled in Europe. Among the Iberian tribes I am confident about the Cunesioi and the Draganum Proles ... I am almost confident about the Tigurini, the Scythians, the Vascones, open-minded about the others. (*TTS* 9)

After unveiling the Vascone-Basque connection in Clare, Butler turns to the Ui Draignech of Connacht, tribal kin to the continental Dragani and known to the Romans as the Draganum Proles, living on the Bay of Biscay beside the Basques and Veneti (*TTS* 80-108, 126-128). Thus, the DNA determination of a 98% Basque association with Connacht further authenticates Butler's work.[12]

As postulated by Darwin, geographical features like mountains, rivers and seas may define genetic borders.[13] Further, the borders of languages and dialects may influence, or reflect, the definition of genetic borders, though less strongly.[14] A recent archaeogenetic survey of European Y-chromosomal diversity favours geography over linguistic affinity.[15] But one cannot ignore the isolated and singular Basque language, Euskara. It closely correlates with their unique blood type and archaeogenetic origins. Descended from Paleolithic and Mesolithic communities, the Basques preceded the Neolithics in Europe.[16] Compression of the Basques into the western Pyrenees, in what is now southwest France and northern Spain, distinctly preserved Euskara. Very likely, this compacting of habitat preserved Euskara much more strongly than the long-term Basque genetic outflow to Ireland and elsewhere, because languages do not have sex.[17] Euskara's local strength in the Pays Basque kept the Gascon variety of Occitan distinct from the other Occitan dialects.

Long before DNA connected the Basque to the Irish, Butler had observed that

very few place and tribal names in ancient Spain contain the *sc* sound and they almost all occur in or near the Pyrenees – Osca, Menosca, Biscargis (Biscay), Muscara, Cascantium, Virovesca, and among the tribes we find the Vascones, Vescitani, Conisci. The Vescitani are obviously a variant of their neighbours the Vascones, and Virovesca must be derived from an amalgamation between the Vescitani and their powerful Celtic neighbours the Verones or Berones. This sound *sc* seems equally rare in Irish proper names. (*TTS* 153)

Butler's *sc* hypothesis concurs with the non-Indo-European elements of Irish vocabulary and the structural relationships between Irish and Euskara.[18] Ancient glossaries; signatures of potters; coin legends; inscriptions; local, regional, ethnic, personal, divine names and placenames – all have been shown to have constituent pre-Celtic and non-Indo-European roots, whether in the Pays Basque, Iberia, Gascony, Provence or Liguria, and Butler traces their use by tribes migrating to and from Ireland. In short, a notable non-Indo-European remnant is this *sc* sound among both the pre-Celtic and Celtic-speaking communities that extended from Iberia north and east into France, Germany, Switzerland and Italy (Liguria), and west into Britain and Ireland.[19]

Butler continues:

> Indeed among the tribes we only meet the *sc* sound among the Basc-, Musc-, Esc- or Uisc- peoples, and evidence of the kinship suggests that all these people belonged to the same tribe, whose name was differently pronounced. Cairbre Bascain, the ancestor of the Dal Bascind was the brother of Cairbre Musc, the ancestor of the Muscraige, and the Dal Bascind are called Dal mBascind and equated with the Dal nOengus Muscae. Among the saints the same picture is apparent. St Mescan (St Patrick's brewer) and St Bresca (St Patrick's chaplain) were both culted on the river Faughan in Co Derry, and certain scholars have said they were the same. (*TTS* 153)

Butler's proposed Ulster Basque descendants have a DNA frequency of 82%.[20] Likewise the lands of the Muscraige Tire tribe, visited by St. Patrick or one of his ninth century successors on a trip through north Munster, lay in northwest Tipperary, opposite the Shannon shore habitat of the Corcu Bascainn tribe, their Basque cousins, whose descendants now share a 94% DNA association with Munster.[21] The French Gascons, just north of the Basques, also preserve the *sc* sound in tribal and place names, and thus invite examination of their DNA contribution to Irish and European genomes. Likewise, other regions of ancient Gaul deserve genetic research where non-Indo-European language residuals exist.[22]

Clued by the *sc* sound, Butler finds further ties between the Basques and Co Clare. Mata Muiresc, daughter of the king of Scotland, "was the ancestress of the Clann Morna of Clare and had seven children, all of them obviously tribal ancestors of Connacht" by Magach, a male not her husband (*TTS* 156). One child, Bascall, "would appear to be a Vasconic hybrid" (*TTS* 156). His glossary indicates that the Vascones include the Basc folk (*TTS* 331). The frequency of the Basque DNA links supporting Butler's work are 98% in Connacht and 94% in Munster. As for links between the Basque lands and Scotland in known Celtic-surname territories, the Basque DNA frequencies of 56% in mainland Scotland and 66% in the Orkneys further endorse Butler's conclusions.[23]

Butler's index in *Ten Thousand Saints* reveals the unique identifying *sc* sound of the Basque language to be present in 45 of 736 names of ancestors and heroes (0.6%); 8 of 392 names of saints (0.2%); 10 of 334 names of Irish tribes and their ancestors (0.3%); and 16 of 265 names of Continental tribes and their ancestors (0.6%) (*TTS* 326-332). *The Ordnance Survey Road Atlas of Ireland* tabulates 3223 names of communities, and its maps mark hundreds more untabulated names for hills, mountains, lakes, bogs and crossroads. The *sc* sound appears in 182 sites: 68 in Munster, 56 in Connacht, 36 in Leinster, and 22 in Ulster. These figures merit cautious interpretation, if read as Basque only, since some *sc* sounds that initiate names possibly descend from Scythian, or tribes other than Basques (*TTS* 154, 157-159). But the possible Basque-Scythian genomic connections to ancient Gaul and Ireland, proposed by Butler (*TTS* 287-295) and Whatmough, should not be overlooked for future DNA analysis.[24]

III

The Irish archaeogenetic survey – which connects the male Y-chromosome (of the haplotype 1 variety) in Connacht, Munster, Ulster and Leinster to the Pays Basque – tracks the contemporary male Y-chromosome back through thousand-year-old Irish surnames, which are presumed to be inherited only through the male line.[25] However, by contrast with Butler's pre-Celtic archaeolinguistics, such DNA-analyzed patrilineal surnames are often younger than the names of prehistoric tribes, ancestors, heroes and saints, in both Ireland and Europe. The linkage of surnames to Y-chromosome-based family histories clearly has important genealogical applications.[26] But Irish archaeogenetic researchers have had to keep family names confidential. This precludes linking surnames to ancestral tribal, heroic and pre-saintly origins. In other words, an individual has both a cultural family and a biological (genetic) family. The two may not be identical, whatever an individual or family may think. Thus DNA testing may confirm an accepted genetic link in a family, or reveal a hitherto unknown, surprising, and perhaps unwanted genetic connection.[27] Balancing which genetic interests to pursue (or honour) presents problems such as, for instance, negotiations among individuals and families with various religious and social mores. Which social or research needs can be pursued – during the course of useful genetic or medical investigations – may depend upon intrusive questions, if precise genealogical knowledge is to be obtained. Thus the simple satisfaction of curiosity about origins may become complicated. American law protects Native American and other human remains, and may therefore prevent archaeogenetic analysis. The needs of anthropologists, archaeologists and archaeogeneticists may clash with religious tenets, other persuasions, or simple prejudice against exploring early origins, particularly if acquiring DNA samples perturbs burial or other sacred sites.[28]

If the reluctance of Irish families to disclose genes and names can be overcome – as it has in Iceland, Sweden, Estonia and Denmark [29] – Butler's linguistic work opens new lines of inquiry for archaeogeneticists to investigate. Irish surnames have discrete, still localizable, ancient tribal origins. For instance, the Draignean tribal name in the Monaghan parish of Donaghmoyne evolved into the surnames O'Drynan and Drennan, as well as many similar local place names. In Cromwell's time, *draighean* (which means *blackthorn* in Irish) was Anglicized to Thornton. The name of the Draignean tribe, Butler continues, connects it to "the familiar nomadic tribes of early Europe …[and] most resembles …the Draganum Proles which lived on the Bay of Biscay before the Celts and traced their descent from Draganes." He further hypothesizes that Draig, Traig or Trega, their Irish ancestor figure, might also be the punned ancestor of the Thracians. If so, the Draganum Proles were not Celtic, but hybrid Thracians (pushed from the northeast by Iberian Celts) who had to leave for Ireland. Later, the Draganum, acculturized by the Irish and their language, kept their draighean name with its blackthorn and Thornton connections (*TTS* 126-128). Since the Draganum Proles were neighbours of the Basques in Iberia, Algarve, Gascony, Gironde and Ireland, the family surnames O'Drynan and Drennan might contribute more genomic data about Irish origins, if families with these surnames consented to DNA sampling.

The Kingdom of Ossory, on the doorstep of Maidenhall, piqued Butler's curiosity especially (*TTS* 20-31). Ossory comprises Co Kilkenny, but enlarged by several baronies in Leix and Offaly. It had a large and unexplained number of dumb and stammering kings, heroes and saints. Butler concludes that Goidelic speakers (Q-Celts) met presumably indigenous and mixed remnants of earlier P-Celtic invasions. The incomprehensible P-Celtic language made Goidels label Ossorians "dumb" or "stammerers." Not all agree with T. F. O'Rahilly, in *Early Irish History and Mythology*, that P-Celts preceded Q-Celts in the same territories.[30] Brythonic-speaking tribes, such as the Cruthin, akin to the Picts of Scotland, dwelt in northeast Ireland, and the Erainn dwelt in southwest Ireland. Since they were earlier immigrants than the Goidels, the Cruthins and Erainns possibly spoke vernacular Q-Celtic, and continuous tribal crossings of the Irish Sea expedited linguistic exchange and innovation.[31]

Butler reported over 30 "dumb" or "stammering" Ossorian chieftains and notable men. Scanlan was the "stammering" king of Ossory. Other eminent stammerers with *sc* names were Cuscraid the Stammerer of the Ulaid (the Ulstermen of the Saga) who once were P-Celts; and Itharnaisc, saint of Clane, Co Kildare.[32] Stammering implies a spoken language different from that of the indigenous or newly dominant tribes in the region. He noted "a tradition in County Kilkenny that the descendants of Scanlan did, in fact, stammer" (*TTS* 27). He further wonders "who was the Scal Balbh and why was his name attached to the Leac an Sceal Bhaildh," the largest dolmen in south Kilkenny (*TTS* 27). One obvious candidate was Lugh, the chief god of the ancient Celts of Gaul – with strong presence in what is now France, Holland, Switzerland, Austria, Silesia, Spain, Wales and Ireland – who was known as a foreign and stammering spirit.[33] Nonetheless, Butler cautions

> it would be premature, though tempting, to build a theory of racial origins on facts such as these. The most one can do is to draw attention to their oddity and to hope that its significance will be better understood (*TTS* 27).

In light of the DNA data shedding new light on Irish origins, present-day Scanlan families in Kilkenny, Leix and Offaly would merit DNA investigation for their possible link to the Basques.

The wanderings of the Frisian tribe and of the four Irish St Fursas also garnered Butler's especial attention. These wanderings covered Munster, Connacht, Ulster and Leinster – now known for high Basque DNA association – and East Anglia, Scotland, northern Gaul, the Low Countries and Germany, likewise with significant Basque DNA association.[34] His description of their movements now concurs with the frequencies of the Basque DNA association with the Netherlands (64%), Scotland (56%) and the Orkneys (66%) – and thus points to the possible genetic spread from (or to) Ireland. [35]

IV

What lies behind Butler's foreshadowing of the DNA Basque-Irish connection and his antecedent, serendipitous confirmation of it? How did Butler ever come to link the Irish with Basques? Always skeptical, Butler's originating line of inquiry is the following:

> Why were there ten speckled saints, eleven leper saints, and fifty called Mo Chua? Why did St. Fintan of Aran in a rage chase the

humble St. Goban right across Ireland to Anglesey? Why did St. Tigernach of Clones breathe alternately white, red and yellow? Why were there holy men and women nicknamed Brocainechbindcorach — Badger-face-sweet-tuneful — and Derbindbelfada — Sweet-tear-long-mouth? Were these real men and women or were they, as antiquarians of 150 years ago insisted, "monkish fictions"? (*TTS* 335)

As a result, Butler came to believe that

there was a hard reality behind these fantasies and that to the patient explorer it will ultimately be revealed … the Irish inherited their saints from the pre-Celtic past, in which they figured as ancestors of half-forgotten tribes. They domesticated them in their mythology, sacred and profane, much as the Greeks assimilated Perseus, ancestor of the Persians and Medea, ancestress of the Medes. They wove their stories as did the Greeks, the Hebrews and all early peoples from the wanderings of tribes and by wordplay with their time-battered, unstable names. These stories were written with humour and imaginative ingenuity and now, if we can interpret them correctly, we shall one day learn who were the first colonists of Britain and Ireland and where they came from. (*TTS* 335)

Butler then connected the Irish and the Basques when he recognized that

From Scythia to Gibraltar, the Celts mingled with all the people they met. Each tribe that reached Ireland carried portmanteau-wise fragments of other tribes and knew that fragments of itself coexisted in other tribal portmanteaus. (*TTS* 81)

Thus, Butler's tribal word-fragments analogously parallel the various DNA fragments used to track the male Y-chromosome haplotype and the female mitochondrial DNA haplotype in Irish and European genomes. Butler's final insight was that

There were Thracian, Iberian, German and Scythian portmanteaus with Celts in all of them and the Celtic portmanteaus will have been as capacious and well-stocked as any. Fighting and merging its way across Europe, each tribe will have lost most of its cultural distinctiveness, as a Finn or a Bulgar does in Massachusetts. Only through their ancestral pedigrees will they have hung on to their identities. So, if we study seriously those long lists of obviously invented beings, the tribal ancestors, every genealogy becomes a table of ingredients in a cookery book. We know how each tribal dish was composed and there are no limits to what we can learn about our past. (*TTS* 81)

On reading Butler's work, Lino Rossi of Milan, an independent scholar of the topography of pre-Celtic and Celtic Liguria – and a non-academic like Butler – agreed with this scenario, precisely because Celtic and Ligurian territory encompassed

> a wide area of southwest Piedmont, Liguria and eastern Provence. Certainly these Celto-Ligurians were great travellers and no wonder their numerous tribes reached Ireland and left their names to be "extrapolated" into "traditional" saint-sages in a way that is completely different from the case of most of Christendom's continental saints.[36]

Indeed, glossaries of ancient Gallic dialects clearly support Rossi's and Butler's views of Irish and European origins.[37]

V

In conclusion, the DNA determination of a similar 89-90 % frequency of the common male Y-chromosome haplotype unites the Basques, Irish and Welsh.[38] As noted above, similar Basque DNA connections occur with Scotland (56%) and the Orkneys (66%). In Ireland, the distribution frequencies are, respectively, 82% in the northeast, 94% in the southwest, 98% in the west and 73% in the southeast.[39] These distributions reflect prehistoric tribal wanderings with consequent swapping and spread of dialects, and were surmised by Butler. They point to the need for more DNA sampling in the Basque, Gallic and other European regions in order to establish links with their identifiable descendants in Brittany, Cornwall and Wales (P-Celts), as well in Ireland, Scotland and the Isle of Man (Q-Celts). The possibility now exists to identify the genomes of the pre-Celtic tribal, heroic, ancestral and hagiographic names that later evolved or migrated into Irish surnames. In short, Butler's *Ten Thousand Saints: A Study in Irish and European Origins* hypothesizes Ireland's pre-Celtic tribal origins from linguistics, and over two decades before the emergence of archaeogenetics. Its compendium of saints, heroes and ancestors – and in particular, its analyses of the "dumb" and "stammering" figures of his locality – provide useful starting points from which to expand research into Irish and European genomes.

Three years after the publication of *Ten Thousand Saints*, W.M.S. Russell, Reader in Social Biology at Reading University, and a member of the British Social Biology Council, publicly recognized the potential for confirmation of Butler's research by blood group tests. He wrote

> in a short article, it is impossible to do justice to the wealth of detail in Butler's book, the multiplicity of examples, the checking and cross-checking, the elaborate catalogues, tables and maps, the glossary of Irish pun-words classified under the relevant tribal groupings. It is the accumulation of interlocking evidence that carries conviction. But quite apart from the evidence Butler has gathered himself, there are many considerations that support his thesis. To begin with, everything we know or can surmise about the prehistory of the British Isles and Europe fits perfectly. Fortunately, Butler's patterns of tribal distribution are so detailed and specific that the cruder sources of error would be automatically controlled, especially if a considerable number of genetic systems were studied at once.

He went on to suggest that Butler's "hypotheses be tested by independent measures of relationship such as blood group frequency distributions" and invited him to lecture.[40] In fact, later population archaeogeneticists like L.L. Cavalli-Sforza have, in this manner, combined linguistics, archaeology, topology, geography, demography and blood group distribution tests with molecular analysis of genes and their frequency.[41] More recently, D.G. Bradley of the Royal Irish Academy's advisory committee on genetic anthropology has affirmed that "drawing of secure inference about the past from genetic research is no easy task and requires the collaborative efforts of many scholars including archaeologists, geographers, linguists and historians."[42] Butler's scholarship encompassed precisely these disciplines, with particular stress on linguistics, whilst lacking only the vital tool of DNA-driven archaeogenetics, a nonexistent science at the time.

When reporting his research, Butler perceived closed-mindedness and indifference among his contemporaries. In the early 1950s, he showed his provisional results to Myles Dillon who was "sympathetic" and to Dan Binchy who was "polite and friendly but absolutely dismissive".[43] He insisted that his hypotheses and conclusions would be confirmed since the data illuminated "fascinating problems, which take us back behind the frontiers of recorded history to the remote wanderings of European peoples, to the clash of tribes and tongues" (*TTS* 335). His plight remarkably resembled that of Gregor Mendel, who experimented well; aired ingenious results at his local natural history society and in its journal; and notified European scientists, who ignored him. Forty years later, and 20 after his death, Mendel's seminal genetic discoveries became recognized.[44] Like Mendel, Butler's data and hypotheses, ignored or doubted by the professional academics of his time, were later verified by the progress of science.

Ten Thousand Saints was published privately by a local publisher, The Wellbrook Press, on the foot of 30 years' work, often up to seven hours daily. To make ends meet, he survived by selling garden and orchard produce, renting rooms and sometimes his house. He persevered with help from Eleanor Burgess and encouragement from his wife, Peggy. Burgess served as contrarian and supporting scholar, and typed the book from Butler's legendary tiny handwriting. Peggy drew maps and illustrated. Damien Harrington designed the cover and Desmond McCheane printed the book. In the Foreword, Butler records that "writing as a country scholar, I am proud that my book is printed and its cover designed by friends and neighbours in my own county" (*TTS* 11). The poignant dedication of his book is to his intellectual and spiritual predecessor, and highlights the background agony of the struggle against indifference towards his work:

TO

JACQUES BOUCHER DE PERTHES

1788-1868

THE CUSTOMS OFFICER OF ABBEVILLE

WHO

GREW PRIZE PEARS

WROTE PLAYS THAT WERE NEVER PRODUCED

JOINED THE KILKENNY ARCHAEOLOGICAL SOCIETY

SHUNNED SCIENTISTS

AND FOUNDED

THE SCIENCE OF PREHISTORY

A few individuals discussed, criticized and supported Butler's research. They included Eric Dorman-O'Gowan, "a solitary scholar of Cavan" who as General Dorman-Smith formulated the winning battle plan for El-Alamein, and

Eleanor Burgess "who both understood what I was trying to say and helped me to say it" (*TTS* 11). John McCormick of Newcastle, Co. Wicklow, wrote that "a symposium on these (Butler's) fascinating topics would be of great interest not only to those professionally engaged in the many disciplines involved, but also to a wider public ever curious about that tantalizing subject, the remote past." [45] Others attracted to his work were David Grene of the University of Chicago; Gerard Hanley, a writer and expert on East African tribes; Lino Rossi, a physician in Milan; and W.M.S. Russell, social biologist. As early as 1956 Butler remarked that "nobody has managed to undermine in the very faintest degree my absolute conviction that my method of approach is the right one and that 20 years from now the general scheme of my argument will be universally accepted." [46] In fact, archaeogenetic research has now vindicated his Basque-Irish and Basque-Irish-Frisian-Scottish connections, albeit three decades after he had to pay to publish *Ten Thousand Saints*. Notwithstanding those "shunned scientists", he would surely have welcomed the archaeogenetic confirmation of his work by the scientific community. Further research on the Irish genome, implicit in his data, may substantiate his other important hypotheses about Irish and European origins.

This is an expanded version of the original address.

ACKNOWLEDGEMENTS

When Butler first showed me his work on the saints in 1963, it greatly impressed me. Prior to the DNA research confirming Irish-Basque genetic links, I detailed Butler's meticulous verbal techniques in a paper presented to the Kildare Archaeological Society at Maidenhall on 19 July 1998. After the appearance of the aforementioned DNA research, Eleanor Burgess made helpful suggestions and stressed Butler's solid research methods. Dr Daniel Bradley of Trinity College, Dublin introduced me to Irish and European DNA archaeogenetics. The late John McCormick gave me source material concerning pre-Celtic sites, glossaries and *sc* names. The late Billy O'Sullivan, Keeper of Manuscripts at Trinity, and an astute friend of Butler's, provided a key reference and several relevant books. When I was outside Ireland, Professor Barbara Wright updated me on new developments in Irish genomic research. I thank her for provocative questions as well as many details of phonetics and tribal origins. I am also grateful to Daniel Bradley's colleagues at Trinity, the geneticists David McConnell and Patrick Cunningham, who improved the text with their comments and suggestions. Finally, I am endebted to Professor Padraic Ó Rián of NUI Cork for his unpublished lecture, "St Patrick in Munster: The Journey That Never Was," delivered at Queen's College, Cambridge University, 6 February 2001.

NOTES

1   Besides *Ten Thousand Saints,* see Hubert Butler (i) "The Dumb and the Stammerers in Early Irish History,"*Antiquity* 23 (1949), pp. 20-31; (ii) "Who Were 'the Stammerers'?," *The Journal of the Royal Society of Antiquaries of Ireland* 80.2 (1950), pp. 228-236; (iii) "Charts of Irish Tribes, Saints and Heroes" (1971), Ms. 10304/75/69-105, Butler Papers, Trinity College, Dublin; (iv) "In the Land of Nod: Puns and Tribal Ancestors" and "Woe unto Thee Bethsaida: Puns in the New Testament" in *In the Land of Nod* (Dublin: Lilliput, 1996) pp. 247-262.

2   See (i) E. W. Hill, M.A. Jobling and D.G. Bradley, "Y-Chromosome Variation and Irish Origins: A Pre-Neolithic Gene Gradation Starts in the Near East and Culminates in Western Ireland," *Nature* 404 (2000) pp. 351-352; (ii) C. Renfrew and K. Boyle, eds.,*Archaeogenetics: DNA and the Population Prehistory of Europe* (Exeter: Short Run Press, 2000) pp. 203-208.

3   See (i) Hill *et al* pp. 203-208, 351-352; (ii) D.J. McConnell, "The Genetic History and Geography of Ireland: A Project of the Royal Irish Academy," *Ceide* 1.2 (1997) pp. 10-11

4   See McConnell, pp. 10-11

5   See Hill *et al* pp. 203-208, 351-352.

6   See Butler, "The Dumb and the Stammerers in Early Irish History," pp. 20-31, "Who Were 'the Stammerers'?," pp. 228-236; and "Charts of Irish Tribes, Saints and Heroes", Ms.

7   See Butler, "Charts of Irish Tribes, Saints and Heroes", Ms.

8   See (i) Hill *et al*, pp. 351-352; (ii) Renfrew and Boyle, *in toto*; (iii) Z.H. Rosser *et al*, "Y-Chromosomal Diversity in Europe Is Clinal and Influenced Primarily by Geography Rather Than Language," *American Journal of Human Genetics* 67 (2000) pp. 1526-1543.

9   See (i) Hill *et al*, pp. 351-352; (ii) Renfrew and Boyle, pp. 203-208.

10 J. Whatmough, *The Dialects of Ancient Gaul* (Cambridge: Harvard University Press, 1970).

11 See (i) Hill *et al*, pp. 351-352; (ii) Renfrew and Boyle, pp. 203-208.

12 See (i) Hill *et al*, pp. 351-352; (ii) Renfrew and Boyle, pp. 203-208.

13 Charles Darwin, *On the Origins of Species* (London: John Murray, 1859).

14 See (i) Z.H. Rosser *et al*; (ii) J.H. Greenberg *et al*, "The Settlement of America: A Comparison of Linguistic, Dental and Genetic Evidence," *Current Anthropology* 27 (1986) pp. 477-497; (iii) L.L. Cavalli-Sforza *et al*, "Reconstruction of Human Evolution: Bringing Together Genetic, Archaeological and Linguistic Data," *Proceedings of the National Academy of Sciences* 85 (1988) pp. 6002-6006.

15   Z.H. Rosser *et al*, pp. 1526-1543.

16   See L.L. Cavalli-Sforza, *Genes, People and Languages*, trans. M. Seielstad (New York: North Point Press, 2000).

17   See M Ruhlen, *The Origin of Language: Tracing the Evolution of the Mother Tongue* (New York: John Wiley & Sons, 1994).

18   See (i) Whatmough, *in toto*; (ii) M. Dillon and N.K. Chadwick, *The Celtic Realms* (London: Weidenfeld & Nicholson, 1967) pp.15-35; (iii) E. Lewy, "Der Bau der Europäischen Sprachen," *Proceedings of the Royal Irish Academy* 48 (1942) pp. 15-117.

19   See Whatmough, *in toto*.

20   See Hill *et al*, pp. 351-352.

21   See Hill *et al*, pp. 351-352

22   See Whatmough, *in toto*.

23   See (i) A. Helgason *et al*, "Estimating Scandinavian and Gaelic Ancestry in the Male Settlers of Iceland," *American Journal of Human Genetics* 67 (2000) pp. 697-717; (ii) J.F. Wilson *et al*, "Genetic Evidence for Different Male and Female Roles During Cultural Transitions in the British Isles," *Proceedings of the National Academy of Science* 98 (2001) pp 5078-5083.

24   See Whatmough, *in toto*.

25   See Hill *et al*, pp. 351-352.

26   See (i) B. Sykes and C. Irven, "Surnames and the Y-Chromosome," *American Journal of Human Genetics* 66 (2000) pp1417-1419; (ii) B. Sykes, *The Seven Daughters of Eve* (London: Bantam Press, 2001).

27   See J. Seabrook, "The Tree of Me: DNA Testing and the Mania for Genealogy," *The New Yorker* 26 March 2001, pp. 55-71.

28   See (i) T.T. Ashburn *et al*, "Human Tissue Research in the Genomic Era of Medicine: Balancing Individual and Societal Interests," *Archives of Internal Medicine* 160 (2000) pp. 377-384; (ii) N. Wade, "A Genomic Treasure Hunt May Be Striking Gold: Hunting for Disease Genes In Iceland's Genealogies," *The New York Times* 18 June 2000, pp. 1&4 (D1); (iii) R. Bonnichsen and A.L. Schneider, "Battle of the Bones," *The Sciences* 40.3 (2000) pp. 40-46.

29   See Ashburn, pp. 377-384 and Wade, pp. 1, 4.

30   See Greenberg, pp. 477-497.

31   See Dillon and Chadwick, pp. 19-20, 36.

32   See Butler, "Who Were the Stammerers?", pp. 228-236.

33   See Dillon and Chadwick, pp. 28-29.

34   See Hill *et al*, pp. 351-352; Helgsason *et al*, pp. 697-717; Wilson, pp. 5078-5083.

35   See Hill *et al*, pp. 351-352; Helgsason *et al*, pp. 697-717; Wilson, pp. 5078-5083.

36   See Lino Rossi, letter to Hubert Butler, 18 July 1981.

37   See Whatmough, *in toto*.

38   See Helgason *et al*, pp. 697-717.

39   See Hill *et al*, pp. 351-352; Helgsason *et al*, pp. 697-717; Wilson, pp. 5078-5083.

40   W.M.S. Russell, "Saints, Tribes and Ancestors," *Biology and Human Affairs* 40.3 (1975) pp. 118-130.

41   See Cavalli-Sforza, *Genes, People and Languages*, *in toto*.

42   D.G. Bradley, "Introduction: The Genetic History and Geography of Ireland," Royal Irish Academy Programme, 8 December 2000, pp. 2-3.

43   Hubert Butler, Maidenhall Commonplace Book, 4 June 1956, pp. 36-38.

44   See J. Cain, "The Prince of Peas," review of *The Monk in the Garden: The Lost and Found Genius of Gregor Mendel, the Father of Genetics*, by Robin Marantz Henig, *The New York Times Book Review* 27 August 2000, p.16.

45   J.O. McCormick, letter to Susan Butler, 1995.

46   Butler, Maidenhall Commonplace Book, pp. 36-38.

FROM THE BUTLER ALBUM

Photographs 1927-1938

Top to bottom: Tyrone Guthrie, wife Judy Guthrie, HMB, Peggy Butler, August 1928

HMB and Peggy Butler, 1931

Annaghmakerrig, Co. Monaghan, left to right: Mrs Norah Guthrie, Tyrone Guthrie, Susan Power, unknown, Peggy Butler holding daughter Julia, HMB, circa 1935

School outing, Alexandria, Egypt, 1927

Peggy Butler with daughter Julia aged 1, Belgrade, 1936

Volga, Russia, 1931

Volga, Russia, 1931

Left to right: unknown, Archie Lyell, HMB,
Volga, Russia, 1931

Left to right: HMB and Archie Lyell,
Leningrad, 1931

HMB, Berlin, June 1930

Riga Strand, Summer 1930

HMB, Riga Strand, Summer 1930

Riga Strand, Summer 1930

Left to right: Julia Crampton and daughter Cordelia, HMB, Peggy Butler, 1962

PART III: BUTLER ABROAD

BUTLER'S WINDOW ON THE WORLD

John Banville

John McGahern and I used to have fun with something someone had said of me – or perhaps I had been foolish enough to say it of myself – to the effect that in my fiction and my literary journalism I was trying to open a window on the world. Yes, McGahern said, with a basilisk look, and while you're trying to open it, I suppose I'm trying to slam it shut. It was a nice image, the two of us struggling at the sash, me pulling and him pushing. Thus do one's pretensions turn to comedy.

Hubert Butler was a very particular kind of Irishman. He liked to describe himself as a Protestant Republican, but Roy Foster has suggested a more accurate formulation would be "Ascendancy Nationalist" or "Anglo-Irish Nationalist." He was also, as a writer and a citizen, a quintessential European figure. Neal Ascherson has described him, accurately, I think as

> a *feuilleton* writer. The word has misleading echoes of leafy lightness and even weightlessness. But for a century and a half it has meant a special kind of intellectual journalism, witty and often angry, elegant but piercing, and revealing great learning lightly borne, interested in "epiphanies" which make currents of social and political change visible through the lens of some small incident or absurdity. (*ILN* x)

The breadth of Butler's interests and concerns is remarkable, even for a writer whose career spanned the greater part of the tumultuous century that has just ended. Yet, as he observed, even when his essays appear to be about Russia or Greece or Spain or Yugoslavia, "they are really about Ireland … this focus for me has never varied" (*EA* 2). Indeed, his focus is narrower still: "I have always believed", he wrote, "that local history is more important than national history". This is one of the many variations on an abiding theme in his essays: the fatuousness of our modern-day concern for the universal at he expense of the particular.

However, he is conscious too of the dangers of blinkered parochialism. In one of his finest essays, "The Invader Wore Slippers", Butler recalls how, during the war, "we in Ireland heard much of the jackboot and how we should be trampled beneath it if Britain's protection failed us", and how "our imagination, fed on the daily press, showed us a Technicolor picture of barbarity and heroism." "We did not ask ourselves: 'Supposing the invader wears not jackboots, but carpet slippers, or patent-leather pumps, how will I behave, and the respectable Xs, the patriotic Ys, and the pious Zs?'" (*EA* 103). Butler harboured very grave doubts as to how Ireland would have behaved if the Germans had invaded. He quotes a telling declaration made in the Dail in 1943 by Oliver J. Flannagan, Fine Gael TD, and self-appointed guardian of Irish faith and morals into the 1980s: "There is one thing", he said,

> "that the Germans did and that was to rout the Jews out of their country." He added that we should rout them out of Ireland: "They crucified our saviour 1,900 years ago and they have been crucifying us every day of the week."

"No one", Butler laconically observes, "contradicted him."

When, after the war, Butler sought to bring to public attention the frightful crimes condoned by, and in some cases committed by, Franciscan priests in wartime Yugoslavia, he found himself ostracized by his own country. The Catholic Church had refused to acknowledge that mass conversions of Orthodox Serbs had been forced, or had involved violence. At a public meeting in Dublin Butler attempted to read a statement on the issue, but after a few sentences the Papal Nuncio walked out, whereupon the meeting was halted. Next morning the Irish edition of the *Sunday Express* carried the headline: "Pope's Envoy Walks Out. Government to Discuss Insult to Nuncio."

> All the local government bodies of the city and county held special meetings to condemn the "Insult." There were speeches from mayors, ex-mayors, aldermen, creamery managers. The county council expelled me from one of its subcommittees, and I was forced to give up the honorary secretaryship of the Kilkenny Archaeological Society, which I had myself rvived and guided through seven difficult years. (*EA* 273-274)

It was, in that place, in those times, a familiar story.

Butler's vision is all of a piece. Whether he is writing about warime atrocities or local history, the slaughter of the Jews or Celtic hagiography, he speaks with complete authenticity. In an age such as ours, marked – indeed, maimed – by inauthenticity, he is to be treasured, listened to, and emulated. It is not a window on the world that he opens, but a wide doorway, through which, if we are bold enough, and if our minds are broad enough, we may follow.

THE STEPINAC FILE

Chris Agee

I

In the summer of 1947, on his first trip to postwar Yugoslavia, Hubert Butler arrived at the reading-room desk of the Municipal Library in Zagreb. Fluent in Serbo-Croat, he obtained his ticket and spent the next few days perusing the newspapers, especially the ecclesiastical papers, published during the 1941-45 Quisling regime of Independent Croatia. He was hoping to make, he would later say, "a study of the Christian crisis in Yugoslavia." [1] He had stumbled on the trail – the very beginning of the trail – of what I shall call, echoing his own phrasing, "the Stepinac File".

At 46, Butler was no stranger to the great events of his period. Already he had firsthand experience of the Russian Revolution, the rise of fascism, and what is surely the matrix for both, the unravelling of four empires on European soil. In 1931, he spent three months teaching English in Leningrad at the beginning of the Stalinist Terror. On the Dalmatian coast in the mid-thirties, he saw early waves of refugees from Hitler and then, working with the Quakers in Vienna in 1938-39, helped expedite the flight of Jews after the *Anschluss.* Closer to home, travelling from Charterhouse during term break, he had passed through the smoking ruins of Dublin in the aftermath of the Rising on Easter Monday and concluded he was an Irish republican.

Unlike many or most nationalists at the time, Butler from an early stage did not view the War of Independence in primarily insular terms. The freedom of Ireland was inextricably bound up with a wider pan-European phenomenon, the disintegration of empires and the emergence of what in the interwar period were known as the Succession States; a dozen small nations, he wrote, "formed at the same time (1918-1921), and under the influence of much the same ideas"(*GWT* 47). From this perspective, which he never abandoned, indeed never ceased refining, the ideals of the Easter Rising were but a spiritual stone's thrown from those that brought forth the new states in the East. Pearse in Dublin was cognate with Princip in Sarajevo.

Notwithstanding the writerly potential of his *wanderlust* through the late twenties and thirties, Butler had not, by the end of the Second World War, written much in his own voice; and, of this, very little had appeared in print. An early interest in Russia and Russian had resulted in book translations of Leonid Leonov's *The Thief* in 1931 and Anton Chekhov's *The Cherry Orchard* in

1934. But his own work, aged 46, consisted of only a handful of essays and reviews. These included "Riga Strand in 1930" and "In Dalmatia", neither of which would appear until the Lilliput volumes, plus several others from the thirties which remain unpublished; two postwar reviews of Soviet literature; and two wartime essays, "The Barriers" (1941) and "The Two Languages" (1943) in which, as from an Indian-summer chrysalis, Butler's prose genius is suddenly glimpsed in full flight. In short, Butler began unusually late.

When he arrived at the Municipal Library in Zagreb, he had, therefore, little in the way of a published literary career behind him outside his considerable gifts as a translator. But although he had barely begun, the virtuosity of that beginning is unmistakable. His prose is already an instrument of unusual richness. It had long been tuned by his notebooks and letters.

Indeed, one wonders if he ever had a literary career in the usual sense; there is something of the urgent Reuters report in all his work, as if from the thick of life and its pressing issues, in a posting far from the literary world, he had found time to dispatch another report from the ethical front. In contrast to much of the professionalized literary milieu, there is never the sense of suborning life's grist to the mill of the next deadline or book; never the heresy of adjusting the course of living to the calculus of literary ambition; never the sacrifice of the passions of the amateur for the royal road of the professional career. That note of the far-flung ethical dispatch – the letter from the literary nowhere – is itself part of the distinction of the style.

To flourish, though, like the proverbial mustard seed, Butler's style still needed, it seems to me, the right soil. The instrument might be ready, mellowed by the years of travel, but what would he play – and what would be the leitmotifs? In the best writing, such themes are never wholly a matter of choice. The X-axis of the individual sensibility intersects the Y-axis of the historical moment. There is a sense in which many of the most indispensable writers – think of Kafka or Wilfred Owen – have been chosen by the themes imposed by the narrow gate of circumstance. Of potential, Ted Hughes remarks that "it is as if one grain of talent – in the right psychological climate – can become a great harvest, where a load of grains – in the wrong climate – simply goes off." [2]

II

What Butler uncovered during those first days in the Municipal Library in 1947 – and subsequent visits to the Library of the University of Zagreb during the same trip and again in 1950 – astounded him. On every plane: ethical, historical, psychological, emotional. "The moment in the library", as I will call his various visits to the Zagreb files, would have a decisive influence on the course of his life and work. If Butler was one of a rare breed of writer, like Swift or Orwell, for whom the source of inspiration is what I have termed elsewhere "the ethical imagination," then we might liken Butler's discovery in that first reading room to the moment before the *madeleine* with which Marcel Proust begins *À la recherche du temps perdu.*

At the very beginning of that novel, the narrator experiences an epiphany as he tastes a small pastry of that name, and it is the pursuit of the significance of this moment of sudden apprehension that informs the whole meandering epic flowing from it. Likewise, metaphorically, Butler's "moment in the library" is the ethical epiphany that would decant into much of his very greatest writing. As Joseph Brodsky observed while the Bosnian war raged,

> For modern readers, Hubert Butler's most valuable insights would be no doubt those that have to do with *Mitteleuropa*. He knew the reality firsthand, and its worst period at that. Which is to say that our understanding of its present conditions logically stands to benefit from what Hubert Butler depicted half a century ago. A man of immense learning, he was interested in this borderline zone, with its fusion of Latin and Slavic cultures, presumably because he sensed in their interplay the future of European civilization. Born where he was, he couldn't help being concerned with the fate of Christendom, whose natural son he was. ("Appendix", *ILN* 268)

We will come to the specifics of the Stepinac case, and "its supreme importance," as he put it, "to all thinking Christians" (*ILN* 137). But let us first register the haunting presence of the Zagreb files in Butler's writing. No other single experience is accorded such a repeated airing. A direct account of the visits to the two libraries is related in seven essays, while the nature of what he uncovered there appears, in varying degrees, in another four, as well as in a dozen or so uncollected letters published in the Irish and English press in the late forties and fifties.

Lining up all this material in the order it issued from his pen gives us Butler's accumulating account of Archbishop Stepinac. Since Butler had not written much before "the moment in the library", the Stepinac file becomes a fugal narrative that runs right through his entire corpus, from the clutch of early Yugoslav essays in the late forties, dealing directly with his postwar visits, to the last paragraphs of his last essay in 1990, "A Three-Day Nation", where the Stepinac theme reappears, and he concludes: "I have always thought that compared with the question of how we behave, what we believe is of little importance" (*ILN* 166).

III

Of what, then, did the epiphany in the reading room consist? For an answer, let us now turn to the man himself, in four extracts.

Extract one, from "The Sub-Prefect Should Have Held His Tongue" (1956):

> I have been reproached several times by sincere and civilized unbelievers for my efforts to find out the details of the vast campaign in Croatia in 1941 to convert two and a half million Orthodox to Catholicism. "Why not let bygones be bygones?" they say. "If we rake these things up we'll merely start trouble at home and play into the hands of the Communists. And anyway, they are always killing each other in the Balkans." I once heard an ambassador in Belgrade argue like that, and indeed I have never heard a British or American official abroad argue in any other way. When in 1947 I went to Zagreb and looked up the files of the war-time newspapers of Croatia in which the whole story was to be read, it was obvious no foreign inquirer had handled them before, and the library clerks regarded me with wonder and suspicion. (*EA* 270)

Extract two, from "Report on Yugoslavia" (an address to War Resisters International, in Shrewsbury, England, in August 1947):

> When I was in Zagreb I spent several days in the public library looking up the old files of the newspapers that were issued in the occupation period, particularly the Church papers. I wanted to see what resistance, if any, was made by organised Christianity to the ruthless militarism of Pavelitch, the Croat national leader, and his German and Italian patrons; I am afraid the results were disheartening. I did not expect to find outspoken criticism or condemnation in the Church papers because, if it had been published, the papers would certainly have been suppressed. But I was wholly unprepared for the gush of hysterical adulation which was poured forth by almost all the leading clergy upon Pavelitch, who was probably the vilest of all war criminals. He was their saviour against Bolshevism, their champion against the

Eastern barbarian and heretic, the Serb; he was restorer of their nation and the Christian faith, a veritable hero of olden time. As I believe that the Christian idiom is still the best in which peace and goodwill can be preached, I found this profoundly disturbing … (*ILN* 106-107)

Extract three, from "The Invader Wore Slippers" (1950):

When an incendiary sets a match to respectability, it smoulders malodorously, but piety, like patriotism, goes off like a rocket. The jackboot was worn by the Croats themselves and used so vigorously against the schismatic Serbs that the Germans and Italians, who had established the little state, were amazed. Pavelitch, the regicide ruler of Croatia, was himself the epitome, the personification, of the extraordinary alliance of religion and crime, which for four years made Croatia the model for all satellite states in German Europe. He was extremely devout, attending mass every morning with his family in a private chapel built onto his house. He received expressions of devoted loyalty from the leaders of the churches, including the Orthodox, whose murdered metropolitan had been replaced by a subservient nominee. He gave them medals and enriched their parishes with the plundered property of the schismatics, and he applied the simple creed of One Faith, One Fatherland, with a literalness that makes the heart stand still. It was an equation that had to be solved in blood. Nearly two million Orthodox were offered the alternatives of death or conversion to the faith of the majority …

Yet, as I read the newspaper files in Zagreb, I felt it was not the human disaster but the damage done to honoured words and thoughts that was most irreparable. The letter and spirit had been wrested violently apart and a whole vocabulary of Christian goodness had blown inside out like an umbrella in a thunderstorm. (*EA* 110-111)

Extract four, from "The Artukovitch File" (1970-88): (Artuković was the Croatian Himmler):

These terrible Church papers, 1941 to 1945, should destroy forever our faith in those diplomatic prelates, often good and kindly men, who believe that at all costs the ecclesiastical fabric, its schools and rules, its ancient privileges and powers, should be preserved. The clerical editors published the Aryan laws, the accounts of the forced conversions, without protest, the endless photographs of Pavelitch's visits to seminaries and convents and the ecstatic speeches of welcome with which he was greeted. Turn, for example, to *Katolicki Tjednik* (*The Catholic Weekly*), Christmas 1941, and read the twenty-six verse "Ode to Pavelitch", in which Archbishop Sharitch praises him for his measures against Serbs and Jews. Examine the Protestant papers and you will find the same story. Is it not clear that in times like those the Church doors should be shut, the Church newspapers closed down, and Christians, who believe that we should love our neighbours as ourselves, should go underground and try to build up a new faith in the catacombs? (*EA* 285)

Returning to my earlier imagery, is this not the soil in which a great crop first flourished?

What crystallizes for the first time in the early Yugoslav writing is an ensemble of characteristic themes the cohesion of which can be felt to descend through the variousness of the entire work. Butler's palette, I have written elsewhere, "is narrow yet profound: he writes out of a compact but interrelated set of preoccupations which over the course of his life he elaborated into a unique terrain of historical, cultural, religious and philosophical reflection." The outline of that terrain first migrates from the cast of sensibility to the temper of the writing in the Balkan work of the late forties. Somewhere Orwell remarks that a writer should never depart too far from his first style, and the same might be said of first themes. Certainly Butler never did so.

To extend the point: Butler not only begins late, he begins, mainly, in the East. By my reckoning, up to and and including 1948, the year after his first visit to Zagreb, Butler's published and unpublished essays and articles (excluding short reviews) have expanded to include only six on an Irish topic, but 16 on the Balkans, nine on Russia, two on the small nations of Europe, and one each on a German and English topic. Thereafter, his output quickens still further and the Irish topics multiply; but even at mid-century the tally is 38 on the Balkans and Eastern Europe and 13 on Ireland.

When the preponderance of the East in the early writing is appreciated, the place of the Croatian genocide in the overall evolution of his work also comes clear. "The moment in the Library" was the first great Reuters report from the historical front; this was where "the ethical imagination" consolidated and embarked. As with Proust's small but momentous pastry, it was the *démarche* that he never quite left.

Spanning five decades, the Yugoslav work is not, therefore, some Ruritanian spur to a more central Irish track. On the contrary, the Croatian genocide is firmly at the centre of his corpus; it is not so much a limb as a backbone. To read the Balkan essays in chronological order is to become aware of the fugal skill with which he broaches and elaborates the matter of the genocide. Themes are introduced and outlined; later they are embellished and extended. He begins by writing of his Balkan time in the thirties, his postwar visits, and the wartime genocide; then the Nuncio controversy in Ireland intervenes; then he interlaces both perspectives; what emerges in the later essays is something more universal, transcending the particulars of either country.

The difficulty is that, scattered through the four volumes, the pattern of the Balkan work, second nature to the author, is lost on the reader not intent on unravelling it. Even when laid out in chronological order the titles have an occasional and even strange air to the English ear (see facing page), and so do not quite do justice to the crafted and supple orchestration that they embody. After all, did he not consider the events in Croatia "the most bloodthirsty religio-racial crusade in history, far surpassing anything achieved by Cromwell or the Spanish Inquisitors" (*EA* 284)? How could a writer like Butler with his ethical and historical and cultural cast of mind, with an intimate knowledge of the country and that defining moment in Zagreb Municipal Library, give the theme short shrift? Indeed, how could he not make it central?

IV

At the heart of the Croatian work is, of course, the figure of Monsignor Alojzije Stepinac, the Archbishop of Croatia during the quisling regime. Although there is no single essay devoted to Stepinac alone, Butler's *J'accuse*, his shrewd and meticulous portrait of a compromised prelate, belongs to one of his quintessential modes: the focus on the single personality through which a wider historical, cultural and/or ethical picture is adumbrated. Most of these figures – such as Anton Chekhov, Boucher de Perthes, Ernst Renan, Carl Ossietsky, Mr Pfeffer of Sarajevo – are drawn from Butler's eclectic pantheon of intellectual heroes, and in his hands they become universal parables for the struggle of the independent spirit against the conformist tide of history, culture or scholarship.

Only in the writing on Stepinac does this pattern vary decisively. The figure of the Archbishop is Butler's great parable for something at odds with the cussedness he extols in his heroes – not something more complex, necessarily, but something more opaque, fluid, unsettling, elusive. The Monsignor's is a

BALKAN ESSAYS
1937-1990
By chronology of subject matter

1   Mr Pfeffer of Sarajevo

2   James Bourchier: An Irishman in Bulgaria

3   Escape from the Anthill (Introduction to the first volume)

4   In Dalmatia

5   The Last *Izmirenje*

6   **In Serbian Macedonia** (typescript)

7   Yugoslavia: The Cultural Background

8   **Croatia and Gaj** (manuscript)

9   The Barriers

10 The Two Languages

11 Fiume, Shusak and the Nugents

12 Nazor, Oroshatz and the Von Berks

13 Maria Pasquinelli and the Dissolution of the Ego

14 The Russian Consul

15 Some Encounters: Zagreb 1947

16 Father Chok and Compulsory Conversion

17 Two Faces of Postwar Yugoslavia: Belgrade and Split

18 **A Trial** (typescript)

19 Report on Yugoslavia

20 Yugoslav Papers: The Church and Its Opponents (with manuscript **Coda**)

21 **A Walk in the Park** (untitled typescript)

22 Memorandum on the Struggle Between Communism and Christianity

23 Ireland and Croatia

24 **"Stewed Eyeballs and Bishops": The Stepinac Case 1946-53** (all but one published in the press):

    A Primate's Trial (1946)
    The Trial of Archbishop Stepinac (1946)
    The Real Issue (1946)
    Archbishop Stepinac (1946)
    Proofs to Editor (with Epilogue) (1946)
    Forced Confessions (1948)

    Prison Interview with Archbishop Stepinac (1950)
    Cardinal Stepinac (1953)
    Tito and Stepinac (1953)

25 **The Compulsory Conversion Campaign of 1941: I-III** (published)

26 **Europe's Troubled Lands** (published):

    Yugoslavia
    Dubrovnik and Cavtat
    On Korcula
    Montenegro
    Macedonia
    Croatia

27 A Visit to Lepoglava

28 The Invader Wore Slippers

29 The Sub-Prefect Should Have Held His Tongue

30 **Andrija Artukovitch**

31 **Artukovitch: A Postscript** (typescript)

32 The Artukovitch File

33 **A Sordid Chapter of Church History**

34 **Cardinal Seper and the Ulster of Yugoslavia: I-II** (typescript)

35 Return to Hellas

36 The Final Solution

37 A Three-Day Nation

Other Yugoslav Texts:

38 **The Yugoslav Correspondence:**

    To his mother in the 1930's
    To Yugoslav friends in the 1940's and 1950's
    In the English and Irish press in the 1940's and 1950's
    Letters under a pseudonym?

Bold denotes uncollected work, whether published or in typescript.

parable about a breakdown in the ethical machinery connected to the absence of that independence of spirit.

Butler does not simply lay charges at the door of the Archbishop. With the forensic eye for inner detail that characterizes all his writing on personality, he is interested in something more important, more exemplary of a social process, than simple moral condemnation. Butler avoids any sense of anathematizing the character of Stepinac, whose courage, piety and personal kindliness he emphasizes. Moreover, there is no suggestion that the Monsignor belongs to the same moral universe as actual war criminals like Pavelić, Artuković and Eichmann.

Nonetheless, Butler does not shirk from making a decisive comparison with them in the matter of *the process of behaviour*. For Butler, Stepinac is another avatar of the Organization Man, subset Ecclesiastical. In a period of Alice-in-Wonderland values, institutional order itself, in a sense, is the problem. "The Organization Man's fatal respect for orderliness"(*GWT* 209) becomes integral to the vastness of the criminal enterprise. In bureaucratic cases like Eichmann and Artuković, who were dutiful cogs in the momentum of the state, the role of the Organization Man is now well-understood. But what I think Butler saw in the figure of Stepinac – what he first saw firsthand in the Municipal Library in Zagreb – is a less obvious form of the phenomenon, a corollary of the first, though perhaps no less essential to that breakdown in the ethical machinery: *the Organization Man in proximity to crime.*

These two faces of the Organization Man are so entwined as to suggest the continuum of human nature itself. If Eichmann and Artuković are instances of what Hannah Arendt called the banality of evil, then Butler on Stepinac concerns what I would call the gentility of evil ... so long as we understand the word "evil" as a moral evaluation of consequences and not an explanation of its metaphysical provenance.

V

Remembrance of things past was, of course, the emotional atmospheric behind Butler's return to Zagreb in 1947. Awarded a Travelling Scholarship to Yugoslavia by the School of Slavonic Studies in London, he had lived the country for three years, from 1934 to 1937. "I think I was first attracted there," he wrote in 1979, "by the fact that it attained its independence at the same time as we did in Ireland and had to confront similar problems of diverse religions, culture, loyalties."[3] Although he took seriously the adjective "travelling" and spent much of the time crisscrossing Croatia, Bosnia, Serbia, Macedonia and Montenegro, his main base was Zagreb, where he taught English for Anglo-

Yugoslav Society and had a wide circle of friends and acquaintances, including several notable literary and ecclesiastical figures.

Several essays tell us, in fact, that he was quite familiar with the public role of Stepinac in the interwar period. A mere four years after his ordination, Stepinac had became Archbishop of Croatia – the youngest in the world – and was soon embroiled in two major political controversies, the Yugolsav King's concordat with the Vatican (which was associated in the public mind with a simultaneous commercial treaty with Fascist Italy) and Catholic opposition to the building of an Orthodox cathedral in Zagreb. In such firsthand and telling detail, we see why Butler has good reason to remark, in the Introduction to *Escape form the Anthill* (1985), that Yugoslavia "is the foreign country I know best"(*EA* 8); those familiar with both this island and the Balkans will marvel at how his command of the cultural geography of the latter is no less magisterial than that of the former.

Butler heard of the terrible events in Croatia at an early stage. In a letter to *The Irish Times* in October 1946, commenting on the recent Yugoslav trial of Stepinac, found guilty of collaboration, he mentions that he read during the war a volume entitled *Yugoslavia at War,* by M. Sudjic. It had been published in 1942 in London on behalf of the exiled monarchist government as part of the *Europe under the Nazis* series. He adds:

> The writer accused Stepinac and other prominent Catholic prelates of collaboration. For example, he asserted that Mgr Sharitch, Archbishop of Bosnia, published under his own name in a Zagreb paper a poem hailing the quisling Pavelitch as "the sun of Croatia". [4]

Having gotten wind of the genocide, his intimate knowledge of prewar Croatia would have given him a vivid image of the nature of the cataclysm engulfing Orthodox, Jew and Roma.

Furthermore, from an unpublished letter of October 1947, declined by the leading Irish Catholic weekly *The Standard,* one can glean the sequence of events that led him to the reading room in Zagreb:

> Before I went last summer to Zagreb, where thirteen years ago I held for a couple of years a scholarship from the School of Slavonic Studies, I made an examination of the large collection of documents dealing with the Churches under occupation published by the Yugoslav Government in 1946 (known as *Dokumenti*) ... A large part of these were photostats of the signed

depositions of witnesses or of letters from prominent people in the Church or the quisling state. I saw no way of verifying these because forgery and moral pressure are not easy for a foreigner to detect.

But in addition to these, there are about 500 newspaper extracts, some photographed, some merely quoted. They are all dated. It seemed quite a difficult thing to fake so many newspapers that had circulated five years before, because as well as the immense labour of editing and printing, it would be necessary to suppress all the genuine copies. Most of the papers were church papers and must have reached Italy, with which Croatia was, at that time, closely associated and possibly even the Vatican. The task of substituting the counterfeit for the genuine would be an impossible one. Therefore, I felt, even before I went to Zagreb, that either a transparent hoax had been perpetrated or the extracts were genuine … [5]

Now we can see the chronology. During the war, he reads that a great crime had befallen the much-loved country where he had lived for three years and where he still had many close friends. Somehow he obtains the postwar book of evidence for that crime, though it is not distributed outside Yugoslavia, and reads it in the original. The tale told seems incredible. Is it really to be believed? He must go back and see for himself.

VI

By the late forties, the trial and imprisonment of Stepinac in Tito's Yugoslavia had become one of those tremendous political issues that is quickly forgotten by later generations. The question of the role of the Archbishop during the quisling regime had fallen foul of the hardening dichotomies of the Cold War. The forcible conversion campaign was barely known outside Yugoslavia, and along with Cardinal Mindszenty in Hungary, Stepinac had shapeshifted into an imprisoned martyr of the struggle between Christianity and Communism. In his 1948 essay, "Ireland and Croatia", Butler remarks:

> Few events in Europe excited such widespread interest in Ireland as the trial of Archbishop Stepinac and the struggle between the Catholic Church in Yugoslavia and the Yugoslav Government. It was as though after six years of discrete silence, we had at last found a subject about which we could safely vent our repressed

> indignation. Croatia is a remote, little-known part of Europe, and
> this made it very strange that our press, our parliament, our
> county council, which had been silent when one country after
> another had been overrun by Germany, should suddenly pass
> resolutions in the strongest and boldest language. (*ILN* 90)

On the first of May 1949, for instance, over 150,000 people gathered in the
centre of Dublin to protest at the treatment of the two prelates. This was the
perfervid background that would later decant into the Nuncio incident.

After his return from Zagreb, Butler gave a talk on Radio Éireann about
postwar Yugoslavia that embroiled him in attacks from several correspondents
in *The Standard,* who criticised him for "whitewashing" the treatment of the
Catholic Church by Tito. In the broadcast Butler had, in fact, mentioned
neither the Communist attack on the Church nor the forced conversion
campaign for, he says, "I could not refer to the Communist persecution of
religion without mentioning the more terrible Catholic persecution which had
preceded it, so I thought silence was best" (*EA* 271). Butler himself gives a
barbed *précis,* in the first paragraphs of "The Sub-prefect Should Have Held His
Tongue" (1956), of the evolution of the controversy that had begun to engage
him in the letters columns after his return from Zagreb.

In retrospect, what is so striking when one sees the texts of these first
attacks on Butler – besides the unpleasantness of the authoritarian tone – is the
degree to which he had already, through his Irish newspaper letters before the
1947 visit to Zagreb, become associated with the Stepinac issue. A subsequent
editorial in *The Standard,* devoted entirely to Butler, proceeds thus: "We
remember every detail of Mr Butler's record: his several attempts to depict
Archbishop Stepinac as a 'traitor', a 'collaborator with the enemy' and the
driving force behind the 'forced conversions ... ' " [6] It goes on to elaborate the
charge sheet for another 21 paragraphs. In a secularizing Ireland, we are
beginning to forget the degree to which the monolithic political Christianity of
both traditions was an organized power across the island. Indeed, it was
precisely "militant and political Christianity" (*ILN* 133), as he puts it, that had
led to the ethical breakdown revealed in the Zagreb files, and he was now
getting a small personal taste of one of its essential flavours.

A fuse had been lit that would smoulder on until in its final flare-up in the
so-called "Insult to the Nuncio". At the end of a Dublin meeting of the Foreign
Affairs Association in 1952, following a lecture on religious persecution in
Tito's Yugoslavia, Butler tried to raise the issue of the wartime persecution of
the Orthodox. Unknown to him, Ireland's Papal Nuncio was in the audience
and, on hearing Butler's opening, walked out. The "slight" had been

unintentional, but the point to grasp here is the charged atmosphere of the meeting. The lecturer was none other than the editor who published the diatribe against Butler in *The Standard*, and there was an attempt by the Chairman to foreclose discussion after the lecture, possibly in anticipation of an intervention by Butler. And after "the Insult" reached the papers and was transmogrified into a furore, there would have been no shortage of people in the press and public life well-aware of Butler's refusal to hold his tongue – and happy for the pretext to give the Kilkenny gadfly a hammering.

VII

Having laid general charges against Stepinac, Butler zeros in on the precise nature of his collaboration with a prosecutor's eye for the damning detail. If the several dozen passages assessing Stepinac are extracted and conflated, the result is an extraordinary *tour de force*, notable for its subtlety on three counts: in the marshalling of primary sources; in the parsing of coded meanings; in the fair-mindedness of his moral delineation.

But one text, above all, stands out as Butler's summary of the Stepinac file. It is the uncollected preamble to a long document that Butler had found and translated himself. The preamble and the entire document, of November 1941, which he titles "An Unpublished Letter from Archbishop Stepinac to Pavelitch," appeared in three instalments in *The Church of Ireland Gazette* in December-January, 1950-51.

The letter is a personal communication that accompanied a formal resolution from the Croatian bishops. In it, Stepinac protests against the barbarities of the conversion campaign; his letter also contains extracts from memoranda of protest from four other bishops. "When I was in Zagreb", Butler tells us, "I discovered that one of the most important of all the documents had never been published in Yugoslavia, let alone translated into English." [7]

For those familiar with the case mounted in defence of Stepinac, this is *the* key document, for extracts of *the accompanying formal resolution* would later often be used to absolve Stepinac of any responsibility for the conversion campaign. Here is part of Butler's preamble, republished for the first time since 1950, in which he dismantles that defense:

> When I was in Zagreb this September (1950) I secured through the Ministry of Justice some documents relating to the Stepinac trial. Most of them were already familiar to me, but the letter which I have translated below (though not the resolution that accompanied it) was new to me. Though it is of great

importance, neither the enemies or champions of Mgr Stepinac have made use of it. The letter is not helpful either for the Communist prosecution or Catholic defence. It reveals a confused human situation, where angels and devils are not easily identified.

The gigantic massacre of 1941, which was linked with Pavelitch's conversion campaign, has often been declared, particularly in Ireland, to be a fabrication of Chetniks or Communists or the Orthodox Church. Mgr Stepinac's letter, once and for all, establishes its actuality. In a more peaceful age, it would have been a great historical landmark, for the dead outnumbered the total of the victims of the massacre of the Albigenses, the Waldenses, and of St Bartholomew's Eve ...

The Archbishop's letter reveals the regret and revulsion which the violent methods used by Pavelitch's missionaries inspired in the Catholic hierarchy. The formal resolution, which was passed in concave in November, 1941, was an attempt to bring the conversion campaign under the control of the Church, and to check the rule of violence. The attempt was belated since the fury had spent itself by July, 1941, three months earlier.

If we exclude Archbishop Sharitch (of Bosnia), the author of the celebrated odes to Pavelitch and the fervent advocate of all his designs, the letters of Mgr Stepinac and the four bishops, whom he quotes, are moderate and humane. Why was the hierarchy so utterly impotent to check this inroad of fanatical barbarians into the purely ecclesiastical domain of conversion? I think the answer can be seen by a close examination of the letters (of the four bishops). Pity for the heretic had always to be qualified, and was sometimes neutralized, by zeal for the extension of the Catholic Church. Never once did they say, "Let there be an end to conversions! There can be no talk of free will and voluntary change of faith in a land invaded by two armies and ravaged by civil war!" Their concern is all for the right ordering of things ... A great opportunity had come to them. They must use it wisely, and not barbarously, for the saving of souls, but use it they must.[8]

In the following translation of Stepinac's personal letter, with its composite quotes, there are many passages in which the Bishops reveal the ambiguity at the heart of their thinking, including one (made famous by the title of one of

Butler's greatest essays) about the protest against the massacres voiced by a Muslim Sub-Prefect in Mostar who nonetheless, according the Bishop of Mostar, "as a state employee should have held his tongue."[9] Throughout, the ecclesiastical have-your-cake-and-eat-it, the careful eye on the future, are unmistakable.

But Butler, in the scrapbook where he kept much of his published Yugoslav writing, highlights in pencil just one passage in Stepinac's unpublished letter. It is the following, also from the memorandum of the Bishop of Mostar (again, because quoted, given Church imprimatur by Stepinac): "Every single person will condemn this irresponsible activity, but in the present circumstances we are letting slip excellent opportunities which we could use for the good of Croatia and the Holy Catholic cause. From a minority we might become a majority in Bosnia and Herzegovina ... "[10] (Bosnia had been awarded to Croatia by the Nazis. Strangely, if everybody condemned the violence, why was it happening? Double-speak here? Pious connivance? *In the present circumstances ...*).

With that, the ethical imagination rests its case.

VIII

There is a final twist to the Stepinac file. The most astonishing of all, perhaps: Butler's visit, during the 1950 trip, to the imprisoned Archbishop himself, recounted in a single brief essay, "A Visit to Lepoglava". If one is not already familiar with the Balkan writings, it is easy to miss the drama of the encounter. In this exemplary moment of the ethical imagination in the 20th century, the writer confronts the object of his writing. Butler and his Quaker companions have only a few minutes to ask the essential questions in French:

> I said I had read a letter he had written to Pavelitch ... protesting against the barbarity with which the conversion campaign had been conducted and that I had never doubted his dislike of cruelty. But why, when he wished to regulate this campaign, had he chosen as one of his collaborators Mgr Shimrak ... Mgr Shimrak's enthusiasm for the disgraceful conversion campaign had been well-known and publicly expressed. I had myself looked up his published address in his diocesan magazine *Krizhevtsi* ... The Archbishop gave the stock reply he had so often given at his trial (which incidentally has become the stock answer among the flippant of Zagreb to any awkward question): *Notre conscience est tranquille. (ILN* 136)

It is an extraordinary moment in the literature of actuality, reminiscent of Chekhov's trip to the penal camp of Sakhalin.

The encounter at Lepoglava gives us a further insight into Butler's persistence in truth-telling that would culminate in the Nuncio incident two years later. What was a spat in Ireland, or even removal from the Kilkenny Archaeological Society, which he had revived, compared to the events he was publicizing?

> I was denounced by special meetings of the Kilkenny Corporation and Kilkenny County Council, and the chain of events began which drew me from all this pleasant constructive planning for the revival of archaeology. I in "The Sub-Prefect Should Have Held His Tongue," Paul Blanchard in *The Irish and Catholic Power*, have told only a very little of it and later on I want to describe all that happened afterwards, a sequel of which I am proud enough, because I have stood by what I believed and hit back at those, who damaged me only a little, but damaged truth a great *deal* ... [11]

That controversy, we can now see, was an exemplary moment in the history of the public intellectual in modern Ireland; one where Butler exemplifies, in the life of the parish as well as the nation, the independent spirit whom Chekhov extols. In the Nuncio controversy, life and work fuse in a moment of ethical courage.

IX

However remote the events in Quisling Croatia may now seem to the Westerner, their influence is still very much alive in the Balkans. The Croatian crusade is deeply connected to its recent Serb doppelganger at Vukovar, Sarajevo, Srebrenica, Kosova and the rest. What might be called "a peregrination of trauma" has occurred: the victim becomes the victimizer; the shame of defeat, the shamelessness of victory; the evil suffered, the evil done. It is a pattern we know well in Ireland. How can we expect better things in a renewed Serbia, if Stepinac is still revered in Croatia, even by the intelligentsia, to say nothing of the Church, as saintly and patriotic?

Since the break-up of Yugoslavia, an effigy of Stepinac, resembling nothing so much as the embalmed Lenin, sits in a glass case on the altar of Zagreb Cathedral. In 1998, the Pope initiated the process of his canonization. Shortly afterwards, in Italy, a small and respected religious press published a book about the conversion campaign entitled *The Genocide Archbishop.* [12] The struggle between hagiography and historiography, "of utmost importance to all thinking Christians", is still engaged. It would appear that the Stepinac file, which Hubert Butler did so much to keep open in the West, cannot soon be closed.

NOTES

1   Hubert Butler, letter to the Editor of *The Standard* (unpublished proof, autumn 1947), Hubert Butler Papers (uncatalogued), Trinity College, Dublin.

2   Ted Hughes, *Winter Pollen* (London: Faber, 1994), p.31.

3   Hubert Butler, unpublished address at the opening of a "Yugoslav Exhibition" in the Art Gallery of Kilkenny Castle (5 November 1979), Butler Papers (uncatalogued).

4   *The Irish Times* 16 October 1946.

5   Hubert Butler, letter to the Editor of *The Standard* (unpublished proof, autumn 1947), Hubert Butler Papers (uncatalogued).

6   *The Standard* 10 October 1947.

7   Hubert Butler, unpublished manuscript, Butler Papers (uncatalogued).

8   *The Church of Ireland Gazette* 22 December 1950.

9   *The Church of Ireland Gazette* 5 January 1951.

10   *The Church of Ireland Gazette* 5 January 1951.

11   Hubert Butler, diary, 1950s, Butler Papers (uncatalogued).

12   Marco Rivelli, *The Genocide Archbishop* (Milan: Kaos, 1998).

NEIGHBOURHOODS

John Casey

In the summer of 1979 there was a postal strike in Ireland, which also meant that the telephone service was out. This was an inconvenience of course, but it also meant that when I drove to Maidenhall to drop off one or the other of Hubert Butler's granddaughters (who occasionally helped take care of my two very young daughters) and Hubert asked me in for tea, there were no phone calls – and so we could talk and talk. A visitor from America forgets how far north Ireland is and how long the summer daylight lasts. I often left with a book Hubert thought I should read – and eventually – near the end of my stay – with a folder of his own essays. The first sentence from the folder:

> I have lived for most of my life on the Nore and own three fields upon its banks, some miles before it turns to the south-east and forces its way under Brandon Hill to join the Barrow above New Ross. (*EA* 88)

It rings just right. Clear and confident – confident but without egotism – the initial "I" soon becomes the mind's eye that follows the river as it makes its way to join the Barrow. The sentence stops short of the sea. The subject of the essay is the neighborhood, not the world.

Mind's eye and neighborhood – the good twins of so many of Butler's essays. But the second essay in the folder was about Butler's long term as an English teacher in Leningrad in 1931. Is there a contradiction here? Is this allegiance to neighborhood, to the local and human scale of things at risk? I think not, but it is interesting to see how Butler is consistent and clear in what he values most.

Butler went for a brief visit and made what appears to be a spur-of-the-moment decision to stay on. He shared a small flat with a Russian friend and the friend's mother, and several other people. He sets up a camp-cot between the stove and the window. He doesn't explain his motives and scarcely mentions his misgivings. It is only by way of some by-the-way sentences we learn that he already speaks Russian.

> Over the whole flat there was that sweetish musty smell of black bread and benzine and scent that Russians seem to carry with them, even into exile. I felt lonely and ill-at-ease. Nina Gavrilovna (the friend's mother) plainly didn't want me there.

> She refused to believe that being foreign I could understand
> anything, unless she shouted at me with plentiful gesticulations.
> (*EA* 309)

Almost all the details about material life are bleak and daunting, but Butler's bright interest in everyone he meets is evident from his sympathetic but clear-eyed summaries of their life stories.

Christopher Isherwood, who was in Berlin in the thirties in a somewhat similar situation, wrote of his own attitude: "I am a camera with its shutter open." This is true of Butler, perhaps even truer – Butler's account is more about the pictures than about the emotional life of the camera.

Butler isn't neutral – not in the sense of indifferent – but he carefully allows others to make the large statements. At a tea party given by his friend Kolya he meets Baroness Garatinsky. He has learned from Kolya that

> She had been an old revolutionary and in 1917 her peasants, who
> had taken over her estates in Central Russia, had made her their
> manager. Five years later her position had become impossible and
> she was now teaching languages in Leningrad...In Goskurs
> where she taught she was the victim of petty persecution.
> "Women are the worst," (Kolya) said. (*EA* 307)

The baroness, just coming in, hears this.

> She paused in the doorway, leaning on her stick, and diverted
> with a smile (Kolya's mother's) effort to introduce us and give
> her a chair. "Later, later, Nina Gavrilovna." To us she said,
> "Women are allowed a bit more license because even here they
> aren't taken seriously. Masculine unreliability matters more ... "
> She always talked rapidly and provocatively when she was
> maneuvering into chairs or difficult positions, as if to distract
> attention. She looked coldly into people's eyes when she talked
> to them. She herself had a lack of personal inquisitiveness that
> was almost unfriendly. (*EA* 307)

Kolya's mother tried to divert the dangerous conversation.

> The baroness, seeing her agitation, said to me, "You mustn't think
> that because we have much to complain of we are enemies of the
> Revolution. The Revolution had to happen, it was the result of

generations of suffering and plotting. It is a historical fact, a great convulsion of human nature. If we are to go on living we must accept it, and I have always done so gladly." (*EA* 308)

After that declaration by the baroness we hear no further overview of the Revolution. Well, a word or two – through clenched teeth. This is partly because, now that the last tourist ships of summer have left, Butler is living inside the Revolution and life is overcoats, galoshes, documents and food.

Butler sees more of the baroness as the months go by, and he also meets a lot of other people and becomes entwined in their lives. Usually the subject of conversation is immediate necessity but occasionally there is a sudden beam of light on how the whole thing works, but the beam is generated by a particular situation.

> One day as (Kolya and I) were queuing up outside the office of the Lensoviet, he tried to explain himself to me: "I am a Caucasian from Georgia like Stalin, with the same theological background. He was a theological student. He believes like the Manicheans that there is Good and Evil, Black and White, a dichotomy. All this which he thinks Good is Evil." He waved his hand at the Lensoviet and the long queue ...
>
> I found his claim to be Caucasian as irritating as he found my claim to be Irish...
>
> After a pause he said, "Darya Andreyevna ... thinks you are a spy and wants the House Committee to turn you out. She has been to the Upravdom. Lyubotchka did her best for you. She said she thought you were a harmless idiot because you smile when you talk to her."
>
> "I only meant to be friendly."
>
> "Yes, but real Russians only smile at jokes." (*EA* 311-312)

There is no apparent ideology in the thirty-year old Butler nor in the older man who wrote the essay, though his attentiveness to personal character, and sometimes, more largely to Russian characteristics as they blend with or modify Soviet life, is a stance, a corrective to mechanical abstraction.

Darya Andreyevna's husband, it turns out, had been a colonel in the Tsar's army and she a famous opera singer.

> After the Revolution she had sung Soviet songs and had been awarded the rank of "Naoochnaya Rabotnitsa" or Scientific

worker. Because of this she had first-category food rations ... she could get, among other things, macaroni. Nina Gavrilovna could never forgive her this. A Tsarist colonel's wife got macaroni while her son, a Marxist professor ..., had to live on vegetable marrow. Incessantly nagging Kolya about this, she made it psychologically impossible for him to get a first-category food ticket ... Whenever macaroni was mentioned, his face went dead and cold and Manichean. (*EA* 312-313)

With such shrewdness and sympathy Butler takes us through the fall and winter. As Neal Ascherson writes in the Forward to *In The Land Of Nod*, Butler is "interested in the 'epiphanies' which make currents of social and political change visible through the lens of some small accident or absurdity" (*ILN* x).

In the passage from Manichean to macaroni – from Stalin's Georgian and theological slant and Kolya's rebuttal, to the new privileges and resentments of the classless society at ground level, and then on to the sad truth about a mother's nagging – there is a reversal of the usual ascension of literary magnitude – instead of lyric, dramatic, and epic we get epic, dramatic, and lyric.

A great deal is said and more implied in this next short paragraph:

One day, as I was walking to my classes in the twilight, I saw a large leather-coated figure lying on the pavement. He had an open dispatch-case beside him with papers scattered about. He was snoring. A woman came from the far side of the Moika river to help me lift him up. "What a shame," she exclaimed, "to see such a beautiful coat lying in the mud." We examined it together – "I bet he's a commissar," she said. "One can only get a coat like that with Valuta." (Valuta is foreign money). We dragged him to the Marinski Theatre and propped him up sitting against one of the columns of the portico – I told her I had Valuta and needed a coat, so she took a piece of paper out of his dispatch-case and wrote the name of the place where I could get one like it. (*EA* 313)

Butler, by the way, never does get a coat like it.

Aside from the brisk matter-of-factness of style and aside from the woman's comically fast remark "I bet he's a commissar", there are two other neatnesses of observation.

The first thing the woman says is not what a shame to see a drunk man in the middle of the sidewalk but what a shame to see such a beautiful coat lying in the mud. First things first. And then the odd reminder of the elegance of the once and future St. Petersburg – the columns of the portico of the Mariinski Theater.

The essay is filled with passages of such visual and audible clarity, and not only from 1931. Butler modestly holds back until the essay is half over his knowledge and appreciation of Russian literature and history as it has sprung from or been at odds with St. Petersburg or Leningrad. And it becomes clear the he has absorbed and been absorbed by the city. I think that it was not simply his knowledge of the Russian language and Russian literature that made this possible. Nor was it simply his temperament, his quality of sympathetic attentiveness, though that counts for a lot. I think he could not have learned and appreciated so much of another place had he not first educated and enlarged his sense of place at home. And I think he had developed here in Ireland a notion of life that is both an element of his style and worldview. No, not worldview – a worldview is a perspective from afar and may be an ideological siren song offering final answers. Butler was skeptical of siren songs and final answers. In our short correspondence the subject of what our parents had taught us came up. I had written that my mother lullabied me along the lines of the world-is-your-oyster optimism. Hubert wrote back, "My parents led me to believe that life is a series of minor duties, most of them unpleasant." He may have been led to believe this, and it may have lingered, but as it turned out his sense of duty was not minor, and, if understanding is the highest pleasure, he had that too.

But a major element in his belief was that it is necessary to see as much as possible face to face, that the epic must be seen on a realistic human scale.

In the epilogue to the essay Butler returns to Russia in 1956. Between 1931 and 1956 there were the Yezhovshchina – the purges of the mid 30s – then the war, the bombardment and 900-day siege of Leningrad. His Intourist guide, Anna, supplements his own knowledge.

> To the north I saw the islands where I had walked with Yegunov and his dog. They were now called the Kirov Islands, and the great highway that led to them was called Kirov Avenue. Thousands of honest men and women died because of Kirov, but their names are nowhere recorded.
>
> I have forgotten much of what Anna told me but I am more inclined to apologize for writing about great events, which touched me not at all, than for tracing again the tiny snail track which I made myself. I was thinking not of the tremendous disasters that had befallen Leningrad and all Russia, but of the

small stupidities, the acts of laziness or greed I had committed myself. Why had I not given the blue rug to Kolya's mother instead of leaving it behind by mistake? Why hadn't I sent Guzelimian his fishing rod? (*EA* 338)

The essay ends with these small self-reproachful questions. I believe in Butler's immediate confessional pangs, but I certainly wouldn't assign him more than a very small penance. What I believe in and accept more completely is the perspective he creates. There is a similar insistence on scale and perspective in the essay "The Children of Drancy". The essay is not just about the Nazi deportation and killing of 4,051 Jewish children in 1942. It is about the response.

The facts are bleak and few ... But no one seems interested. I believe we are bored because the scale is so large that the children seem to belong to sociology and statistics. We cannot visualize them reading Babar books, having their teeth straightened, arranging dolls' tea parties. (*CD* 186)

When Butler writes of the real details of his Russian friends' lives or of the imagined details of the unlived lives of the children of Drancy, he refused either to let them be reduced to statistical miniatures or to let them be swept up into the blurred majesty of epic. What Butler does is to write so well about particulars that they fix themselves in memory: the overcoat, the wave of Kolya's hand at the Lensoviet, the macaroni. Small things – but they become "ciphers to this great account" – a record not only of themselves but intimating other – so many other – unrecorded incidents that are the threads of our most necessary history.

BUTLER IN AMERICA

Christopher Merrill

It is significant that *Independent Spirit*, Hubert Butler's only selection of writings yet to appear in America, contains just one essay – and a glancing one at that – about my country. "Little K," a compassionate meditation about Butler's severely handicapped granddaughter who is confined to a hospital in New York, becomes a vehicle for a sober look at natural law, euthanasia, and the role of the Church in establishing social norms. It is a fine example of his ability to articulate difficult questions gracefully, for his moral compass is true, his powers of empathy wide. Little K, he suggests, "is one of nature's mistakes and left to herself nature might have taken her away" – the starting point for a relentless examination of his own heart, conscience, and beliefs. "To me God is the assurance that the world of men is not purposeless or evil," he writes,

> and that we can trust ourselves to it and that, when old laws lose their significance, new ones will slowly shape themselves to take their place. As for Christ, he is the assurance that a man can learn when and how to free himself from the power of the law, however strongly it may be reinforced with venerable traditions and popular approval. The show bread may have to be eaten, the sabbath profaned, the prostitute exalted. "GOD" is the promise that out of this disorder a better order will ultimately ensue. (*IS* 541)

This passage alone might earn Butler an honored place among those whose lifework is in behalf of that better order; and this final essay in *Independent Spirit* concludes with a poignant vision of his coming death, in which he hopes to meet at the top rung of her ladder Little K, "the companion that (he) would choose above all others to travel back with (him) into nothingness."

Meantime he travelled throughout the United States, writing about unusual subjects like the Oneida Community, Mary Baker Eddy, and Bob Jones University. Unaccountably these essays do not figure in *Independent Spirit*. Perhaps his New York editor was embarrassed by his take on our experiment in democracy, his curiosity (which, he says elsewhere, does not stagnate, unlike knowledge) about what the majority of my countrymen view with apprehension, if not outright disdain. Yet it is precisely in these works that Butler reveals his genius for capturing, in quick strokes, the essence of a place.

He understands that what at first glance is most eccentric about this land is indeed what is most in the American grain. "How can one protect oneself from the ravages of secondhand experience?" he asks (*EA* 3). Direct experience, tough questioning, hard thought – these are his antidotes to received opinions. And what he discovered in his travels, particularly in the 1960s, was a country foreign to much of its citizenry.

"American Impressions," a suite of four seemingly unconnected pieces, presents in fact a provocative argument about the origins of several currents in contemporary American life. Butler flies into "the apocalyptic landscape" of Salt Lake City, where he "can see how it must have appeared to Brigham Young and his followers as a final refuge, a sanctuary so inhospitable that no one would wish to violate it" (*GWT* 230, 232). Then comes an objective account of the Mormons, "a proud, ignorant people who are persecuted for their convictions" – victims in their own land, that is, of the same kinds of bigotry that brought the Puritans, and so many other peoples, to these shores. Salt Lake is only the latest and, in Butler's view, most fascinating city on the hill: an example, bizarre as it may seem to mainstream Americans, of the revolutionary impulse at the heart of our experience.

In the second and third sections of "American Impressions" Butler finds different versions of that impulse at work. First he travels by bus through the Deep South, following the route of the Freedom Riders – black and white – who brought an end to segregation, and then he covers the student revolt at Columbia University. Unlike other campus rebellions against the war in Vietnam, which accentuated divisions between students and townspeople, at Columbia the protesters were joined by blacks from the neighborhood, who were about to lose their housing to a university development project. Butler believes these revolutionaries could thus "claim an intellectual licence that (had) not existed since the War of Independence." And he reminds us that as a student at this very university Alexander Hamilton plotted revolution, with this difference: "He was worse than a draft-dodger because he was ready to fight his own countrymen in defence of natural rights" (*GWT* 245).

The final section of this essay takes place at Bob Jones University, a fundamentalist bastion dear to certain Republican politicians – and to Ian Paisley. The Protestant leader wrote a book with Bob Jones himself, *America's Debt to Ulster*, which traces the contributions Ulstermen made to the United States, fighting in the Revolution, then helping to enshrine in the Constitution the civil and religious liberties first promulgated by William of Orange. And what Butler sees in this depressingly normal university is a ferocity of belief, the sort of faith upon which this country was founded – and which still exists in pockets, here and abroad.

The Perfectionists, for example, who founded the Oneida Community in upstate New York. It is true that the history Butler narrates of this religious society is strange in the extreme, at least by conventional lights. Led by the charismatic John Humphrey Noyes – a divine madman, according to one of his biographers – the Perfectionists believed that the Kingdom of Heaven had arrived on 1 June 1846, that angels have sex, that they themselves had been freed from sin. They shared husbands and wives, they raised their children communally, they created the famous brand of silverware – and then they were hounded out of existence. "Pioneers," Butler writes, "who find causes by examining their hearts inevitably assume that what they find there comes from some source that transcends reason" – a source that in the end proved to be too threatening to the local authorities. Yet when Butler visited Oneida in 1962, long after the community had dissolved, he was struck by the industry displayed by the descendants of the Perfectionists, the people turning out forks and knives. "Even when the principles are rejected," he decides, "the memory of the cohesion remains and acts as an inspiration to the survivors."

That is a fair description of the United States, where the desire for religious freedom often spurs revolutionary change. And lest you think that Butler's interest in the Oneida Community *et al* is another species of antiquarianism let me explain that although my Midwestern town has more writers per capita than anywhere else in America I cannot forget that I am surrounded by utopians of another sort: south of Iowa City is an Amish community, to the north are the Amana Colonies (which only recently traded communal kitchens for building refrigerators), and to the east and west are farmers in air-conditioned combines which can harvest sixty acres of corn in a matter of hours – exactly the kind of juxtaposition that Hubert Butler would have appreciated.

BUTLER AMONG THE SAINTS

—

Tim Robinson

Hubert Butler grew up, as he has written, in sight of the old castle of Kilbline, named from a St Blaan, the round tower of Tullaherin, associated with St Ciaráin, the glow in the night sky of Kilkenny, the city of St Canice or Cainnech (*TTS* 13-17). He evidently felt that to enquire into these memorials, verbal and physical, which predate even his own long-settled family's historical implication with the neighbourhood, was one of the duties of consciousness, the application of the mind to one's surroundings, so as to inhabit them with one's best attentions. And being a country scholar with the impetuous energy of such, he undertook among all his multifarious works a task any specialist would blench at, a general inquisition into the claims of the saints of Ireland to our memorious respect. The main outcome was the book Dick Crampton spoke about yesterday: *Ten Thousand Saints*, which considers saints by the bushel and the metric tonne; but there is also an essay in which Butler hunted down those saints particularly associated with *Ára na Naomh*, Aran of the Saints, itself. Since this session is devoted to Butler Abroad, I'll turn very soon to the Aran Islands material, Aran being as far abroad as one can get, not only from Ireland but from the world in general. But let me begin here with Butler at home.

His thesis, in both book and essay, is that the thousands of saints mentioned in ancient sources – the twenty-seven St Fintans, the fifty-eight St Mochuas, the forty-three St Molaises, the saints with bizarre epithets to their name like "dirty-fist" or "badger-faced", or whose vomit turns to gold, who slay enemies with a blow from an eyelash, and who are, collectively considered, incredible – never existed as individuals; instead, he claims:

> ... the saints were the fabulous pre-Christian ancestors of pre-
> Celtic and proto-Celtic tribes and amalgamations of tribes, and
> that in their pilgrimages and pedigrees and in the multiplicity of
> their names, nicknames, cult-centres, we can read the true story
> of the wandering of tribes. But since on this early pattern of
> history-writing later patterns have been superimposed, we have
> a palimpsest that is very hard to decipher. (*GWT* 126)

Also, since the names of many of these population groups would have been in some non-Celtic language, they were interpreted by the Celts of a later time through word-play; the names and epithets of the saints and the weird biographies concocted to explain them are, Butler suggests, elaborate puns on the underlying tribal names. In support of this he drew up a huge glossary of the name-elements associated with all the well-known Celtic tribes and many that only the specialist would ever have heard of, with maps showing where they all had their being.

Although two or three saints, most notably St Brigid, are generally admitted to have originated in Celtic mythology rather than in Christian history, Butler is the first to cast such a disillusioned eye on the whole lot of them. The clue to his interest is, I think, that through these pairings and transformations of names an obscure picture emerges of Ireland's prehistoric politics, a topic more congenial to Butler than the traditional tale of fifth and sixth-century religious fanatics thrashing their way through the forests of paganism. He is even brave enough to apply his pun-craft to such eminences as St Fursey, well-known in Ireland, England and Gaul, whose Life was written only a decade or two after his death, according to the traditional view; Fursey, he asserts, was Forseti, the ancestor-god of the Frisians (*TTS* 300-316). He does not undertake to repaganise St Colm Cille though.

I'll take his home-saint, St Cainnech, as an example of his method (*TTS* 163-167). There are foundations attributed to him in Ireland, Wales and Scotland, where he is supposed to have helped Colm Cille in converting the Picts. Every year Kilkenny celebrates him, Butler says, "as a busy Irish prelate with widespread diocesan responsibilities". However Butler claims that he and his colleagues are not "a dim foreshadowing of a bench of bishops but the dying echoes of an immemorially old world ... pre-Roman, pre-Greek, almost certainly pre-Celtic and it is in the most fabulous passages, which the modern hagiographer rejects, that the features of that world can be most plainly distinguished" (*TTS* 16). St Cainnech is sometimes known as Ceanneich, which appears to mean "horsehead", and there are legends linking him with magical horses and with heads; for instance when a fellow saint was decapitated St Cainnech put his head back so perfectly that the only trace was a circular scar round his neck. There are many other saints with the element *ceann* in their names; but according to Butler, the association with heads is an attempt to make sense of a pre-Celtic tribal name; St Cainnech, he thinks, originated as the ancestor of the Cianachta, a people inhabiting Derry and other parts who, he surmises, themselves were an amalgamation of two tribes of names involving *ceann* and *ech*.

The danger in such speculation is that of erecting a convincingly self-supporting scaffolding all made up of weak links. Donncha Ó Corráin's book on Irish names indicates that Cainnech was a fairly common name both for males and females; it doesn't seem to call for any particular explanation.

Professor MacEoin of NUI Galway thinks that the cult of St Cainnech arose from a dedication of a certain church to Colm Cille, which was shortened to "Cainnech"; if so, St Cainnech is a clone, or a virtual clone, of Colm Cille, whose name means what it says, dove of the church, and who has as much of a historical identity as can be demanded of a personage of a millennium and a half ago.

Turning to the saints of Aran, let us follow Butler at work on St Gregory or Grióir (*TTS* 206-210). This saint, celebrated in the Aran Islands on either side of Gregory's Sound, is said to be a native of Kerry, where the strait between the Blasket Islands and the Dingle Peninsula is another Gregory's Sound. Butler writes:

> Opposite Aran on the Clare coast were the Grecraige or Crecraige, with one ancestor called Grecus and another called Grec mac Arod. There are Grecraige on Lough Gara in Co. Sligo, and their territory is called the Gregories, so obviously Grecraige turns easily into Gregory and makes St. Grigoir-Gregory look like a Christian incarnation of the pagan ancestor Grecus. (*GWT* 130)

I consulted our leading hagiographer, Padraic Ó Riáin of NUI Cork, about the Grecraige. It appears they were a peripatetic family of hereditary scholars associated with Emly and other ecclesiastical centres, and Professor Ó Riain doesn't think they have any connection with St Gregory. So perhaps we have to consign poor Gregory to the realms of shadowy unprovables. But of course Gregory has no imposing Life, no *Vita Sancti Gregorii*, to back his claim to existence, and everything we read or hear of him is fabulous. What of the most famous of Aran's saints, St Enda himself, then, whose Latin life was written down in the 14th century? Butler writes:

> I have noted nine or ten saints called Enna or Eanda, but no doubt there are many more; the most illustrious of them is St. Enda of Aran ... At the moment he enjoys considerable favour, and jet-planes have been named after him ... No modern scholar has questioned the existence of St. Enda, and Fr. Ryan attributes to him a certain originality of method. "He followed a rule of astonishing severity." This is to be inferred from the story that on Aran he used to send out his monks in curraghs without any hide covering and that they all came back bone dry, except one, who had stolen some food. Thought on such lines is "corrupting to the mind." Enda did not exist ... (Butler goes on:) I suggest that

Enda's travels by sea might be echoes of the voyages of the Veneti of Brittany, who were the most famous sea-travellers in Gaul. And there may be more distant echoes from the Eneti of Venice and Paphlagonia, from whom the Veneti were supposed to be descended, and whose travels were celebrated in Homeric legend. Some say that Aeneas was the ancestor of their tribe. (*TTS* 189-192)

Julius Caesar claimed to have put to death all the "senate" of the Veneti and sold the rest for slaves after defeating their fleet of two hundred ships at Bordeaux, but as Hubert Butler points out it is possible that many of them escaped to Britain and Ireland, and mentions that the place-names of Fanad in Donegal and Fenit in Kerry have been said to reflect their presence here (*GWT* 127).

What is the current opinion, if such exists, on this topic? I lifted the telephone – my favorite research implement – and made some spot checks. Dónal Mac Giolla Easpaig of the Placenames Department tells me that no etymology is known for Fenit, but it could be Scandinavian; Fanad is just Old Irish *fánaid*, a slope, the "aid" being a "petrified" dative ending. These are complicated matters and, as I have discovered to my own cost, one needs more than "ad-hoc" Irish to speculate fruitfully in them. As to Ireland's pre-Celtic languages, Professor MacEoin says that virtually nothing is known of them, which surely implies that a theory of saints' names and epithets arising from Celtic puns on pre-Celtic tribe names is, to say the least, unverifiable. Professor Ó Riáin tells me that he likes to start his lecture course by quoting Butler's fine passage about St Canice and the other saints of his neighbourhood, and accepts his general thesis that the majority of saints originated as tribal ancestor-figures, but only an expert Indo-Europeanologist would be able to say more about their particular affinities.

Of course Butler was well forearmed against what he called "the fine finicky methods" of the academics. The essay I mentioned, dated 1987 and published in the collection *Grandmother and Wolf Tone*, describes a visit to Aran, most of which he spent ill in bed; it is called "Influenza in Aran" – a typically self-deprecating title, with its hint that his head was stuffed with matter of no consequence. Behind this cover, and in his habitually witty and genial style, he deals with deep questions. While bedridden he read the only two sources of local information he could lay his hands on: a pious pamphlet by a Fr Scantlebury, *Saints and Shrines of Aran Mór*, and a romanticising history, *Aran, Islands of Legend*, by P.A. Ó Síocháin, according to which Aran was once "the greatest spiritual storehouse the world has ever known." Butler's attitude to these works is generous and open-minded. An amusing subplot of the Aran essay is Butler's meetings and discussions with a Dr. Simpson of Galway, an expert in Early Irish, who dismisses the naive writings of Fr. Scantlebury and Ó Síocháin with scorn and talks of the Latin *Life of St. Enda*, its conflations, collations, recensions, dodges the issue of its historicity by mumbling something about folklore and the charms of innocence, leaving Butler with the impression "that Enda is sliding gently out of history ... and that the whole 'spiritual storehouse' is in danger of collapsing" (*GWT* 124). No one wants this to happen, he says, but it will, and without any sort of explosion – which is proof that learning is dead, for real learning is dynamic, dangerous, built of curiosity, and is now being replaced by Dr Simpson's brand of textual criticism, philology, etc.

Now – perhaps the question is as naive as that of who was St Enda, but one wants to know – who was this Dr. Simpson? Is this English-sounding academic a stuffed figure set up for Butler to knock down in his amiable and disarming fashion, or did he exist? Once again I phoned professors with long memories in NUI Galway (the Aran visit was in 1964, I am told by Eleanor Burgess, who accompanied Hubert and Peggy). The consensus is that Dr Simpson could have been the late Tomás Ó Máille, born and bred in England, who spoke Irish with a Manchester accent. However, Eleanor thinks that no such person met them in Aran or Galway – and that much of Hubert's essay is fictional; he didn't even have influenza, just a cold; but "Influenza in Aran" is of course a more euphonious title than "A head-cold in Aran."

So the question of the identity of Dr Simpson has much in common with that of the saints, it seems. And I fear that a resignedly syncretic agnosticism is the only rational attitude to the truth-value of the Lives of the Saints. They surely contain echoes of the origin-myths of hundreds of early tribal groups, but so hopelessly entangled with stories of other sorts including adventures of the rivalrous missionaries who founded Ireland's early churches, and then exaggerated to magnify the prestige of much later religious establishments, moralized to edify the credulous and fantasticated to entertain the simple, that no historical actualities can be deduced from them.

However, I am reluctant to reduce the miraculous history of St Enda to such tepidity. And perhaps there is a more positive way of interpreting Butler's work on the saints, and of understanding the saints themselves. For, ultimately, Hubert Butler, even if he were wrong in detail, would be right in essence: the saints are too important to us as symbols, to be let slip into nonentity. To echo a famous question: What are saints for, in this desacralised age? In the *Life of St. Enda* we read that when Enda and his colleagues were on their way to Aran, they found no boat available, so eight of his monks pushed a big stone into the sea, on which they sailed across. Let there be no doubting that fact: the stone currach is still to be seen on Aran, near the end of the runway. How are we to understand this miracle? The arrival of St Enda in Aran is the inauguration of its history – a history the very foundation stone of which is already afloat on the seas of meaning. Only a true miracle can float an endless future of weighty reinterpretations, and then only if we disbelieve in it. By excluding it from the constraints of reality we make the miracle a believable symbol of the unbelievable potentialities latent in any fragment of reality. Similarly for the saint, the miracle-worker. From his tower of legend the necessarily inexistent saint rings his bell to wake us to the endless surprise of human invention. Some new interpretation can always be written in the dust on long-neglected books; that is the lesson of Butler's efforts. On this metaphorical view of the saints their affinities do not lie back in the foggy realms, the impenetrable alphabet-souper of prehistory, but with the creative spirits of our own time, one of whom we are celebrating today. Thinkers and rethinkers would be our saints, if saints there were; and when they go marching in, Hubert Butler will surely be of their number.

UNFINISHED IRELAND: HUBERT BUTLER'S CONTEMPORARY RELEVANCE

Neal Ascherson

What a conference this has been! The Butler and Crampton families, above all, should be congratulated by us. This was in many ways a rare occasion. In European history, it has not been uncommon to bring back the bodies or hearts of exiled writers to their native land, as the body of Adam Mickiewicz was brought back to be buried in the Wawel at Krakow in 1895. Much more special is the rescue and commemoration of writers neglected even in their own countries.

But this conference, at which the long 15-year process of honouring and establishing the work of Hubert Butler has reached its culminating moment, is much more than a commemoration. This is the planting-out of a strong young tree, nursed up from seed since 1985, which from today stands in the middle of Ireland to give fruit and shade to readers and thinkers and other writers all over the world.

It's good, though, that this meeting has not been anything like a "beatification" (and neither, as Edna Longley said yesterday, was it "some sort of revisionist retreat!"). There has been contention here. At times I was put in mind of Butler's sketch about "The Last *Izmirenje*", the Montenegrin ceremony he once witnessed which put an end to a blood-feud between two families. That essay shows how very difficult it is to forgive and to ask for forgiveness. And this leads me to the most astounding and moving moment in the conference, right at its outset: the speech of Mayor Paul Cuddihy in which he told the Butler family and this large public gathering that the city had wronged Hubert Butler and that on its behalf he wanted now to apologise.

In all my life as a journalist, up and down the world, I never heard a public official speak like that. He spoke with utter candour and out of deep emotion; there was no reservation or qualification in what he said. It seems to me that Mayor Cuddihy did himself honour, and did his city honour.

I begin this talk with a quotation not by Hubert Butler, but from an article written in Vienna in November 1914 about the outbreak of war.

What is the press? Only a messenger? One who also importunes us with his message? Torments us with his impressions? Insists on adding to the fact he brings us his conception of it? ...

No, (the press report) is the event. Is it discourse? No, it is life. It not only claims that the true events are its news about the events, it also brings about the uncanny identity that makes it come to seem that deeds are first reported and then done ... Thus it is that I don't mind being told that I am for ever exaggerating the importance of the press. It is no mere messenger – how could a messenger demand so much and get it too? – it is the event itself ...

Once again, a mere instrument has got the better of us ... With many years' practice, (the reporter) has reduced mankind to such poverty of the imagination as to make it possible for man to wage a war of destruction against himself. (from *Das Weltgericht*, Vienna 1919).

Much can be drawn from those sentences. One point is that it took half a century before these ideas reached the anglophone world. A second point is that Hubert Butler seems always to have understood about messengers who are the event themselves. He was fastidious about words to the point of being laconic, often, and he knew from long experience that the reporting of an event can be more momentous, and can require more critical energy, than the event itself.

The writer of those words was Karl Kraus, the – what shall we call him? – culture-critic of late-Habsburg and wartime Vienna. Any label understates his many-sided anger. There is a peculiar plaster statue of him which occupies what may well not be his old table at the Café Central, and it was proposed that a plaque should be put up inscribed: "Here Karl Kraus sat every day, reading the newspapers he loathed." Some people have suggested that Hubert Butler and Kraus had much in common. I think that this is only true up to a point. Chris Agee has written that Butler's most characteristic literary or polemic form can be described as the parable, something for which Kraus seldom had the patience. It's fair to say, though, that both men excelled at what in central Europe is called the *feuilleton*, a particular kind of intellectual journalism which is witty and biting, elegant but piercing, and which reveals deep learning lightly borne. The *feuilleton* writer (I am quoting here from my own Foreword to *In The Land of Nod*) is "interested in the epiphanies which make currents of social and political change visible through the lens of some small accident or absurdity" (*ILN* x).

Café society in Vienna may seem a long way from Bennettsbridge. Maybe so, but for me the difference between Kraus and Butler is one of sophistication. And here I want to turn the easy assumption around. It is Kraus who was the provincial visionary, and Hubert Butler who was the man of the world with a much broader grasp of international politics and human motivation. Butler does not approach Kraus's quality of apocalyptic satire, or his nervous, dialectic brilliance at turning cliché inside out. He could never have written "The Last Days of Humanity", and I think he could never have treated those around him with the unpredictable, inconsequent nastiness of which Kraus was capable. But he was as tough and obstinate as Kraus in the fight with his adversaries, and rather more consistent.

Adversaries are not simply the censors and the gendarmes, of course. Both men, the Austrian Jew and the Irish Protestant, had to cope with what you might call aggressive emollience, in shapes peculiar to their societies. For Kraus, it was the fatuous good nature of the Viennese, who assumed that this tense little chap could be disarmed by asking him to dinner and by the suggestion that it would all be the same in a hundred years. Butler, for his part, had to cope with what he unforgettably called being "up to the neck ... in this soft sweet-smelling porridge that has everything in it and tastes of nothing" (*ILN* 54). The editors, for example, who would print mendacious attacks on him and then somehow just fail to publish the letters he sent in reply; challenged, they might send an affable, intimate note suggesting that it had all been set up in type but somebody went off with the proofs on holiday and forgot to tell somebody else ... you know how it is here! The subtext here is the warning that to persist carries penalties: not arrest or confiscation but exclusion as an unclubbable, sad outsider. Both Kraus and Butler ignored the penalties. They pressed on.

Kraus never really went anywhere. Butler, as we have heard, lived in many foreign countries, often in times of extremity or crisis, and he experienced them in depth by living among their ordinary inhabitants and learning their languages. He, not Kraus, was the cosmopolitan intellect. Kraus, not he, was the metropolitan intellect. What was Sub-Carpathian Ruthenia to these two critics? Kraus, if tidings of any kind reached him from Uzhhorod or Mukachevo, would have simply milled them to extract radioactive particles which might have meaning for humanity in general or for the Habsburg state in particular. Butler, in contrast, actually knew something about what he called "Carpatho-Russia". He had spent much time listening patiently and respectfully to Carpatho-Russians as they told him their own feelings about their small country.

In New York, he became a friend of the exiled Sub-Carpathian politician (or church diplomat) Alexei Gierowski. His knowledge of Jugoslavia helped him to grasp the significance of Orthodox Christianity in that luckless territory and to appreciate the unexpected fact that "Carpatho-Russia" was in the Orthodox see of Sremski Karlovac in Serbia. In this, there was not a trace of that "English" stamp-collecting glee about the possession of obscure knowledge which is so patronising, so repellently metropolitan. Why is it thought sophisticated to dismiss the arrangements of small, far-off peoples as faintly comic? As the Auschwitz survivor said to the Red Cross when they asked him why he wanted to settle so far away in New Zealand: "Far away from what?"

Hubert Butler took other nations, other societies, on their own terms. He instinctively respected their sense of priorities, and did not attempt to distort them through a lens "made in Dublin" or London or anywhere else. (Only the very best of foreign correspondents take this approach now, and they exasperate their news editors by doing so). He understood that allegiance to Karlovac and to Bishop Dositheus, an ethnic Serb, was a serious thing for the Orthodox community trying to survive the policies of Benes, Hitler and Stalin in "Podkarpacki Rus", comically exotic as it might seem to strangers in the West. When Dositheus died of his injuries, kicked and beaten to death by a Catholic mob in Zagreb, Butler was one of the very few foreigners who could hear the distant, manifold resonances across Eastern and Central Europe of that small tragedy.

I am supposed to be discussing Hubert Butler's relevance to the 21st century. Before talking about how his thoughts may make an impact on this knock-kneed young millennium in its pimply first decade, it's worth pointing out that Butler was not primarily a prophet. Butler did not sit down in Kilkenny and write a work entitled "Ireland: Testbed for the End of the World". That was the sort of thing Kraus did, because Vienna in his time really was such a testbed, or at least a range on which all the explosives to be used in the Nazi cataclysm were already being tried out. Butler, in contrast, abstained from cosmic pessimism about the future and concentrated on diagnosing the present. But that was worrying enough to him, and he expressed some terminally gloomy views about the landscape he eyed.

For instance, he was fond of saying that something was "dead", by which he often meant that it had lost its memory. From time to time, in the days when this country was perhaps Celtic hedgehog rather than tiger, he would claim that Ireland was dead. This was almost always a reference back to passages of history when Ireland lived more energetically and dangerously, for example when people sought to live under "the common name of Irishman." But he could also recognise corpsehood in entire professions. "Unlike archaeologists", he wrote in 1984, "anthropologists have shown themselves ready to admit that their science is dead" (*EA* 245). This too is a puzzling observation, taken on its own.

Anthropology is flourishing, while archaeology in Britain or Ireland or the United States has more practitioners and a bigger public than ever in its history. But he was talking about the heartlands of Europe, as he often did: not just about the monstrous abuse of those two professions by Hitlerism – with the enthusiastic assistance of most of their German scholars – but about the postwar refusal to admit the truth about that past. "I think myself that archaeology did not really die until all international scholars decided that it would be wise and generous to let bygones be bygones" (*EA* 244). The new generation of German archaeologists under 40 would know exactly what he meant by that, and they have decided, 50 years on, that the only way to resurrect their discipline is indeed to dig it up and display the remains in the hope that life will return to them again.

He thought that any intellectual surrender to any state brought with it the risk of moral death. This opinion was part of his hostility to the very specialisation of learning itself. Hubert Butler preserved a view which can now seem archaic: that learning, to survive, had to be universal, "an integral part of an educated man, transfusing everything" (*EA* 244). What he called "departmentalisation" cut off the moral view, and left the scholar defenceless against the powers who coveted his or her skills in order to abuse them. "In this way archaeology, which had been born beside ruined abbeys and whose purpose had not been knowledge but to keep alive in a small community the sense of the past and the continuity of history, became one of the whore sciences whose poxy favours can be bought by any government prepared to pay for them" (*EA* 244).

This is one of my favourite Butler passages. But isn't this merely the nostalgia of the last country gentleman, whose ancestors went on the Grand Tour, acquired "polish" and flourished before the intellectual division of labour? And what has this reckless, Gothic declaration of love for amateur antiquarianism got to do with professional scientific archaeology? What is the contemporary relevance of any of this?

More than might at first appear. To start at the narrow end first, the re-humanising of archaeology is now proceeding fast. While few would agree that its purpose is not knowledge, "post-processual" archaeologists would now agree that their discipline has to be "multi-vocal" – including the voice of the small community which uses the material relics of the past to enhance its "sense of the past and the continuity of history". This voice cannot be patronised away by the claim of a professional trained élite to superior knowledge. In the United Kingdom, museum strategy is reluctantly coming back to the idea of the local museum, or at least to returning many objects from capital-city vitrines to the localities where they were found. I don't know that Hubert Butler ever wrote about it, but I assume that he would have disliked the strongly centralised and authoritarian streak in the Heritage boom, the element which simply imposes on all citizens a list of sites or monuments which they are ordered to cherish on trust for posterity. What he would certainly be welcoming are signs that the monolithic version of Heritage is now beginning to break up, and that local people – farmers, teachers, shopkeepers, contractors, New Age wizards, even men with metal-detectors – are now able to contest the uses to which a scheduled cultural landscape can be put.

He believed in the priority of local communities; he believed in small nations. But not just because he was an apostle of smallness for itself, like Leopold Kohr. Butler was a nationalist, with a steady faith in the virtues of national statehood and independence. It has already been asked, the obvious question: would the post-1989 disasters in south-eastern Europe, the Jugoslav wars, have made him change his mind? After Vukovar, Srebrenica and Racak, can small-state nationalism be regarded as anything but a ticket to the fiery furnace?

The reply must be a double No. Butler understood, as the English still find very difficult to understand, that nationalism is never entirely good or bad, "civic" or "ethnic", but – as Tom Nairn famously taught, with his image of the two-faced nationalist Janus – always contains elements of both. The point is in the proportions of the mix. For Hubert Butler, who had seen independence struggles, successful or doomed, all over Europe from the Baltic to the Adriatic, the modernising and liberalising element was inherently stronger. He condemned "the new passionate racism – the disease of the twentieth century". But he did not shy away from the self-assertiveness of nationalism, so long as it was not distorted by xenophobia.

> Germans were ejected from the Tyrol and Slavs from northern Italy. What has this to do with nationalism, which is comprehensive and based on neighbourliness and a common devotion to the land in which you live? (*ILN* 35)

Looking at the struggles for Jerusalem or for Sarajevo, you might ask: What have they to do with anything comprehensive or neighbourly? Here Butler, uncharacteristically, was twisting language to suit his purposes. He was trying to redefine nationalism so narrowly that the word excluded bad behaviour. The brutality of General Mladić, he might have said, disqualified him for the honourable title of nationalist.

Hubert Butler, as we have heard, admired Wolfe Tone for his inclusive patriotism, open to all who lived in the land whether they were Catholic or Protestant, Irish, Scottish or English, but not invoking the overseas diaspora.

This especially appealed to Butler, who felt that "diaspora nationalism" was akin to racism. On this point, he differed from President Mary Robinson, whose open-hearted outlook in certain other ways resembled his own (indeed, she was the first public figure to show obvious Butlerian influence in her official pronouncements). I wish that he could have lived to savour the intriguing commemorations of 1798 and of the Famine, with their subtle re-inventions of public memory. Mary Robinson, as you will all remember better than I, expertly steered the Famine recollection away from thoughts of mass graves, Trevelyan or "soupers" and endeavoured to re-brand the occasion as a festival of the Irish diaspora. I cannot think that Hubert Butler would have liked this, although it might have made him laugh.

There is, in short, nothing dated about Butler's interest in the small free nation – in or out of a supranational confederation of states. Nationalism may be out of fashion in London and Washington – when has it ever been anything else in those capitals, except during the brief flowering of President Wilson's Fourteen Points? But the comfortable little polity grows more and more attractive in the age of globalisation, attractive both to ordinary people and to global corporate investors. Most members of the UN are small, and a great number of them are micro-states with tiny populations, whose independence would have been dismissed as a joke only a few decades ago. Meanwhile nationalism, with all its faults and crimes and failures, still remains the vehicle onto which most oppressed people in the world load their hopes for a better life and for justice.

And there is nothing dated, either, about Hubert Butler's dislike of rhetoric about broad horizons, higher unities and unanimities, "global communities" and all the sub-Hegelian verbiage which Prime Minister John Major, in his own neck of the woods, used to refer to as "Eurocrap". Butler was not in the least insular. But he had a passionate loyalty to the "real" world which he loved as a permanent jostling of small or large differences and contradictions. He agreed with Alexei Gierowski, the Carpatho-Russian, that ecumenists were on the wrong track. "We have to venture out from the well-kept museum of symbols on to the junk-heap of cast-off clothes, broken crockery and maggoty corpses which is history" (*ILN* 158). (Günter Grass has written much the same). He wrote with affection about the New Ireland Forum in 1985, but gently sent up its high-mindedness:

> The Forum failed of its effect but left a lingering sweetness in the air. The desire for unity and harmony is something like the desire for sleep. (*ILN* 51)

What mattered was the reality of physical neighbours, not distant fantasies. There was nothing Hubert Butler could do about the power of modern communications, but it worried him that even letters (for he was worrying long before email and the mobile permeated our homes) encouraged us to ignore the neighbour who lived a few yards away. In a well-known passage he complained:

> Christianity was born in a small community …Today the idea of neighbourly love has been diluted until it covers all humanity. We grieve for distant events and people with sympathy as thin and ephemeral as the newspaper in which we read about them. We suffer from a disease so widespread as to seem incurable. Yet where the diagnosis is obvious, the cure cannot be for ever beyond our reach. (*EA* 144)

The writings of Hubert Butler help to dissolve the ill-defined fuzz of anxieties and advertising that we call globalisation. He is not always helpful. For example, Butler's doubts about a "diluted" neighbourliness which covers all humanity do not accommodate the shrinking of distance by cheap air fares and new media of communication, changes which allow a growing number of genuine "neighbourships" to be established in other continents. But I think that he would identify the vanity of the "globalisation" word, seeing that this was only one more attempt to bluff good people into an illusion of impotence. After all, the Reaganite or Thatcherite appeal to "world market forces" amounted to only one more suggestion that unemployment and crushing foreign debt are also – in Butler's phrase – "a disease so widespread as to be incurable."

What remains for me a puzzle is what Hubert Butler would have thought of the universal "culture of human rights" which is now arising. He might have detected a sort of blasphemy in the assumption that everything that goes wrong must be somebody's fault, requiring compensation. That sue-for-all society creates its own piggish dependency, running quite contrary to his notion of "the Right of Private Judgement" which he trusted to be the heart of Protestant ethics.

But I am sure that he would have been delighted by the coming of something like a universal criminal jurisdiction, in the matter of crimes against humanity. His special intimacy with Croatia allowed him to see what hypocrisies, what spiritual betrayals of trust are required before a Christian society can bless its sons and send them out to butcher innocent men, women and children of other faiths. What frightened him at least as much as the crimes of the Ustashe was his discovery that those crimes had provoked hypocrisy and spiritual betrayal in his own country as well. I count "The Artukovitch File", the story of his investigation into how and why Ireland came to hide the chief organiser of sectarian genocide in Jugoslavia, as one of the most enthralling true tales of detection I know. But it is a sad tale as well, sad and humiliating about Irish real or feigned ignorance of what went on in the world. This is why I feel certain that Hubert Butler would have rejoiced to see the emergence of International Tribunals like those at The Hague, whose warrants run all over the world, or the *Lex Pinochet* which means that no government will ever again be able to shelter an Ante Pavelić or an Artuković by pleading ignorance.

Lastly, Ireland. Or to put this more tactfully: lastly, Europe and Ireland-in-Europe. Hubert Butler wanted a proud and easy intimacy with Europe – with all of Europe, and not just its West End. He wanted to live in a society which was in every way open to the outside world. But just suppose something entirely improbable – that Síle de Valera had invoked the thoughts of Hubert Butler when she made her recent speech in Boston about political union as a threat to Ireland's "unique identity, culture and traditions". Could she legitimately have appealed to passages in his political creed?

After the Union of 1707 between England and Scotland, the Scottish Whigs were quite certain that enlightenment, modernity and prosperity could only flow in from the south, from London. To keep the inrush going, they were prepared to let it wash away a great deal of native identity, culture and tradition. The Scots Tories, like Walter Scott, thought differently, sometimes for good reasons. The division of opinion about Europe in Poland today, a vigorous but in some ways highly traditional society, is between radical urban reformers and conservative rural patriots. Reading "Brussels" instead of "London", it reminds me of those old Scottish arguments about England and Empire. So do the arguments I read in *The Irish Times*, in which enthusiasm for Europe sometimes reaches a Whiggish, new-broom intensity.

Hubert Butler's works warn that a debate about whether Ireland should become American or Swedish is missing a point – his point. Beware of enthusiasm for distant abstractions, at the cost of close and familiar details. Never mind America and Sweden: Ireland has not yet become Irish, until the alienation between majorities and minorities has been overcome in a new sense of community. There is a world to win. But there is also a family of neighbours down the road, and unfinished business with them. Hubert Butler enjoyed history's poxy ironies. But not that Irish history should now repeat itself inside out: that one part of Ireland should again march away and sign up under the flag of some vaster identity – and leave the other part forgotten in the rain. Yes, there is a threat to Ireland's "unique identity" – but it's to the identity which has not yet been created.

FROM THE BUTLER ALBUM

Photographs 1939-1991

*Family picnic, Annaghmakerrig, right to left: HMB, Florrie (nurse),
Mrs Guthrie, Julia Butler, Peggy Butler, three unknown,
Summer 1939*

*Left to right: HMB, James Delahunty, daughter Julia,
Peggy Butler, Benedict Kiely, 1955*

Maidenhall lawn, houseparty, left to right: Eleanor Arkell (later Burgess), Tommy Arkell,
Julia Butler, HMB, Joe Hone, Rhoisin Harrison, Philippe Fouchois, Clodagh Harrison,
Peggy Butler, Brigid Harrison, 1949

Left to right: Eleanor Arkell (later Burgess), Julia
Butler, Joe Hone, Peter Strunz, Tommy Arkell,
Melosina Lenox-Conyngham, Vere Lenox-
Conyngham, 1949

HMB and Peggy Butler, circa 1970

Elizabeth Bowen Commemoration, Dublin
Left to right: Maurice Craig, HMB, Bruce Arnold, 1987

HMB, porch of Maidenhall, September 1990
Photograph by Suzanna Crampton

EPILOGUE

ON HUBERT BUTLER

Joseph Brodsky

The epilogue to In the Land of Nod, *Butler's fourth collection of essays, published posthumously.*

In less than six years our criminal century will be over, and the United Nations will no doubt appoint a commission to estimate the loss of life owing to political violence in the past hundred years. The estimate will be rough; perhaps it will also be negligible in view of the year 2000's global census. Still, it may run up to a hundred million in Europe alone.

One can choose to be sanguine about this simply by citing survivors' lack of alternative *vis-à-vis* the past, or the majority's *vis-à-vis* the minority. The grip of this sort of ethics gets tighter and tighter with every next headline. So ours seems to be an odd time for Hubert Butler's book of essays. However, no other time thus far has turned out to be congenial.

Which is to say, for most of Hubert Butler's life since he was born in 1900; which is to say, also, for most of this century, since the first collection of his essays was published by a small press in his native Ireland only in 1985, five years before his death in January 1991.

He lived a much longer life than most of these essays' subjects. However, before he gained this advantage, he was their contemporary, and it is the contemporary of victims inexorably growing into the contemporary of villains – for the latter tend to outlast the former – that you find in these pages.

Small wonder that Hubert Butler shows an extraordinarily keen eye and ear for every shade and whisper of demagoguery. The events he happened to witness left him no choice if he wanted to retain his sanity and self-esteem. Apparently, this desire in him was stronger than in the bulk of his compatriots and those of his generation elsewhere. One can put this down to the particularity of his family background, which went back to the twelfth century, but that would amount to extolling the Irish aristocracy. Given Butler's own views on the subject, that route should be avoided. But Ireland is partly the reason, and one can safely paraphrase here Wystan Auden's line on William Butler Yeats – "Mad Ireland hurt you into poetry". All we have to do is replace "poetry" with "essays" and we'll have our man.

For all its extraordinary beauty, Butler's island is an extremely divided place. Because of its size, loyalties and animosities there get incestuously tangled and hurtful; in a place so small, it's hard to miss a target. And the divisions themselves, be they political (into Unionists and Nationalists) or religious (into Catholics and Protestants) are all articulated in English and equally oblivious of the Commandment: Thou shall not kill.

"Mad" is perhaps a bit too strong. Schizophrenic is a better word. Ireland indeed could be likened to a brain dissatisfied with the body it belongs to and craving autonomy. The body's enemy is therefore this brain's friend. This sort of predisposition can be easily exploited, as it was in Hubert Butler's lifetime, and still is, resulting now and then in bad dreams and very strange mental bedfellows.

Also, because the place is relatively rich in history, evocation of it is nearly relentless. Uncertainty always seeks to provide itself with a pedigree of causality, and Ireland's politicians for the better part of the century indeed could qualify as parvenus of uncertainty. Given the almost vengeful Irish mastery of the English language, the level of public rhetoric is as high as it is venomous. Small wonder that a word translated into a deed often results in spilled blood.

Smaller wonder still that someone who grew up in such a mental climate and ventured into the large world eastward would find its weather, in the thirties and forties especially, quite familiar, although a good deal more frightening. That, however, would have to do with the size of the place and with the masses falling prey left and right to the divisive rhetoric of rectifying history's mistakes, not with its substance. That also had to do with the physical existence of strange bedfellows exploiting that rhetoric and overtaking those places and masses. Indeed, what the thirty-year-old Butler saw in the Balkans and in Russia must have felt to him like the Irish brain's dream coming nightmarishly true.

History makes no mistakes because it has no purpose – that much Hubert Butler must have known by that time if only because at Oxford he read the Greek and Roman classics. In any case, the dishonesty, self-deception, and self-aggrandizement of those evoking history to pull the trigger didn't escape him, nor did their utter humanness. His knowledge of Russian (he is the best English translator of Chekhov's *The Cherry Orchard*, among other things) and of Serbo-Croatian, not to mention his French and his German, helped him along the line, no doubt, enormously. The detection of humanness in those whose words and deeds obscure it is, however, his own feat. On the other hand, this must have been easier for him, an Irishman, since schizophrenic uncertainty is humanness' integral part.

Yet observed by Hubert Butler as well as not, the large world kept at turning his contemporaries into victims, mounting up data for that would-be UN commission. No single man could stop this, certainly not an Irish gentleman living in his ancestral house and translating Russian novels. His sense of impotence must have been overwhelming, but not unique. This was the time for the armies, which were slowly and inevitably piling up a lot of similar data in the process. Those upon whom their roofs were not falling and under whose feet the earth didn't burn had to take the long view, and that's what Hubert Butler presumably did.

He was, one imagines, a man of phlegmatic disposition, fond now and then of quoting Horace, and the distinctly Horatian equipoise that marks his writing wasn't a posture. As early as the age of fourteen he resolved to live where he was born, and for all his languages and travels he stuck to this resolution to the end of his days. Which is to say, he knew his place on this earth, and this was what enabled him to provide us with a unique commodity: a perspective which is steady.

In this perspective the world as it emerged from the Second World War, the world where to all intents and purposes the just cause seems to have prevailed, didn't appear entirely attractive. At least, it didn't appear to Hubert Butler to be the subject for his automatic embrace. For one thing, the rhetoric of division, instead of dying in the flames of war, has emerged from them as the physical reality of divided Europe. Living in its better part, Hubert Butler now and then would notice in the crowd of cheerful survivors the familiar faces of those who diminished that crowd substantially.

He registered his observations, and you'll find some of them in this book. Made where they were made, *i.e.* in the Irish press, they caused a substantial stir, since they concerned the role played by the Catholic Church in wartime. Made when they were made, *i.e.* in the fifties, when the free world's chief nemesis was Communism, opposed by the Catholic Church, they seemed as well to recall that the old adage "my enemy's enemy is my friend" still can be played to the gallery with reasonable success.

Make no mistake, Hubert Butler was no Nazi-hunter or Protestant crusader against the Vatican: he was a dishonesty hunter. He just happened to know Serbo-Croatian better than the gentlemen in the Roman curia, and was more aware of the bloody record of some of the Croatian prelates retained by Rome for an otherwise worthy cause. But then he happened to know several things better than others did, apart from languages. Small wonder that he came to regard the postwar world's ethics as "dirty-grey".

For modern readers, Hubert Butler's most valuable insights would be no doubt those that have to do with *Mitteleuropa*. He knew the reality first hand, and in its worst period at that. Which is to say that our understanding of its present conditions logically stands to benefit from what Hubert Butler depicted half a century ago. A man of immense learning, he was interested in this borderline zone, with its fusion of Latin and Slavic cultures, presumably because he sensed in their interplay the future of European civilisation. Born where he was, he couldn't help being concerned with the fate of Christendom, whose natural son he was.

It's too bad that he wasn't listened to earlier. And it's too bad that he is not with us now, although he would feel badly dismayed and impotent once more. On the other hand, he might have again taken the long view. Still, this book is here, and it should help you cut through the verbiage and mental garbage of the trigger-happy swine whose faces you no doubt will be able to espy in any future crowd of cheerful survivors.

Amsterdam, September 1994

This essay is published coutesy of The Lilliput Press.

AFTERWORD FROM THE BUTLER SOCIETY

Eleanor Burgess

The Butler Society is pleased to be associated with this publication because Hubert Butler, with Lord Dunboyne and the late George Butler, was responsible for its foundation. The Society now has worldwide membership, triennial rallies, a substantial journal and a much-visited website.

Hubert belonged to the Dunboyne branch of the Butlers. His family first came to Kilkenny when his great grandfather was appointed rector of Burnchurch. Nevertheless, since his teens he had been interested in his "ancestors" and the important role Butlers had played in the neighbourhood. He had had visions of setting up a museum or local archive in Kilkenny Castle and, in the 1940s, he had broached the subject with the 5th Marquess of Ormonde.

In 1965, Hubert invited Lord Dunboyne to give a talk on the history of the Butlers in Ireland at Kilkenny Castle to The Arts Society. "It is a very crucial year in the history of the castle and the talk would be opportune." Lord Dunboyne, the chief historian and genealogist of the Butler family, came and camped on the tennis court at Maidenhall with his teenage son John, now the Society's webmaster. His talk, which was much appreciated, is still available as a booklet entitled *Butler Family History*. On the strength of its success, George Butler, who had recently retired as Chief Superintendent of the Waterford Gardaí and who also had a comprehensive knowledge of Butler history, suggested they should hold a Butler rally and pressed for the formation of a Butler Society.

In 1949 the 6th Marquess of Ormonde inherited Kilkenny Castle, which had belonged to the Ormonds for over five centuries. The castle ceased to be their residence in 1936 when the contents were sold by auction. Its subsequent deterioration was inevitable; but the 6th Marquess was keen that the Castle should be preserved and that it should be an asset to Kilkenny City. After much thought and investigation, he decided to give it to the people of Kilkenny.

A restoration committee was formed that included representatives of the city and of the national government. Sacrificing the personal fortune that an auction would have raised, the Marquess "sold" the castle to them for the nominal sum of fifty pounds. He added to his generous gift by buying the adjoining parkland from the trustees to give to the city also. Thus he ensured that this beautiful space would not be built over and the castle would continue to be seen in all its dignity and grandeur. The Marquess would formally hand over the castle to the restoration committee on behalf of the people of Kilkenny on 12th August 1967. This seemed a propitious moment to launch the Butler Society and hold its first rally.

In 1963 Hubert had attended an O'Mahony rally at Dunmanus Castle, a ruin on a windswept peninsula in West Cork. The invitation had been sent by his friend, Eoin O'Mahony, affectionately known to all as "The Pope of Dublin". Hubert greatly admired him as "the man who tried to change the quality of life." He was inspired by Eoin's vigorous and successful championship of the O'Mahony family. He was impressed by the rally's wild spontaneity: "a happy confident chaos that must have had years of practice, megatons of spiritual buoyancy, behind it." Eoin had sent out hundreds of gold-embossed invitations in the name of the Vicomte and Vicomtesse O'Mahony to come to Dunmanus Castle at 11 am and, tongue in cheek, had written "dancing" in one corner. When we arrived, the clansmen were assembling with their banners to the discomfiture of an English family, who thought they had found a quiet romantic spot to camp, and a *Daily Express* journalist, who had packed his dinner jacket as he thought he had been invited to dance at a château. Eoin translated the Vicomte's account of O'Mahony history after apologising good humouredly for the state of the castle. His magic pervaded the whole scene. Hubert fully understood and empathized with Eoin's aims. He wrote later that Eoin "had seen in the extended family, a blueprint for what life might one day be like. Perhaps some generations or centuries from now groups of people, linked together maybe as kinsmen, maybe as neighbours, will feel a special responsibility for each other, based on closer knowledge and affection than is possible in our faceless centralised society." Unlike the O'Mahonys, a closely-knit Irish clan, the Butlers are "merely a group of families, sometimes closely, sometimes remotely, sometimes not at all related." In spite of their differences Hubert recognised that the two societies were pointing in the same direction.

As founder editor of *The Journal of the Butler Society*, he wrote in its first foreword: "We aim at being a family society and the bonds we recognise, however tenuous they may be, are the same as any family recognises. We have elected to be brothers and sisters, if not ascertainably by blood, then by adoption ... we inherit a number of built-in political enmities of long standing but, if we take our kinship seriously, we inherit also the means of overcoming them." His vision and ideas for the Society, which in many cases have come true, can be found in his forewords.

Encouraged by his experience with the O'Mahonys, Hubert believed the Butlers could emulate them. He set to work to contact Butlers worldwide and the word spread that there was to be a Butler rally in Kilkenny. Enquiries were coming in from all corners of the earth as well as, naturally, from Ireland and

England. Elizabeth Smith, who succeeded Peter Smithwick as Honorary Secretary, offered to help with the correspondence. Hubert was delighted to find there was already a society of the close-knit von Buttlar family in Germany.

Horst Freiherr Treusch von Buttlar Brandenfels and his son wrote an account of the first rally for the first journal. Most of the four hundred participants were from Ireland and England but, as well as from Germany, some had gathered from such scattered places as France, South Africa, Australia, Cyprus, Kuwait, Nigeria, Portugal, Spain, Sweden and many from America including Charles Butler from Chicago who would become the seventh and last Marquess of Ormonde. The Mayor of Kilkenny and Charles Haughey, the Minister of Finance, were present when Lord Ormonde handed over the keys of the castle. The rally lasted a week and included visits to various Butler castles, opportunities to explore the city, and evening entertainments, including dinner in the elegant picture gallery of Kilkenny Castle.

At a well-attended General Meeting, the draft rules for the Society, carefully prepared by Lord Dunboyne, were diligently debated and approved. It all augured well for the future of the society whose objects are:

1   To bring together the scattered branches of the Butlers and their kinsmen and to renew old ties that are in danger of breaking.

2   To preserve the records of our family, its manuscripts, its history, its still living traditions.

3   To establish in Kilkenny a focal point of friendliness and family lore and to arrange reunions during which, for a few days, the ties of blood and family tradition will count more than the national and political differences which inevitably divide.

Indeed, since those heady days in August 1967, full of hope and enthusiasm, there have been regular triennial rallies in Kilkenny and occasional ones in various parts of the world, starting with the von Buttlar's invitation to their family gathering in Hesse in 1968. That year Hubert could confidently start *The Journal*: "It is pleasant to be associated with a society, which is plainly flourishing and expanding." He went on to describe it: "Our society was founded from a mixture of motives, scholarship, idealism, sociability. Our critics would add 'nostalgia, sentimentality, snobbery and commercialised romanticism'. Some want to use the society to keep things as they are, arresting the process of oblivion and decay; others see it as a way of breaking up the stagnation of the present and recovering some dynamism, which we have lost. For our ancestors, even the worst of them had an independence of mind, which we poor organisation-men of the sixties have almost lost. That is to say, our society is a lot of very respectable things in embryo, a historical society, a society for genealogical research, a society for recording and preserving buildings, books, pictures, traditions. As well as that we are a society for entertaining each other with the informality, which is only possible among people who know each other."

The Butler Society gave Hubert the opportunity to participate again in local history that he had lost when he was forced to resign the Secretaryship of the Kilkenny Archaeological Society. Perhaps he also saw it as a practical concrete way to escape from the anthill, the title of his first book of essays published in 1985. Still confident when he gave up the editorship of *The Journal* in 1979, he wrote: "We know our approach is the right one. All round us men are rebelling against the civilisation of the anthill and wish to be individuals not units, humans not machines, and are juggling in different ways with the old human constants which are under threat, neighbourhoods, kinships, beliefs, skills, traditions."

CONTRIBUTORS

JULIA CRAMPTON is Hubert Butler's daughter. She divides her time between the United States and Ireland.

PAUL CUDDIHY was Mayor of the City of Kilkenny for 2000-2001. He is currently a Fine Gael member of Kilkenny County Council and Kilkenny Corporation. He teaches History and Geography at Kilkenny College.

ROY FOSTER is Carroll Professor of Irish History and Fellow of Hertford College at Oxford. His most recent books are *W.B.Yeats, A Life, I: The Apprentice Mage, 1865-1914* (1997) and *The Irish Story: Telling Tales and Making It Up in Ireland* (2001). The second and final volume of his authorized life of Yeats, *The Arch-Poet, 1915-1939* will be published in 2003.

JOSEPH HONE, who grew up at Maidenhall, is a novelist, travel-writer and broadcaster. His most recent volume is *Firesong* (1997). He currently lives and teaches in Oxfordshire.

ELEANOR BURGESS farms in Essex in England and is active in Green politics. She spent many childhood holidays at Maidenhall. She is currently working on a biography of Butler and is the Editor of *The Journal of the Butler Society*.

CHRISTOPHER FITZ-SIMON is a director and author. For many years he was the Literary Manager and Artistic Director of the Abbey and Peacock Theatres in Dublin. His principal books are *The Arts in Ireland* (1982), *The Irish Theatre* (1983) and *The Boys* (1994).

PETER SMITHWICK, a native of County Kilkenny, is President of the District Court at the Four Courts in Dublin. He knew Butler for many years and attended the Kilkenny Debates in the 1950s.

ANTONY FARRELL is the Founder and Editor-in-Chief of Butler's publisher, The Lilliput Press, Dublin. He was the first editor to publish Butler's essays in book form. He is currently editing a fifth volume of Butler's essays.

ROBERT TOBIN is in his final year at Merton College, Oxford, where he is writing a doctoral thesis on Hubert Butler and Southern Irish Protestant intellectual life after Independence.

TERENCE BROWN is Professor of Modern English Literature and Fellow at Trinity College, Dublin. His most recent publications are *Ireland's Literature* (1988) and a literary biography of W. B. Yeats (1999).

EDNA LONGLEY is Professor of English at The Queen's University of Belfast. Her latest volume of criticism is *Poetry and Posterity* (2000). She has edited *The Bloodaxe Book of Contemporary Poetry from Britain and Ireland* (2000) and is co-author, with Declan Kiberd, of *Multiculturalism: The View from the Two Irelands* (2001).

PROINSIAS Ó DRISCEOIL is the Arts Education Officer of the Kilkenny Vocational Education Committee. He is currently completing a study in Irish of the 19th century scribe and diarist Humphrey O'Sullivan/Amhlaoibh Ó Suilleabháin, and is a regular reviewer for *The Irish Times*.

RICHARD CRAMPTON, who married Julia Butler in 1959, is Professor of Medicine Emeritus at the University of Virginia. He divides his time between the United States and Ireland.

JOHN BANVILLE is a novelist, and Chief Critic and Associate Literary Editor of *The Irish Times*. His most recent novels are *Eclipse* (2000) and *Shroud* (2002).

CHRIS AGEE is the Founder and Editor of *Irish Pages*, a journal of contemporary writing, as well as a publishing imprint. His third book of poems, *First Light*, appeared in 2003. He has also edited *Balkan Essays: 1937-1990* (forthcoming), the first Serbo-Croat translation of Butler's work.

JOHN CASEY is the Henry Hoynes Professor of English at the University of Virginia. He is the author of the novels *Spartina* (1989) and *The Half-Life of Happiness* (1998). He has also translated, from the Italian, the novel *You're an Animal, Viskovitz*, by Alessandro Boffa.

CHRISTOPHER MERRILL is the Director of the International Writers Program at the University of Iowa. His most recent books are a collection of poems, *Brilliant Water* (2001), and a Balkan memoir, *Only The Nails Remain* (1999).

TIM ROBINSON worked as a visual artist in Vienna and London before moving to the Aran Islands where he lived from 1972 to 1984. He now lives in Roundstone, Connemara. His publications include the two-volume *Stones of Aran* (1987, 1995), *Setting Foot on the Shores of Connemara* (1996), as well as maps of Connemara, the Aran Islands and the Burren. His most recent publications are a collection of essays, *My Time in Space* (2001), and his accumulated fictions, *Tales and Imaginings* (2002).

NEAL ASCHERSON, a native of Edinburgh, has spent most of his life as a journalist, much of it as a correspondent in Central and Eastern Europe, and later as a columnist for *The Observer*, *The Scotsman* and *The Independent on Sunday*. He now lives in London as a freelance writer, and edits the journal *Public Archaeology* at University College, London. His most recent books are *Black Sea: The Birthplace of Civilisation and Barbarism* (1995) and *Stone Voices: The Search for Scotland* (2002).

APPENDICES

HUBERT BUTLER: A BIBLIOGRAPHY

I
Essay Collections, Translations, Book Contributions and Pamphlet

Leonid Leonov, *The Thief*. Trans. Hubert Butler. London: Martin Secker, 1931.

Anton Chehov, *The Cherry Orchard*. Trans. Hubert Butler. London: H.F.W. Deane & Sons, 1934.

Hubert Butler, "The Teaching Brigade." *Irish Harvest*. Ed. Robert Greacen. Dublin: New Frontiers Press, 1946.

Hubert Butler, "The Country House – The Life of the Gentry." *Social Life in Ireland, 1800-45*. Ed. R.B. McDowell. Dublin: Cultural Relations Committee of Ireland in association with Radio Éireann, 1957.

Hubert Butler, *Ten Thousand Saints: A Study in Irish and European Origins*. Kilkenny: The Wellbrook Press, 1972.

Hubert Butler, *Wolfe Tone and the Common Name of Irishman* (Lilliput Pamphlet 5). Mullingar: The Lilliput Press, 1985.

Hubert Butler, *Escape from the Anthill*. Mullingar: The Lilliput Press, 1985.

Hubert Butler, *The Children of Drancy*. Mullingar: The Lilliput Press, 1988.

Hubert Butler, *Grandmother and Wolfe Tone*. Dublin: The Lilliput Press, 1990.

Hubert Butler, *The Sub-prefect Should Have Held His Tongue And Other Essays*. Ed. Roy Foster. London: Allen Lane / Penguin, 1990.

Hubert Butler, *L'envahisseur est venu en pantoufles*. Trans. Philippe Blanchard. Paris: Anatolia Editions, 1994.

Hubert Butler, *In the Land of Nod*. Dublin: The Lilliput Press, 1996.

Hubert Butler, *Independent Spirit: Essays*. Ed. Elisabeth Sifton. New York: Farrar, Straus and Giroux, 1996.

Hubert Butler. "Little K." *The Anchor Essay Annual: Best of 1997*. Ed. Philip Lopate. New York: Doubleday, 1997.

II
Previously Unpublished Essays and Articles
First Appearing in the Lilliput Volumes

Escape from the Anthill

> "Introduction"
> "Peter's Window" (expanded version of "The Teaching Brigade")

The Children of Drancy

> "Riga Strand in 1930"
> "In the Adriatic": Sections I and II
> "A Visit to Oneida"
> "A Reply to Silence"
> "The Kagan Gruppe"
> "A Fragment of Autobiography"
> "Aunt Harriet"

Grandmother and Wolfe Tone

> "The Auction"
> "The Two Languages"
> "Crossing the Border"
> "Abortion"
> "The Decay of Archaeology"
> "Influenza in Aran"
> "James Bouchier: An Irishman in Bulgaria"
> "*Mein Kampf*, Mr Eliot and Mr Forster"
> "Yugoslavia: The Cultural Background"
> "Yugoslav Papers: The Church and Its Opponents"
> "Father Chok and Compulsory Conversion"
> "Some Encounters: Zagreb 1947"
> "Two Faces of Post-War Yugoslavia: Belgrade and Split"
> "The Final Solution"
> "American Impressions, IV: The Bob Jones University"

In the Land of Nod

> "Down the Parade"
> "Fichte and the Rise of Racialism in Germany"
> "In Dalmatia"
> "Ireland and Croatia"
> "Report on Yugoslavia"
> "Memorandum on the Struggle Between Communism and Christianity"
> "A Prayerful Project"
> "Irish Literature"
> "The Writer as Independent Spirit"
> "*Romae Kremlin amem*"
> "In the Land of Nod: Puns and Tribal Ancestors in the Old Testament
> "Woe unto Thee Bethsaida: Puns in the New Testament"

III
Essays and Articles Published in Newspapers, Magazines and Periodicals

This list includes both collected and uncollected work. If the title was changed when the piece was collected, the subsequent title is listed in parentheses after the original version.

1940s

"The Barriers." *The Bell* Vol 2, No 4 (July 1941).

"A Lady's Child" (Books) *The Bell* Vol 3, No 5 (February 1942).

"Hanrahan's Daughter" (Books). *The Bell* Vol 5, No 4 (January 1943).

"The Desire to Please" (Books). *The Bell* Vol 8, No 4 (July 1944).

"A Keeper of Swans" (Books). *The Bell* Vol 9, No 5 (February 1945).

"Public Opinion: Censorship" (a response to Monk Gibbon). *The Bell* Vol 9, No 6 (March 1945).

"Soviet Literature." *The Irish Times* 25 May 1946.

"A Plea from the Country." *The Bell* Vol 12, No 3 (June 1946).

"That Lady" (Books). *The Bell* Vol 12, No 5 (August 1946).

"Archaeology and Native Culture." *Iris Oda: A Kilkenny Review* (Samrad 1946).

"Russians Remember." *The Irish Times* 14 December 1946.

"The Kilkenny Theatre 1801-1819." *The Dublin Magazine* Vol 21, No 4 (October-December 1946).

"A Kilkenny Survey." *Old Kilkenny Review* No 1 (1946-47).

"The Last *Izmerenje*." *The Irish Press* 28 February 1947.

"New Geneva in Waterford." *Journal of the Royal Society of Antiquaries of Ireland* Vol 57 (December 1947).

"The Deserted Sun-Palace" (later Section I of "Midland Perpsectives"). *The Irish Press* 20 July 1948.

"Istria and Maria Pasquinelli" (later under the title "Maria Pasquinilli and the Dissolution of the Ego"). *The Dublin Magazine* Vol 23, No 1 (January-March 1948).

"Otway Cuffe." *The Dublin Magazine* Vol 23, No 4 (October-December 1948).

"Report on Yugoslavia." *Peace News* 8, 15, 22, 29 October 1948.

"Letter from Ireland." *Peace News* 4 March 1949.

"The Truth and the truth!" *The Church of Ireland Gazette* 11 March 1949.

"Pacifism in Ireland." *Peace News* 13 May 1949.

"Wanted: Unofficial Travellers." *Peace News* 1 July 1949.

"Dangan Revisited" (later Section II of "Midland Perpsectives"). *The Irish Press* 8 July 1949.

"Friendship: Personal or Official." *Peace News* 22 July 1949.

"The County Libraries and the Censorship" (later under the title "The County Libraries: Sex, Religion and Censorship"). *Irish Writing*, No 8 (July 1949).

"Henry Flood of Farmley." *The Kilkenny People* 27 August 1949.

1950s

"Life and Leisure in Kilkenny." *Irish Monthly* Vol 58 (April 1950).

"Henry and Frances." *The Dublin Magazine* Vol 25, No 2 (April-June 1950).

"Materialism without Marx." *Envoy* Vol 3, No 9 (August 1950).

"The Statue and the Calvary: Ernest Renan" (later under the title "Ernest Renan: The Statue and the Calvary"). *The Listener* 31 August 1950.

"The Invader Wore Slippers." *The Bell* Vol 6, No 2 (November 1950).

"Prison Interview with Archbishop Stepinac." *Peace News* 29 December 1950.

"Who were the 'Stammerers'?" *Journal of the Royal Society of Antiquaries of Ireland* Series 7, Vol 20 (1950).

"In Europe's Troubled Lands." *The Irish Times* 26, 27, 28, 29, 30, 31 March 1951.

"The Compulsory Conversion Campaign of 1941" (preamble, with episcopal documents translated from the Croatian). *The Church of Ireland Gazette* 15, 29 December 1950 and 5 January 1951.

"Shaw." *The Bell* Vol 16, No 4 (January 1951).

"The Mango on the Mango Tree" (Books Section). *The Bell* Vol 16, No 5 (February 1951).

"A Lively Russian" (later under the title "Pushkin and Dostoevsky", Section I). *The Irish Times* 17 March 1951.

"The Slav Mind" (later under the title "Pushkin and Dostoevsky", section II). *The Irish Times* 7 April 1951.

"A Visit to Lepoglava." *The Church of Ireland Gazette* 20 April 1951.

"Autoantiamericanism: 2" (a response to Sean O'Faolain). *The Bell* Vol 17, No 2 (May 1951).

"Old Irish and Highland Dress" & "By the Rivers of Babylon" (Book Reviews). *The Bell* Vol 17, No 2 (May 1951).

"Two Travel Books" (Book Reviews). *The Bell* Vol 17, No 4 (July 1951).

"Nurseries of Writing." *The Bell* Vol 17, No 5 (August 1951).

"Penguins and Pelicans" & "The Weed Problem" (Book Reviews). *The Bell* Vol 17, No 5 (August 1951).

"*Envoy* and Mr. Kavanagh." *The Bell* Vol 17, No 6 (September 1951).

"Croce the King and the Allies" & "The Arts in Ulster" (Book Reviews). *The Bell* Vol 17, No 6 (September 1951).

"The Last of the Irish RM's" (Book Reviews). *The Bell* Vol 17, No 7 (October 1951).

"The Masters (later under the title "Forster, Gerhardi and Snow", Section III)." *The Bell* Vol 17, No 8 (November 1951).

"The Sense of Evil and the Sense of Guilt (I)." *The Bell* Vol 17, No 8 (November 1951).

"The Sense of Evil and the Sense of Guilt (II)." *The Bell* Vol 17, No 9 (December 1951).

"Horace Plunkett: An Anglo-American Irishman" (Book Reviews). *The Bell* Vol 17, No 9 (December 1951).

"The Old Kilkenny Archaeological Society and Its Successors" (a reprint from a Radio Éireann broadcast). *Old Kilkenny Review* No 4 (1951).

"The Dividing Stream" (Book Reviews). *The Bell* Vol 17, No 10 (January 1952).

"Canon James" (Book Reviews). *The Bell* Vol 17, No 11 (February 1952).

"A King's Story" (later incorporated into "Reflections on Royalty"). *The Bell* Vol 17, No 12 (March 1952).

"Two Great Critics" (later under the title "Two Critics: E.M. Forster and Edmund Wilson"). *The Bell* Vol 17, No 12 (March 1952).

"British Royalty and Ireland" (later incorporated into "Reflections on Royalty"). *The Bell* Vol 18, No 3 (June 1952).

"On the Way to Limerick." *The Countryman* (Spring 1953).

"Kilkenny Classical." *Ireland of the Welcomes* (July-August 1953).

"Stocktaking in the Irish Provinces." *The Twentieth Century* Vol 154, No 920 (October 1953).

"Trieste." *Peace News* 20 November 1953.

"I … I suppose so: *Maria Cross* Reconsidered." *The Bell* Vol 19, No 2 (January 1954).

"Letters to the Editor." *The Bell* Vol 19, No 5 (April 1954).

"Portrait of a Minority." *The Bell* Vol 19, No 7 (June 1954).

"Saints, Scholars and Civil Servants." *The Bell* Vol 19, No 10 (November 1954).

"We Are the People of Burke." *The Twentieth Century* Vol 156, No 933 (November 1954).

"A House of God" in *The Twentieth Century* Vol 157, No 939 (May 1955).

"No Petty People?" *The Irish Times* 13-14, 16-18 May and 7-8 June 1955.

"Ireland and Neutrality." *Peace News* 17 June 1955.

"The Minority Voice." *The Church of Ireland Gazette* 26 August 1955.

"Reflections of an Unjustified Stay-at-Home" (a response to Iain Hamilton). *The Twentieth Century* Vol 158, No 944 (October 1955).

"The Ascertainment of Truth." *Pax* (Journal of the Irish Pacifist Movement) Christmas 1955.

"The Human Beast." *The Irish Times* 4 April 1956.

"Slieve Bloom" (later Section III of "Midland Perspectives"). *The Irish Times* 10 May 1956.

"Croats in the Irish Republic." *The Twentieth Century* Vol 159, No 952 (June 1956).

"In County Cavan" (later section IV of "Midland Perspectives"). *The Irish Times* 27 July 1956.

"In County Monaghan" (later Section V of "Midland Perspectives"). *The Irish Times* 6 August 1956.

"A Visit to Yasnaya Polyana" (later Section I of "In Russia"). *The Irish Times* 6 November 1956.

"A Visit to China" (later Sections I-IV of "In China"). *The Irish Times* 16-17, 20-21 November 1956.

"A Siberian Journey" (later Section II of "In Russia"). *The Irish Times* 7-8 January 1957.

"Journey to Shanghai" (later Section V of "In China"). *Peace News* 30 August 1957.

"Protestantism and Unionism: Are They the Same Thing?" *The Plough* Vol 1, No 1 (September 1957).

"Boycott Village." *The Twentieth Century* Vol 163, No 971 (January 1958).

"Spanish Protestants (I)." *The Irish Times* 27-28 May 1958.

"Zhivago's Creator (I)." *The Irish Times* 27 September 1958.

"Escape to Spain (I)." *The Irish Times* 1-2 December 1958.

"Early Christian Ireland." *The Irish Times* 9 December 1958.

"Without the Bible in Spain." *The Twentieth Century* Vol 164, No 982 (December 1958).

"Zhivago's Creator (II)." *The Irish Times* 18 July 1959.

"The One That Got Away." *The Irish Times* 11 November 1959.

1960s

"The Bishop." *The Twentieth Century* Vol 167, No 126 (February 1960).

"Mr. Pfeffer of Sarajevo." *Nonplus* No 4 (Winter 1960).

"By-products." *The Kilkenny Magazine* No 1 (Summer 1960).

"The Eggman and the Fairies." *The Twentieth Century* Vol 168, No 1001 (July 1960).

"Return to Hellas." *The Twentieth Century* Vol 169, No 1007 (January 1961).

"American Impressions (I)." *The Irish Times* 4-5 June 1962.

"The Honorary Foreign Corresponding Member." *The Kilkenny Magazine* No 7 (Summer 1962).

"Grandmother and Wolfe Tone." *The Kilkenny Magazine* No 9 (Spring 1963).

"The Final Solution." *The Irish Times* 3-6 June 1963.

"On Loving Bulls" *The Irish Times* 2 March 1964.

"Carl von Ossietzky: A Hero of the German Resistance" (later under the title of "Carl von Ossietzky") *The Irish Times* 6 June 1964.

"Postscript to Prague" (later under the title "A Prayerful Project"). *The Irish Times* 24 August 1964.

"An Irish Ecumenical Movement." *The Irish Times* 18 December 1964.

"The Sunset of Parlourdom" (later under the title of "Forster, Gerhardi and Snow", Section I). *Hibernia* Vol 28, No 5 (May 1964).

"Am I an Irish Republican?" *The United Irishman* December 1965.

"Andrija Artukovitch." *Le droit de vivre* (Paris) May 1966.

"The Writer and Independence." *The Irish Times* 28 July 1966.

"The Polyglots" (later under the title "Forster, Gerhardi and Snow", Section II). *The Irish Times* 17 January 1967.

"The End of Satire." *The Irish Times* (Jonathan Swift commemorative supplement) 22 March 1967.

"Thalburg Revisted." *The Kilkenny Magazine* No 15 (Spring-Summer 1967).

"American Students in Rebellion." *The Irish Times* 18-21 June 1968.

"A Visit to Hesse and Some Thoughts on Princes." *The Irish Times* 20 September 1968.

"A Sordid Chapter of Church History and Cardinal Seper." *Grille: The Irish Christian Left* No 2 (Autumn 1968).

"The Kilkenny Castle." *The Journal of the Butler Society* Vol 1, No 1 (December 1968).

"Czech Religious Persecution." *The Irish Times* 6 May 1969.

"Protestant Timidity." *Hibernia* Vol 33, No 21 (7-20 November 1969).

1970s

"Nore and Barrow" (later under the title "Beside the Nore"). *Ireland of the Welcomes* May-June (1970).

"Ten Thousand Saints." *Journal of the County Kildare Archaeological Society* Vol 14, No 5 (1970).

"Walter Butler." *The Journal of the Butler Society* Vol 1, No 3 (1970-71).

"Eoin O'Mahony." *The Journal of the Butler Society* Vol 1, No 3 (1970-71).

"Eoin 'Pope' O'Mahony." *The Irish Times* 21 February 1971.

"Whatever Became of Artukovitch?: Reflections on a Croatian Crusade" (later under the title "The Artukovitich File"). *New Blackfriars* (Journal of Oxford Dominicans) February 1971.

"From Peenemunde to Youghal." *Hibernia* Vol 36, No 12 (11-24 June 1971).

"Escape from the Ant-hill." *Treblin Times* No 1 (September 1973).

"Kilkenny in the Days of the Dukes." *The Journal of the Butler Society* Vol 1, No 5 (1973-74).

"Butler's Island in Georgia." *The Journal of the Butler Society* Vol 1, Vol 5 (1973-74).

"The Butlers of Priestown." *The Journal of the Butler Society* Vol 1, Vol 5 (1973-74).

"Leavis on Lawrence." *The Irish Times* 4 September 1974.

"From Kilfarboy to Kilkenny." *Hibernia* Vol 39, No 1 (10-23 January 1975).

"A Protestant Predicament." *Hibernia* Vol 39, No 15 (25 July-14 August 1975).

"Topical Thoughts on Shaw." *The Irish Times* 8 January 1976.

"Peter and Paul." *The Irish Times* 1 May 1976.

"*The Bell*: An Anglo-Irish View." *The Irish University Review* (Spring 1976).

"Black Lamb and Grey Falcon." *The Irish Times* 17 September 1977.

"The Charles II Charter." *The Journal of the Butler Society* Vol 1, No 7 (1977).

"Lady Morgan of Kilkenny." *The Journal of the Butler Society* Vol 1, No 7 (1977).

"Anglo-Irish Twilight, the Last Ormonde War." *The Journal of the Butler Society* Vol 1, No 8 (1978-9).

"A Visit to Hesse and Some Thoughts About Princes" (reprint). *The Journal of the Butler Society* Vol 1, No 8 (1978-79).

"Kiltinan Castle." *The Journal of the Butler Society* Vol 1, No 8 (1978-79).

"Lament for Archaeology." *The Irish Times* 31 July-1 August 1979.

"Divided Loyalties." *An Cosantóir,* (The Irish Army Journal) August 1979.

1980s

"Little K." *The Freethinker* June 1981.

"Martin Luther King: Delicate Balance." *The Irish Press* 20 November 1982.

"Who Was Bernard Biragra?" *The Journal of the Butler Society* Vol 2, No 2 (1982).

"The Member for Kilkenny." *The Journal of the Butler Society* Vol 2, No.3 (1984).

"The Pope and the Innocent Englishman." *Books Ireland* No 93 (May 1985).

"A Future for Kilkenny Castle." *The Journal of the Butler Society* Vol 2, No 4 (1985).

"Ireland in the Nuclear Age." *The Irish Review* No 1 (1986).

"Boucher de Perthes: The Father of Prehistory" in *Social Biology and Human Affairs* (Journal of British Social Biology Council) Vol 51, No 2 (1986).

"The Butlers." *Ireland of the Welcomes* Vol 35, No 6 (November-December 1986).

"Mount Juliet, Kilmurry and the Carricks." *The Journal of the Butler Society* Vol 3, No 1 (1986-87).

"The Children of Drancy." *The Irish Review* No 4 (Spring 1988).

"The Duke of Ormonde and the Huguenots." *The Journal of the Butler Society* Vol 3, No 2 (1988-89).

Posthumous

"In Europe's Troubled Lands." *Irish Pages* Vol 1, No 1 (Spring 2002).
"Specialists in a Soviet School." *The Dublin Review* No 9 (Winter 2003).

IV
Translations Published in Newspapers and Periodicals

"The Chronicles of Narovchat" (a translation from the Russian of Constantin Fedin). *The Bell* Vol 15, No 6 (March 1948).
"The City" (a translation of a poem from the Greek of C.P. Cavafy). *The Irish Times* 10 April 1948.
"Sachalin Island (I)" (a translation from the Russian of Anton Chekhov). *Envoy* Vol 4, No 13 (December 1950).
"Sachalin Island (II)" (a translation from the Russian of Anton Chekhov). *Envoy* Vol 4, No 14 (January 1951).

V
Published Radio Broadcasts

"A Journey to Split" (later under the title "The Russian Consul", Section III of "In the Adriatic"). BBC Radio, The Third Programme, 17 October 1947.
"The Old Kilkenny Archaeological Society and Its Successors", Radio Éireann (later under the same title in *Old Kilkenny Review* No 4, 1951).
"Maria Edgeworth." Radio Éireann, Thomas Davis Lecture, January 1954.
"The Country House – The Life of the Gentry" (later under the title "The Country House After Union"). Radio Éireann, Thomas Davis Lecture, 1957.

VI
The Hubert Butler Papers

The Hubert Butler Papers are held in Trinity College, Dublin. They include manuscripts, diaries, notebooks, correspondence, scrapbooks, and a large body of research on the Irish Saints.

A SELECTED CRITICAL BIBLIOGRAPHY

By chronological order within each section

I
Book

Chris Agee, ed. *Unfinished Ireland: Essays on Hubert Butler*. Belfast: Irish Pages, 2003.

II
Chapters/Essays in Books

Maurice Craig. "Foreword." *Escape from the Anthill*. By Hubert Butler. Dublin: The Lilliput Press, 1985.

Roy Foster. "Foreword." *The Children of Drancy*. By Hubert Butler. Dublin: The Lilliput Press, 1988.

Dervla Murphy. "Foreword." *Grandmother and Wolfe Tone*. By Hubert Butler. Dublin: The Lilliput Press, 1990.

Roy Foster. "Introduction." *The Sub-Prefect Should Have Held His Tongue and Other Essays*. By Hubert Butler. London: Penguin, 1990.

Andrée Sheehy-Skeffington. "The Liberal Ethic 1950-53." *Skeff: A Life of Owen Sheehy-Skeffington 1909-1970*. Dublin: The Lilliput Press, 1991.

David Stephens. "Religious Ireland (II): Protestants in the Republic." *Culture in Ireland: Division or Diversity?* Ed. Edna Longley. Belfast: Institute of Irish Studies, 1991.

Edna Longley. "Defending Ireland's Soul: Protestant Writers and Irish Nationalism after Independence." *The Living Stream: Literature and Revisionism in Ireland*. Newcastle upon Tyne: Bloodaxe Books, 1994.

Tim Robinson. "Origin and Vanishing Point." *Stones of Aran: Labyrinth*. Dublin: The Lilliput Press, 1995.

Neal Ascherson. "Foreword." *In the Land of Nod*. By Hubert Butler. Dublin: The Lilliput Press, 1996.

Joseph Brodsky. "Appendix." *In the Land of Nod*. By Hubert Butler. Dublin: The Lilliput Press, 1996.

Roy Foster. "The Salamander and the Slap: Hubert Butler and His Century." *The Irish Story: Telling Tales and Making It Up in Ireland*. London: Allen Lane, 2001.

III
Scholarly and Literary Journals

Ten Thousand Saints: A Study in Irish and European Origins (1972)

>Author unavailable. Title unavailable. *Journal of the English New Dominicans* May (1973) pp. 238-239.
>
>F. E. Dixon. Title unavailable. *Journal of the Old Dublin Society* (1974) p. 117.
>
>W. M. S. Russell. "Saints, Tribes and Ancestors." *Biology and Human Affairs* 40.3 (1975) pp. 118-130.

Escape from the Anthill (1985)

>Patricia Craig. "Valorizing Valentine Brown." *The London Review of Books* 5 September 1985.
>
>Chris Agee. "Culture." *The Linen Hall Review* Fall (1985) pp. 32-33.
>
>Roy Foster. "For the Meeting of Hearts." *The Times Literary Supplement* 6 September 1985, p.980.
>
>W. J. McCormack. Title unavailable. *Irish Slavonic Studies* 7 (1986).
>
>Marianne Koenig. "Reviews." *The Irish University Review* (1986).
>
>David Krause. "Ireland's Libertarian Conscience." *The Irish Literary Supplement* Fall (1987).

The Children of Drancy (1988)

>John Bayley. "A Lifetime of Rocking the Boat." *The Times Literary Supplement* 18 November 1988.
>
>Florence O'Donoghue. "Lived in Foul Concubinage." *The Literary Review* October (1988).

Grandmother and Wolfe Tone (Ireland, 1990)

>Thomas McCarthy. "Documents of Exclusion." *The Irish Review* May-June (1990) pp. 138-142.

In the Land of Nod (1996)

>Geoffrey Wheatcroft. "Messages from a Gentle Protestant." *The Times Literary Supplement* 18 June 1996, pp.13-14.
>
>Bill Tinley. "The Inconvenience of a Conscience." *Irish Literary Supplement* 16.1 (1997) p. 3.

Independent Spirit (1996)

> Alfred Kazin. Title unavailable. *The New Republic* 3 February 1997.
> John Banville. "The European Irishman." *The New York Review of Books* 12 June 1997, pp. 38-41.
> Julian Moynahan. "Hubert Butler: *Independent Spirit*." *The Recorder* (journal of the Irish-American Historical Association) Spring-Fall (1997).
> Chris Agee. "Poteen in a Brandy-Cask: The Ethical Imagination of Hubert Butler." *The Yale Review* Spring (1998), pp. 129-142.

IV
Newspapers and Magazines

Ten Thousand Saints: A Study in Irish and European Origins (Ireland, 1972)

> Dervla Murphy. Title unavailable. *The Irish Times* 13 January 1973.

Escape from the Anthill (Ireland, 1985)

> Dervla Murphy. "Anglo and Irish." *The Irish Times* 1 June 1985.
> K.M.L. Title unavailable. *The Kilkenny People* 7 June 1985.
> Jack Reynolds (pseudonym of Eoghan Harris). "Hubert Butler — Indomitable Irishry." *Image* June (1985).
> Unsigned. Title unavailable. *The Irish Post* 6 July 1985.
> Ulick O'Connor. "Catholic Ireland Through Protestant Eyes." *The Sunday Independent* 7 July 1985.
> Monk Gibbon. "Wrath of the Fairy Rath." *The Sunday Press* 7 July 1985.
> Tony O'Riordan. "Cross Voice from the Big House." *Irish Independent* 13 July 1985.
> John McKenna. "Books." *In Dublin* July (1985).
> Liam Robinson. "Escape into the World of Mr. Butler." *New Hibernia* July (1985).
> Ulick O'Connor. "Protestant View on the State of the Nation." *The Irish Press* 22 September 1985.
> Edna Longley. "Anglo-Irish Resurrection." *The Honest Ulsterman* Winter (1986).
> Hugh Bredin. "A Rare Treasure of Essays." *Fortnight* 24 February (1986).
> Kieran Nally. Title unavailable. *Irish Independent* 6 December 1986.
> Peter Costello. Title unavailable. *The Sunday Independent* 21 December 1986.
> Henry Cummins. Title unavailable. *The Sunday Press* 1 February 1987.
> Roy Foster. Title unavailable (on the Ewart-Biggs Special Citation). *The*

Irish Times 26 March 1987.

Kevin Myers. "An Irishman'sDiary." *The Irish Times* 7 September 1987.

Jack O'Connell. Title unavailable. *The Southern Star* 7 November 1987.

Patrick Mason. "Books of the Year." *The Irish Times* 10 December 1988.

The Children of Drancy (Ireland, 1988)

Eamon Timmins. "Hubert Butler – New Book Will Mark His 88th Birthday" (interview). *The Kilkenny People* 19 August 1988.

Proinsias Ó Drisceoil. "An Irish Essayist." *The Irish Times* 10 September 1988.

Brian Trench. "Towards a Protestant Identity." *The Sunday Tribune* 25 September 1988.

Dervla Murphy. "Brave Man's Record of Our Times." *Irish Independent* 5 November 1988.

J. Anthony Gaughan. "Anglo-Irish Pieties." *The Irish Press* (date unavailable).

David Hanly. "Hubert Butler's Traits." *The Sunday Tribune* 18 December 1988.

Donal Harrington. "Hubert Butler: Acute Moral Sensitivity." *Alpha* 30 March 1989.

Conor O'Clery. "On Riga Strand, 1989, Pollution Is Master." *The Irish Times* 3 April 1989.

Author unavailable. "Irish Book Awards 1989." *The Sunday Tribune* 10 September 1989.

Grandmother and Wolfe Tone (Ireland, 1990)

Kevin Myers. "An Irishman's Diary." *The Irish Times* 9 May 1990.

A.T.Q. Stewart. "Breathing Deep of the Native Air." *The Irish Times* 19 May 1990.

Sean McMahon. "He's a Bit of a Saint Himself." *Independent Weekender* 19 May 1990.

Unsigned. "Double Celebration for Noted Author." *The Kilkenny People* 11 May 1990.

Terence Brown. "What the Sensitive and Robust Butler Saw." *The Sunday Tribune* 2 June 1990.

Domhnal Mitchell. "Book Review." *Andersonstown News* 9 June 1990.

Fintan O'Toole. "Loyal Dissenter." *The Irish Times* (Weekend) 23 June 1990.

Vincent Lawrence. "Still Writing After All These Years." *The Sunday Press* 8 July 1990.

Bill Maxwell. "The Two Traditions." *Cara Magazine* September-October (1990).

Patrick Gallagher. "The Sage of Maidenhall." *The Sunday Independent* 23

October 1990.

Unsigned. "A Very Irish Voice." *Image Magazine* (October 1990).

Edna Longley. "No Rootless Empiricist." *Fortnight* (Supplement) July-August (1991) pp. 13-14.

The Sub-Prefect Should Have Held His Tongue: Selected Essays (Britain, 1990)

Mark Archer. Title unavailable. *The Financial Times* 11 November 1990.

Robert Kee. Title unavailable. *The Independent on Sunday* 30 December 1990.

Edna Longley. "Close-cropped Grass Comes Up Sweet." *The Times Literary Supplement* 1 February 1991, p. 8.

John Grigg. Title unavailable. *The Times* (Saturday Review) 16 March 1991.

Geoffrey Stokes. Title unavailable. *The Boston Sunday Globe* 22 September 1991.

In the Land of Nod (Ireland, 1996)

Neal Ascherson. "The Strength of Loyalism May Crumble into Dust." *The Independent on Sunday* 25 February 1996.

Robert Graecen. "Scholar and Gentleman." *The Irish Independent* 1 June 1996.

Thomas Kilroy. "Last Words from a Champion of Freedom." *The Irish Times* 1 June 1996.

Eugene McCabe. "The Long View of an Angel." *The Tribune Magazine* 9 June 1996.

Robert Nye. "Keep Mind Wide Awake." *The Times* 13 June 1996.

Sam Gallagher. "Bookshelf." *Xchange* June (1996) p. 13.

Rory Brennan. "Irish Europeans." *Books Ireland* September (1996).

L'envahisseur est venu en pantoufles (France, 1995**)**

Phillipe Petit. Title unavailable. *L'Evenement du Jeudi* 12 April 1995.

Bernard Féron. "Hubert Butler, lucide voyageur." *Le Monde* 30 June 1995.

Independent Spirit (USA, 1996)

Unsigned. Title unavailable. *Kirkus Review* 15 June 1996.

Alice Joyce. Untitled. *Booklist* 1 November 1996.

Thomas Flannagan. Title unavailable. *The Washington Post* 10 November 1996.

Peggy O'Brien. "An Ireland Not Heard." *The Boston Globe* 24 November 1996.

Ann Mundow. "An Irishwoman's Diary." *The Irish Times* 29 November 1996.

Richard Elder. Title unavailable. *The Los Angelos Times* 1 December 1996.

Thomas R. Edwards. Title unavailable. *The New York Times Book Review* 1 December 1996.

V

Miscellaneous Essays, Articles, Appreciations and Mentions

Sean O'Faoláin. "On a Recent Incident at the International Affairs Association." *The Bell* 28 (1953), pp. 517+.

Paul Blanchard. *The Irish and Catholic Power: An American Interpretation*. Boston: Beacon, 1953, p.189+.

Brian Inglis. *West Briton*. London: Faber, 1962, p. 203.

Sean O'Casey. *Sunset and Evening Star*. London: Pan books, 1973, p. 211+.

Geraldine Collins. "Artist (90) in Medal Coup" (on the Irish Book Award). *Irish Independent* 8 September 1989.

Dervla Murphy. Title unavailable (interview). *The Sunday Telegraph* 4 November 1990.

Antony Farrell. "Appreciation." *The Irish Times* 12 January 2001.

Fintan O'Toole. "Inventing a Sense of Being Irish." *The Irish Times* 10 January 1991.

W. J. McCormack. "Prophet Without Honour" (obituary essay). *Making Sense* May/June (1991).

Damian Smyth. "Illegitimate Aspirations." *Fortnight* July-August (1991) pp.31-32.

Seamus Deane, ed. "Autobiography and Memoirs 1890-1988." *The Field Day Anthology of Irish Writing*. Derry: Field Day Publications, 1991, pp.381-382.

W. J. McCormack. "Far-seeing Gifts: Hubert Butler, 1900-1991." *Éire-Ireland* Autumn (1991) pp. 95-100.

Robert Greacen. *Brief Encounters*. Belfast: Lagan Press, (1991), p.35.

Fintan O'Toole. Title unavailable. *The Irish Times* 21 April 1993.

Prionsias Ó Drisceoil. "Dateline 1954: Kilkenny Debates Partition." *Causeway* Spring (1994) pp. 40-45.

Allan Massie. Title unavailable. *The Daily Telegraph* 17 December 1994.

Chris Agee. "Now That the Rye-Crop Waves Beside the Ruins/Sad kad se zito talasa pored rusevina." *Zidne Novine/Wall Pages* (Sarajevo: Irish Issue) December (1996), pp. 1-2.

Fintan O'Toole. Title unavailable. *The Irish Times* 5 December 1997.

Roy Foster. "On the Shelf." *The Sunday Times* (Books) 27 September 1998.

Chris Agee. "The Balkan Butler." *Graph* Vol 1, No 3 (1999) pp. 12-15.

Eoghan Harris. "Escape from the Anthill Mentality." *The Sunday Times* 29 October 2000.

Chris Agee. "The Ivy Room" (poem on Hubert Butler). *Orion* (USA) Autumn (2000).

Chris Dooley. "Kilkenny to Honour Courageous and Prolific Essay Writer." *The Irish Times* 18 October 2000.

Chris Dooley. "A Voice of Real Passion." *The Irish Times* 24 October 2000.

Sean Keane. "Apology Accepted by Hubert Butler's Daughter." *The Kilkenny People* 27
    October 2000.

Geoffrey Wheatcroft. "Letter from Kilkenny" (on the Hubert Butler Centenary
    Celebration). *The Times Literary Supplement* 29 December 2000, pp. 12-13.

Neal Ascherson. "Unfinished Ireland: Hubert Butler's Contemporary Relevance." *Irish Pages*
    Vol 1, No 1 (Spring 2002), pp. 169-177.

Martin Earl. "Interruptions." *Irish Pages* Vol 1, No 1 (Spring 2002), pp. 234-237.

VI
Electronic Magazine

Richard Jones. "Independent Spirit: An Appreciation of Hubert Butler." *Archipelago* Vol 1,
    No 2 (Summer 1997): n. pag.
    Online: http://www.archipelago.org/vol12/appreciation.htm

Chris Agee. "The Balkan Butler." *Archipelago* Vol 5, No 1 (Spring 2001): n. pag.
    Online: http://www.archipelago.org/vol5-1/agee.htm

Chris Agee. "The Stepinac File." *Archipelago* Vol 5, No 1 (Spring 2001): n. pag.
    Online: http://www.archipelago.org/vol5-1/agee.htm